Milwaukee Through History

Milwaukee Through History

A Young Reader's Guide to the People and Events That Shaped a City

James K. Nelsen

Wisconsin Historical Society Press

Published by the **Wisconsin Historical Society Press**
Publishers since 1855

The Wisconsin Historical Society helps people connect to the past by collecting, preserving, and sharing stories. Founded in 1846, the Society is one of the nation's finest historical institutions.

Join the Wisconsin Historical Society: **wisconsinhistory.org/membership**

Publication of this book was made possible in part by a grant from the Jane Bradley Pettit Foundation. Additional funding was provided by a grant from the D.C. Everest fellowship fund.

Printed in Canada

Interior Pages Designed by Shawn Biner

29 28 27 26 25   1 2 3 4 5

Library of Congress Cataloging-in-Publication Data
Names: Nelsen, James, 1975–   author.
Title: Milwaukee through history : a young reader's guide to the people and events that shaped a city / James K. Nelsen.
Other titles: Young reader's guide to the people and events that shaped a city
Description: Madison, WI : Wisconsin Historical Society Press, [2024] | Includes bibliographical references and index. | Audience: Ages 12 and up | Audience: Grades 7–9
Identifiers: LCCN 2023038660 (print) | LCCN 2023038661 (e-book) | ISBN 9781976600036 (paperback) | ISBN 9781976600043 (e-book)
Subjects: LCSH: Milwaukee (Wis.)—History—Juvenile literature.
Classification: LCC F589.M657 N45 2024 (print) | LCC F589.M657 (e-book) | DDC 977.5/95—dc23/eng/20231214
LC record available at https://lccn.loc.gov/2023038660
LC e-book record available at https://lccn.loc.gov/2023038661

♾ The paper used in this publication meets the minimum requirements of the American National Standard for Information Sciences—Permanence of Paper for Printed Library Materials, ANSI Z39.48-1992.

The author thanks the following people for their feedback:
Kevin Abing, Sophonisba Franecki, Kathleen Hazen,
Stephanie Nelsen, Amanda Seligman,
Tiffany Smith, and Tyne Turner.

This book is dedicated to Charlotte Nelsen.
I am looking forward to reading it with you someday.

Contents

Introduction

Milwaukee has been called lots of things over the centuries: Willawaky. Cream City. Brewtown. The Machine Shop of the World. A Great City on a Great Lake. How did Milwaukee earn all of these nicknames? How did it become the biggest city in the state of Wisconsin? What people, places, and events helped shape the city that exists today? In this book, you will find the answers to all of those questions and a lot more. At the beginning of each chapter is a short list of questions to guide your reading. Use them to spark a classroom discussion or to reflect on what you have read on your own. This book is primarily intended for young people who are learning the history of the United States and Wisconsin, either in school or on their own. But the book is also for anyone who is interested in learning the fascinating history of a diverse northern city. Milwaukee is a city that has had its share of triumphs and troubles, successes and failures. It is a city that has survived and strived for better things.

Milwaukee Through History begins thousands of years ago and ends in the twenty-first century. The first chapter introduces the Native peoples who have lived in the place we now call Milwaukee. The second chapter concentrates on the decades Milwaukee spent as a rough frontier town in the 1700s, after the arrival of Europeans. The remaining eight chapters highlight some of the biggest changes Milwaukee has experienced over the past two hundred years.

If you live in or near Milwaukee, or if you plan to visit, pay attention to the "History in Person" sidebars throughout the book. They feature spots you can visit today to get a glimpse of Milwaukee's past. It is a diverse collection of landmarks that includes the city's biggest and smallest public parks, a mural, a museum/memorial, a burial mound, a mansion, and more.

Finally, each chapter of *Milwaukee Through History* ends with a collection of primary source excerpts. These come from books, newspapers, speeches, oral histories, interviews, and letters. (The spelling, grammar, and punctuation in these source documents are just as they appeared in the originals.) Examining primary sources will allow you to listen to the voices of people from Milwaukee's past. Reading their words will help you better understand their perspectives, the ways they disagreed, and the issues that mattered to them. As you read the primary sources, compare them to the perspectives, disagreements, and issues of today. You will find many differences. But you may be surprised at the number of similarities you find as well.

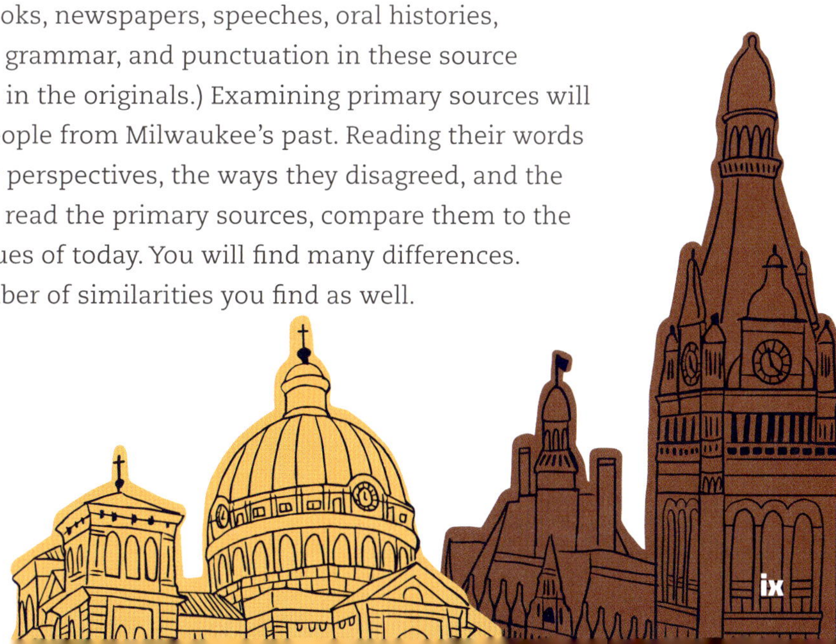

HISTORY IN PERSON SITES

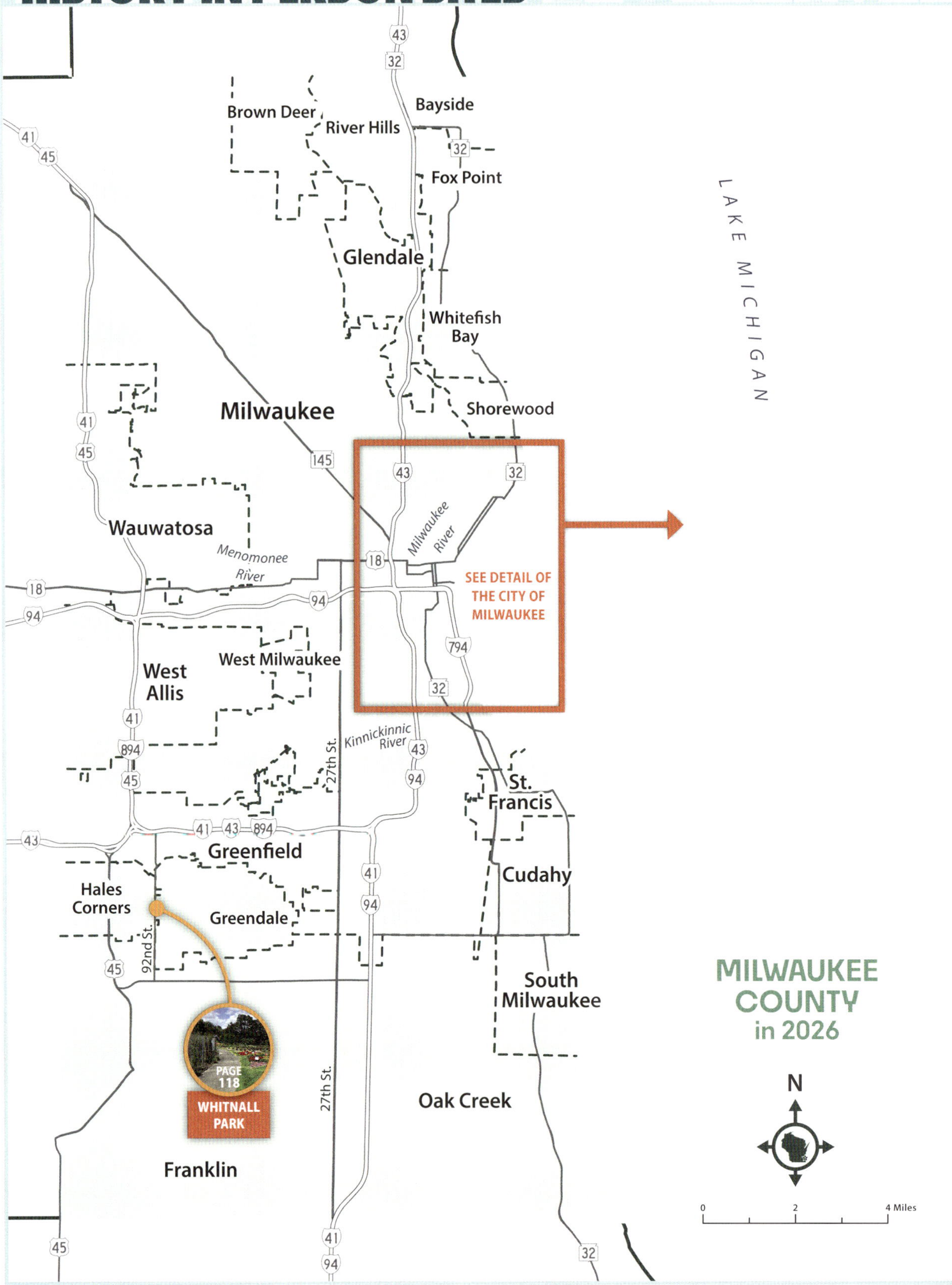

Maps by Colter Sikora

CHAPTER 1

Before It Was Milwaukee

Up to 1814

CHAPTER QUESTIONS

- What were some of the reasons Indigenous peoples came to Milwaukee? How did these reasons change or stay the same over time?
- How do you think Native peoples viewed the early Europeans they met? What did Europeans think of the Native peoples?
- How did trading with the French affect American Indian communities in good or bad ways?
- How did relations between American Indians and European settlers change as a result of the wars that occurred in the 1700s and 1800s?

Milwaukee has been known as *Milwaukee* for only a few centuries. Long before that, the area was home to different groups of American Indians. These groups were drawn to some of the same features that make Milwaukee an attractive place to live today, such as the lake now known as Lake Michigan and the rivers that flow through the area. Native peoples worked the land, raised families, and told stories. They established trade networks and political alliances with other Native nations and later with Europeans. But the arrival of Europeans in the 1600s changed the lives of those Native peoples forever. These changes started slowly with trade and accelerated after the French and Indian War and the American Revolution.

Long before Europeans arrived in this region, many Indigenous cultures lived here. This drawing, made in the 1850s by a white artist, depicts Ho-Chunk people. | *WHI Image ID 10001*

Early Peoples

Before the last Ice Age, southeastern Wisconsin probably resembled the Driftless Area, a region of southwestern Wisconsin known for its high hills and deep valleys. But then, about twenty-six thousand years ago, a huge sheet of ice moved through much of Wisconsin, including the southeast. As the glacier moved, it reshaped the landscape. The glacier flattened land, carved deep basins, and dropped boulders, sand, and gravel. When the climate warmed and the glacier melted, it left behind a rolling plain. Over time the land became covered with dense forests and prairies. The forests were filled with large animals such as white-tailed deer, wolves, and big cats. Basins filled with water and became lakes and ponds. The forests, wildlife, and bodies of water have made southeastern Wisconsin attractive to humans for thousands of years. Although each group that lived in the area had its own traditions, all were tied to the land.

Some Native nations living in Wisconsin today have lived here since time began. The **oral histories** of the Menominee people, for example, say that their people were created near the mouth of the Menominee River and that they have always lived here.

This Paleo-Indian spear point, uncovered in Milwaukee County, was made between ten thousand and fourteen thousand years ago. | *Museum object #1985.2*

Archaeologists have assigned names to early Native peoples to indicate the time period during which they lived. These are not names that the people they refer to ever called themselves. Archaeologists estimate that the people they call Paleo-Indians arrived in this region at least fourteen thousand years ago. The climate here was much colder then, and the people moved with the seasons to follow large game animals such as mastodons and bison. Archaeologists have found and studied spear points made by the Paleo-Indian people. Based on these spear points, scientists think Paleo-Indian people were present in Wisconsin until about 8500 BCE. As the climate warmed, people stayed in one place for longer periods of time. In addition to hunting and gathering, they also fished and planted crops such as corn, beans, and squash. They made pottery and new tools for hunting, such as bows and arrows. Archaeologists call the many Native peoples who lived during this time (about 800 BCE–1200 CE) Woodland people.

Later Woodland Indians are also called Mound Builders because of the large number of earthen mounds they built. Southern Wisconsin had more mounds than any other place in the United States. Some mounds were more than 250 feet long. Some of them were used as burial grounds. Others may have been used for ceremonies or to mark the territory occupied by certain groups. Many of the mounds in the Milwaukee area were built in the shapes of birds, panthers,

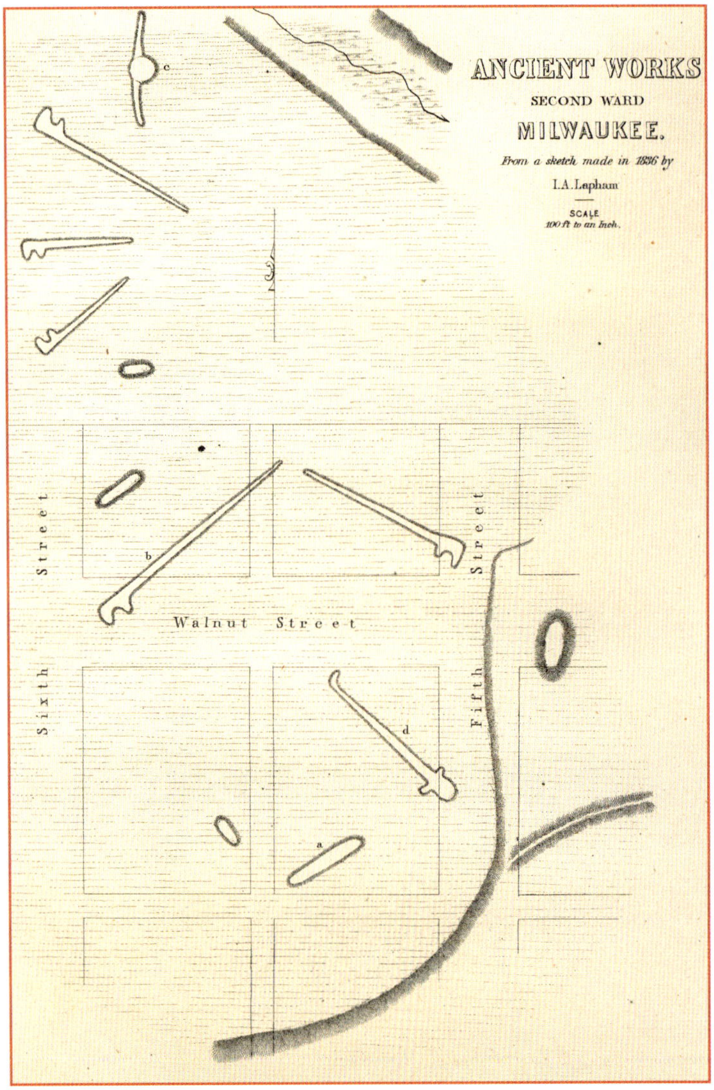

This map shows the location of Indian mounds in Milwaukee's Second Ward. The map was made by Increase Lapham, a white scientist and naturalist, in 1836. Some of the mounds may have been burial mounds and contained tools or items such as the ones shown in his sketch. | *WHI Image ID 100495*

and turtles. Mounds built in shapes like these are called effigy mounds. The Mound Builders may have moved on to other places or combined with other groups over time. The Mounds Builders are the ancestors of many Native peoples who live in the region today.

Starting around the year 1100, the Oneota people spread across the Midwest. The Oneota settled in large villages in southern Wisconsin along rivers and near Lake Michigan. They hunted game, fished, gathered wild rice, and planted crops. They built dwellings called longhouses, which were long, narrow homes built large enough to hold multiple families. Some people believe the Oneota are ancestors of the Ho-Chunk and several other Indian nations. The Oneota ceased to exist as their own culture sometime between 1650 and 1700.

HISTORY IN PERSON

Milwaukee's Last Mounds

Most of the estimated two hundred mounds built by Woodland people in the Milwaukee area were destroyed to make way for farmland, buildings, or parks. One of the few remaining mounds can be seen at Lake Park, 3233 E. Kenwood Blvd. The low, round mound is about forty feet across and two feet high. Experts believe it was constructed up to two thousand years ago. It used to be part of a grouping of several similar mounds. The Wisconsin Archeological Society decided in 1910 to protect the last remaining one.

By the 1600s, the Ho-Chunk people occupied the western shore of Lake Michigan, including the area now known as Milwaukee. French diplomat Jean Nicolet landed on the shores of Wisconsin in 1634, possibly near Marinette in the northeastern part of the state. Ho-Chunk, Menominee, and Potawatomi people met him as he journeyed. They learned about his mission to encourage trade between France and American Indians.

The Ho-Chunk were familiar with European goods due to their trade with eastern Native nations. These eastern peoples acquired kettles and beads from Europeans and traded them to the Ho-Chunk. Unfortunately, contact with Europeans also spread European diseases, including cholera, influenza, measles, scarlet fever, smallpox, and typhus. By the 1660s, those diseases, as well as wars between Native nations, had reduced the Ho-Chunk population from thousands of people to hundreds. The Ho-Chunk left the Milwaukee area and much of the lakeshore. They continued to live in inland areas from what is now the Illinois border to the edge of Wisconsin's North Woods.

This painting was created by Edwin Deming, a white artist who frequently painted Indigenous people. It illustrates a popular story about Jean Nicolet's arrival in Wisconsin. According to the story, Nicolet was searching for a passage to Asia and greeted local Indians wearing a Chinese robe. Historians now know that Nicolet was a diplomat looking to establish trade with American Indians. | *WHI Image ID 1870*

Jolliet and Marquette's traveling party on the Mississippi River
| WHI Image ID 2344

Louis Jolliet followed Nicolet in 1673. Jolliet was a French fur trader and explorer who wanted to follow the Mississippi River. Father Jacques Marquette and five other men accompanied Jolliet. Marquette was a French **missionary** whose goal was to spread Christianity. Their party canoed along Lake Michigan's western shoreline from what is now the Upper Peninsula of Michigan to Green Bay. Following the Fox and Wisconsin Rivers, they reached the Mississippi. On his return trip to Green Bay, Marquette made a brief stop in the area of Milwaukee in 1674 and met the Indigenous peoples living there.

Meanwhile, new groups arrived from the east. The six nations that were part of the powerful Haudenosaunee Confederacy lived in what would become the states of New York and Pennsylvania. These nations were the Mohawk, Oneida, Onondaga, Cayuga, Seneca, and Tuscarora. They went to war with their neighbors over the fur trade and pushed them west. These groups included the Potawatomi, Ojibwe, Ottawa, Kickapoo, Mascouten, Meskwaki (Fox), and Sauk. Members of these nations lived in southeastern Wisconsin in the late seventeenth century on land that had been occupied by the Ho-Chunk.

The place that became Milwaukee was known for its good land. The Milwaukee, Menomonee, and Kinnickinnic Rivers meet in Milwaukee near Lake Michigan. The rivers created wetlands and a large marsh in what are now downtown and the Menomonee Valley. The wetlands extended south to the land now occupied by the Third Ward, Jones Island, Walker's Point, and part of Bay View. Wild rice grew in the marsh and was an important part of Native peoples' diets and cultures. In fact, the Menominee people refer to themselves as *Omeaqnomenewak*, meaning "People of the Wild Rice." The Menominee and other Indigenous peoples gathered reeds from the marshes. They wove the reeds into baskets and mats. The Menominee mainly lived on what is now the north side of Milwaukee. The Potawatomi lived in the area bordered by the Milwaukee River, the Menomonee River, and Lake Michigan. Nearby forests provided branches and bark for small, domed homes called **wigwams**.

Milwaukee continued to be home to people from several Native nations, as it is today. By 1800, the Potawatomi were the largest

Native nation living there. They grew corn, beans, and squash in prairies near what is now the downtown area. The men hunted with bows and arrows for black bear, deer, and elk in the forests that surrounded the prairies. The people tapped maple trees for sap that they turned into maple sugar. Also in that season the Potawatomi set up camps in valleys that protected them from harsh winter weather. They came back together into larger groups in spring to hunt bison on the prairies or fish in streams that emptied into Lake Michigan. The women collected a variety of plants, including berries, nuts, roots, and wild greens. As Native peoples increased food supplies through gardening, the population grew quickly. One white observer estimated that four thousand American Indians lived in the area in the late eighteenth century.

History in Focus

The Good Land

According to a popular story, the name *Milwaukee* comes from a word meaning "good land" in the language spoken by the Potawatomi, Ojibwe, and Ottawa people. But the exact origins of the name are more complicated and mysterious than that. The several Native groups living in the area had different ways of saying the name. Newcomers to the area also used a number of names, some similar to *Milwaukee* but not quite the same. Some of the names included *Milwogues, Miskoumina, Melecki, Wilakie, Willawaky,* and *Milwacky*. European traders, missionaries, and mapmakers struggled to agree on a spelling and a translation when they recorded the name. Some said it meant "gathering place by the river," "wet land," or "stinking river." Others said it referred to a medicinal plant that grew there.

Wild rice was once a plentiful food source in the Milwaukee area. Native peoples harvested the rice by knocking the grains with paddles into canoes. People continue this tradition today in the northern Great Lakes region. | *WHI Image ID 9023*

Potawatomi Cultural Traditions

The word *Potawatomi* translates to "Keepers of the Sacred Fire" in their language. They also call themselves *Neshnabek*, which means "the True People" or "Original People." In traditional Potawatomi culture, the people are organized into **clans**. Men and women were expected to marry into other clans. The married couple lived in the husband's village. The intermarriages of the clans created links among villages. These connections encouraged trade and other cultural ties.

Each village was led by a senior man who was a member of that village's major clan. He was respected but did not have absolute authority over the other villagers. Major decisions, such as going to war, were made in groups. Village leaders gathered for long discussions of the pros and cons. After the decision was made, they would hold a feast to confirm the people's commitment to the decision. Village leaders occasionally selected a single man to speak for all of them.

The Potawatomi people's spiritual life was also organized around the clans. Each clan had a sacred bundle, which held medicines and religious objects. The bundles were also associated with the songs, dances, and origin stories of that clan. Spiritual leaders performed religious rituals and healed the sick. The Potawatomi are among the Native cultures who buried their dead. Though most of the burial grounds were destroyed as cities and towns developed, the Forest Home Cemetery, at the intersection of Forest Home and Lincoln Avenues, was originally a burial ground for a Potawatomi village.

Artist Andrea Hoffman beaded these Potawatomi moccasins in 2008.
| *WHI Image ID 56023*

Colonization and War

As more European traders and settlers arrived in the region, American Indians had increasing contact with them. Archaeologists who have studied Native burial mounds have found that European goods began appearing in the mounds in the 1650s. Both groups had something valuable that the other group wanted. American Indians traded food, canoes, and information about travel routes to Europeans. But the Native peoples' most desirable trade items were beaver and other animal pelts. Europeans made hats and other clothing out of the furs. The demand for beaver furs was so strong that beavers were hunted almost to extinction by 1800. Europeans traded metal tools to American Indians, including knives, awls, kettles, and traps. Europeans also traded steel flints for starting fires, guns and ammunition, wool fabric, porcelain beads, and alcohol.

The French were the major trading partners of Native peoples in the area. By 1712, the French had, without the Native peoples' consent, claimed territory between Newfoundland and the Rocky Mountains, from Hudson Bay to the Gulf of Mexico. This land included the Mississippi River and the St. Lawrence River. These rivers connected the French trade to the rest of the world.

While France claimed large portions of North America, Britain was beginning to form thirteen colonies on the Atlantic coast. In 1754, these two countries went to war over the land between the Appalachian Mountains and the Mississippi River. Most Native nations involved in the conflict sided with the French, who were their business partners. This is why the conflict is often called the French and Indian War. The French needed support from the American Indians because the British outnumbered them. Potawatomi people from Milwaukee joined the French at several locations, including near Fort Duquesne, located at the present site of Pittsburgh, Pennsylvania. The French and American Indian forces defeated the British at this battle. Future first president of the United States George Washington was one of the leaders of the British forces.

As the war continued, the British won most of the battles. The British had several advantages over the French. They had more fighters and could draw on resources from their thirteen colonies. The British overtook Fort Montreal in 1760, which allowed them to move into the Great Lakes area. They made it to Green Bay by 1761. The war ended two years later. The French had lost nearly all their North American territories. Britain took control of the land between the Appalachian Mountains and the Mississippi River, a large area that included present-day Wisconsin. The British blocked the supply of trade items that Native peoples had come to depend on.

After the war, British colonists crossed the Appalachian Mountains to establish new homes for themselves. Native nations in the Great Lakes area feared they would lose their land. Some Ojibwe and Potawatomi people joined with members of other Native groups in the region to fight back. They rallied around Pontiac, an Ottawa leader, in 1763. Pontiac led thousands of troops against British forces at forts near Green Bay, Detroit, and Mackinaw City.

Ottawa chief Pontiac | *Library of Congress 2016886688*

Pontiac's War ended with the British agreeing to enforce the Proclamation of 1763. The proclamation forbade colonists from settling on American Indian territory west of the Appalachian Mountains. It was the first time that a European government recognized that Americans Indians had rights to any land. But many colonists ignored the proclamation. They resented this restriction on their freedom of movement. This resentment toward the British was one of many factors leading to the American Revolution.

Relations between the colonies and Britain worsened in the 1770s. The colonists complained that they had to pay taxes to the British government, but they had no representatives in that government. This meant they had no say in the laws that they had to follow. Britain forbade the colonists from trading directly with Indian nations. Colonists could trade only among themselves or with Britain. The British also threatened to close colonial churches. Many colonists wanted to escape British rule and form their own government. The war we now call the American Revolution broke out in 1775.

Most of the American Indians, including some Potawatomi groups, sided with their new trading partners, the British. But Siggenauk, a Potawatomi chief in Milwaukee, decided to support the colonists. Siggenauk convinced Potawatomi communities along Lake Michigan not to support the British. Potawatomi led by Siggenauk raided British outposts in Michigan. British colonel Arent Schuyler de Peyster, the commander at Fort Michilimackinac at Mackinaw City, was outraged. He referred to the Potawatomi as "those runegates [likely meaning *renegades*] in Milwakie, a horrid set of refractory Indians," meaning they resisted British laws. This statement is believed to be the first time a version of the word *Milwaukee* appeared in print. The colonel ordered a British navy ship to sail to Milwaukee to arrest Siggenauk. The soldiers brought some Potawatomi people onto the ship and tried to bribe them into capturing Siggenauk for them. The Potawatomi took the gifts but refused to hand over their leader.

The American Revolution ended in 1781 with the British surrender, although fighting continued until 1783. The thirteen colonies became thirteen independent states bound together as the United States of America. The Mississippi River became the new country's western boundary, defined by the **Treaty** of Paris of 1783. The British, however, did not completely leave the Great Lakes region. They maintained some forts and once again supplied American Indians with trade items including guns and gunpowder. They also encouraged American Indians to raid American settler communities.

The War of 1812 began because of these raids and trade conflicts between Great Britain and the United States. American Indians understood that white Americans were trying to force them off their lands. Therefore, most American Indians in the Great Lakes region sided with the British. British and American Indian forces seized Detroit, Green Bay, and Mackinaw City. A group of as many as six hundred Potawatomi people, some of whom were from Milwaukee, joined the conflict. The war ended in a **stalemate** in 1814. Neither side had won, but the fighting ceased. The US government took control of the fur trade.

Primary Sources

Potawatomi Oral Tradition

For centuries, Indigenous peoples have passed on their culture through oral storytelling. These stories are a way to preserve culture and share history from one generation to the next. Similar to written records, the stories are a valuable historic record. Over time, some of these stories were written down and published by white people. Therefore, the written versions of the stories are often told through a white person's perspective. The two Potawatomi stories below were recorded by white scholars in the first half of the 1900s. As you read them, think about what they tell you about the Potawatomi people and their ancestors. Then answer the questions that follow.

THE STORY OF WINTER SNOW

Once, two Indian boys lived with their grandmother in a wigwam. One day, the boys went hunting to get some meat for their grandmother. While they were gone, a stranger came and asked for them and waited for their return. When they came back late at night, they brought a large buck deer which they had killed. Their grandmother cooked some of the venison, and the stranger ate with them. When they were finished, the stranger asked the grandmother's permission to stay with them for the winter. She agreed. He was a shaman or medicine man, and whenever they went hunting, he gave them hunting medicine and they were always very successful.

This man's name was Winter Snow. When spring came, he thanked the grandmother for her hospitality and went away. The young men wanted to go with him and followed him into the woods. One morning after this, the old woman heard a moaning sound outdoors and found that the snow was melting. This sound was made by her grandsons who had been transformed into snow when they followed their friend Winter Snow.

Source: Adapted from Dorothy Moulding Brown, "Indian Winter Legends," *Wisconsin Archeologist* 22, no. 4 (1941): 49–53.

THE ORIGIN OF CORN AND OTHER CROPS

After man was created, he was lonely, so the Creator gave him a sister to keep him company. The man dreamed that five spirits would visit his sister and want to marry her. The dream told him that she should reject the first four and marry the fifth suitor. The first four suitors to arrive were Tobacco, Squash, Melon, and Bean. On being rejected by the girl, they each fell dead. The fifth and last suitor was Mandamin, or Corn. The girl took him for her husband, and he buried the other four suitors. From their bodies grew tobacco, squashes, melons, and beans. All Indian people are descended from the marriage of the Indian girl and Corn.

Source: Adapted from Dorothy Moulding Brown, "Wisconsin Indian Corn Origin Myths," *Wisconsin Archeologist* 21, no. 1 (1940): 19–27.

- **How do these Potawatomi stories help us understand the past?**
- **What do you think was important to the Potawatomi people who lived on this land before it became Milwaukee? How did they use stories to explain natural occurrences?**
- **What is the main idea of each story?**

CHAPTER 2

CHAPTER QUESTIONS

- How did Milwaukee's early white settlers view the town? What influenced those views? What might their lives have been like?
- How did the changes that white settlers brought to the area affect the American Indian population?
- How did Milwaukee's founders and their decisions shape the city of today?

A Frontier Town
1795–1845

At the end of the eighteenth century, many French Canadian men who worked for the fur trade came to the Milwaukee area. It was not long until many more people from Europe and the eastern United States arrived to claim land and build homes. These colonists pushed most American Indian peoples out of the region.

As the Wisconsin Territory took shape, so did the city of Milwaukee. Three French Canadian men began to put their differing visions for the city into practice. Soon, conflict brewed among the white settlers. Eventually, though, they managed to come together to draft a city charter, which was approved in 1846.

This illustration, called "View of Milwaukie," appeared in a book published in 1848, the year Wisconsin became a state. | *WHI Image ID 54629*

Fur Traders and Voyageurs

French Canadians were the largest group of white settlers in Milwaukee after the American Revolution ended in 1783. They came to Milwaukee to trade with American Indians and hoped to make a fortune or at least a decent living. Not everyone was successful, however. Life on the frontier had many challenges.

This illustration, from an 1879 issue of *Harper's Monthly*, shows voyageurs with the Hudson's Bay Company portaging along a river. | *WHI Image ID 7009*

Jean Baptiste Mirandeau and Jacques Vieau of La Baye (Green Bay) were the first white settlers in Milwaukee. They were French Canadians who established a fur-trading post in 1795 on the Chicago–Green Bay trail in what is now Mitchell Park. The post was part of the American Fur Company, which had branches in the United States and Canada. Mirandeau remained in Milwaukee all year, and Vieau came every spring with supplies. Mirandeau died in 1820 or 1821. He was the first white person to be buried in a Milwaukee cemetery. Vieau spent more time in Milwaukee after Mirandeau's death. He married Angelique Roy, the granddaughter of a Potawatomi leader, and they had twelve or thirteen children.

Vieau was one of about two hundred white people who lived in Wisconsin in the 1820s. Many of the men involved in the fur trade married American Indian women who lived in the area. **Voyageurs** also traveled in the area. Voyageurs worked for fur companies and transported goods and passengers between the trading posts by boat. It was hard work. They woke up before dawn. They typically paddled fourteen hours per day in canoes that were almost forty feet long and carried eight men. Each man was expected to carry at least two bales of fur (about 160 to 180 pounds) when moving overland from one body of water to another. For meals, they often only had pea soup or corn chowder, lard, and bannock, a type of bread. They would turn over their canoes and sleep under them at night.

Solomon Juneau was Milwaukee's most famous voyageur. Like Mirandeau and Vieau, Juneau was French Canadian. An imposing figure, Juneau was at least six feet tall with the body of a wrestler and eyes that "seemed to pierce your very soul," according to one observer. In 1817, he left Montreal and arrived in Prairie du Chien, a city in southwestern Wisconsin. There, he worked for the Hudson's Bay Company, a Canadian fur-trading company. He moved to Milwaukee the following year and got a job as Vieau's clerk. Juneau also started to court Vieau's daughter Josette. They married in 1821. He was twenty-seven years old, and she was seventeen. (At that time, that kind of age difference was common in married couples.) Milwaukee was so small that it did not yet have a priest, so the couple traveled to Green Bay in a canoe for their wedding ceremony.

Solomon Juneau | *WHI Image ID 47831*

When Solomon and Josette Juneau returned to Milwaukee, they moved into their own trading post. It was at what is now the corner of Water Street and Wisconsin Avenue.

Illustration of the Juneau fur-trading post at Milwaukee in 1833 | *WHI Image ID 4714*

Solomon's first language was French. During the 1820s, he learned the Potawatomi and Menominee languages. He also started to practice English in 1831 so he could become a US citizen. Josette spoke several Native languages as well as French. She sometimes served as an interpreter. She played a role in building relationships between the French Canadian settlers and the local American Indian communities. For these reasons, she is known as the "founding mother of Milwaukee." Solomon and Josette Juneau had at least thirteen children who survived infancy. Some of their children attended boarding schools in Green Bay and Detroit.

Milwaukee's fur traders fell on hard times in the 1830s. The fur trade had greatly reduced the beaver population, which meant there were fewer furs to sell. Then both Native and non-Native Milwaukee residents experienced a food shortage and a smallpox epidemic during the winter of 1831–1832. The Juneaus' children and Josette's father were infected with the disease. They survived, but eighty-five American Indians living in Milwaukee did not. The deaths included twenty-five hunters, which then contributed to the food shortage.

Josette Juneau
| *WHI Image ID 163908*

This painting of Black Hawk by Robert M. Sully shows the Sauk leader wearing European clothing. Other images of Black Hawk show him in traditional Sauk clothing. | *WHI Image ID 11706*

Forced Movements of Native Peoples

Disease and food shortages were not the only threats that American Indians in Milwaukee faced during the early 1800s. They also had to deal with colonists who wanted the American Indians to leave so they could transform Native lands into farms. American Indians resisted, but most were ultimately forced to give up their land.

The Sauk and Meskwaki were among the first peoples to **cede**, or give up, land in what is now Wisconsin. Members of those nations signed a treaty with the US government in 1804 that resulted in a loss of more than 50 million acres of tribal lands in Wisconsin, Illinois, and Missouri.

The push to remove American Indians from land colonists wanted grew stronger starting in 1825. The Erie Canal opened in New York state that year. The canal made it easier to travel from the East Coast to the Great Lakes. This led to a flood of white settlers arriving in Wisconsin. They demanded more of the American Indians' land. In 1825, the US government convened leaders from all the Native nations in the Great Lakes region. Leaders from the Dakota, Ho-Chunk, Iowa, Menominee, Meskwaki, Ottawa, Ojibwe, Potawatomi, and Sauk nations gathered in Prairie du Chien. The purpose of the conference was to draw up borders for each nation in Wisconsin, Illinois, Iowa, and Minnesota. After the boundaries were established, government representatives could negotiate treaties for each Native nation to give up land to the US government. But these treaties didn't convince all of the Native peoples to leave.

Many American Indian nations resisted being removed. In 1832, Black Hawk, a Sauk leader, led a group of about one thousand American Indians from the Sauk, Meskwaki, Ho-Chunk, and Potawatomi nations back to their ancestral lands. White settlers organized a militia force of about seven thousand, who killed more than half of the Native people, many of whom were women, children, and elders who were unable to defend themselves. The survivors were forced to move west.

Some of Milwaukee's American Indian residents considered attacking white settlements in the summer of 1835, when most of the white men were in Green Bay on business matters. Josette Juneau stayed on guard duty on the night of the proposed attack, walking up and down Water Street. The warriors abandoned their plan. Most American Indians in Milwaukee gave in to the US government and colonists and left the area.

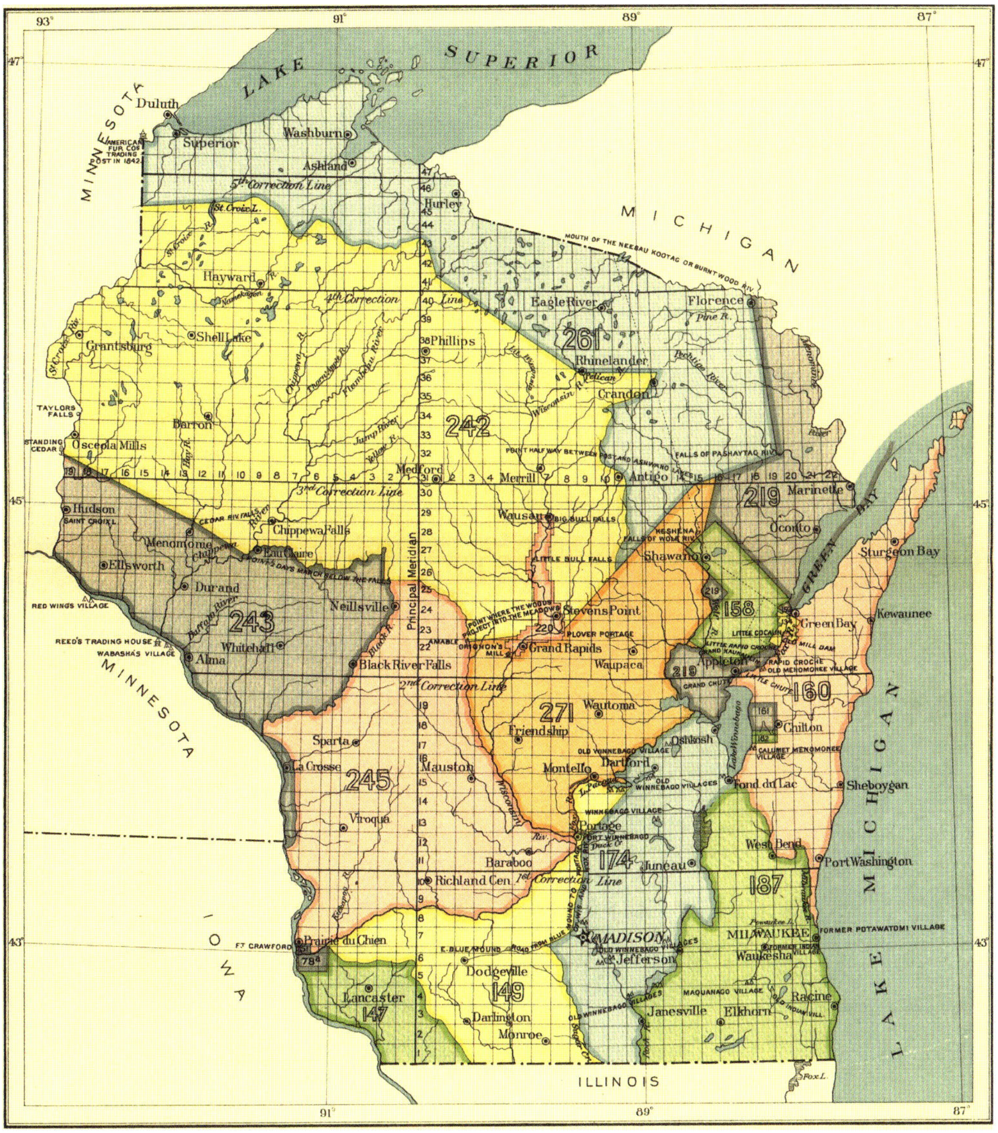

In 1829, the Menominee ceded the land in the pink area to the US. The Ojibwe, Ottawa, and Potawatomi ceded the land in green to the US in 1832. | *Law Library of Congress 13023487*

In 1833, the Ojibwe, Ottawa, and Potawatomi traded five million acres of land east of the Mississippi for five million acres west of the Mississippi. The federal government gave them three years to move. When they did not move, the government forced them to walk to Iowa and Missouri, a journey that took more than a month. Many people died on the way, and the journey would later be called the Trail of Death. White settlers, with the support of the US government, eventually pushed most of the survivors farther west to Kansas. Meanwhile, at least two thousand Potawatomi people moved to northern Wisconsin until white settlers encroached on that part of the state. They then left for the Upper Peninsula of Michigan and Ontario. Other Potawatomi people managed to stay in the Milwaukee area. They continued to trade with the white settlers. Their population in Milwaukee would dwindle until the 1930s, when more Potawatomi people began making their home again in the city.

The Wisconsin Territory

The Wisconsin Territory took shape during the 1830s. According to the original plans, its southern boundary was supposed to be in Illinois. It was also supposed to include the western two-thirds of the Upper Peninsula of Michigan and part of Minnesota. Over time, the Wisconsin Territory lost pieces of land to surrounding states.

The United States was a collection of thirteen semi-independent states from 1781 until 1789. The new nation was governed by the Articles of Confederation, the country's first constitution. Congress had very little power under the articles. However, it successfully passed the Northwest Ordinance in 1787. The ordinance created the Northwest Territory and declared it would be divided into three

THE CHANGING NORTHWEST TERRITORY, 1800–1858

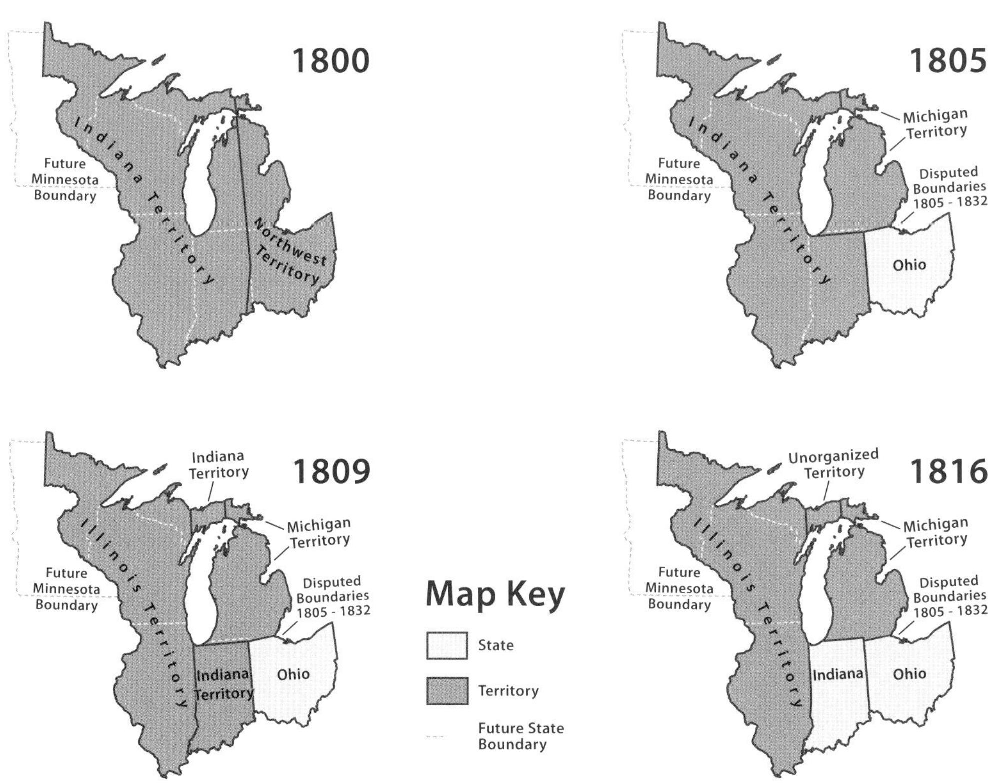

to five states. The ordinance specified that a line should be drawn from Lake Erie to Lake Michigan's southern tip. Two states would be created north of that line, and three would be south of the line.

But the mapmakers did not know exactly where the southernmost tip of Lake Michigan was. Therefore, when Ohio became a state in 1803, its northern border was too far north. It was eight miles too far north on its east end and five miles too far north on its west end. The disputed area became known as the Toledo Strip. By the 1830s, the European and American settlers of Michigan and Ohio engaged in an armed conflict over the Toledo Strip. Congress intervened and gave Michigan the entire Upper Peninsula. Michigan leaders agreed to drop their demands on Ohio. The Upper Peninsula was considered a wasteland at the time. Later, rich supplies of iron, copper, and other ores were discovered there.

Meanwhile, the Europeans and Americans who had settled in Indiana and Illinois asked for and received borders north of the ordinance line. In Illinois's case, the border was adjusted by thirty-one

Map by Colter Sikora

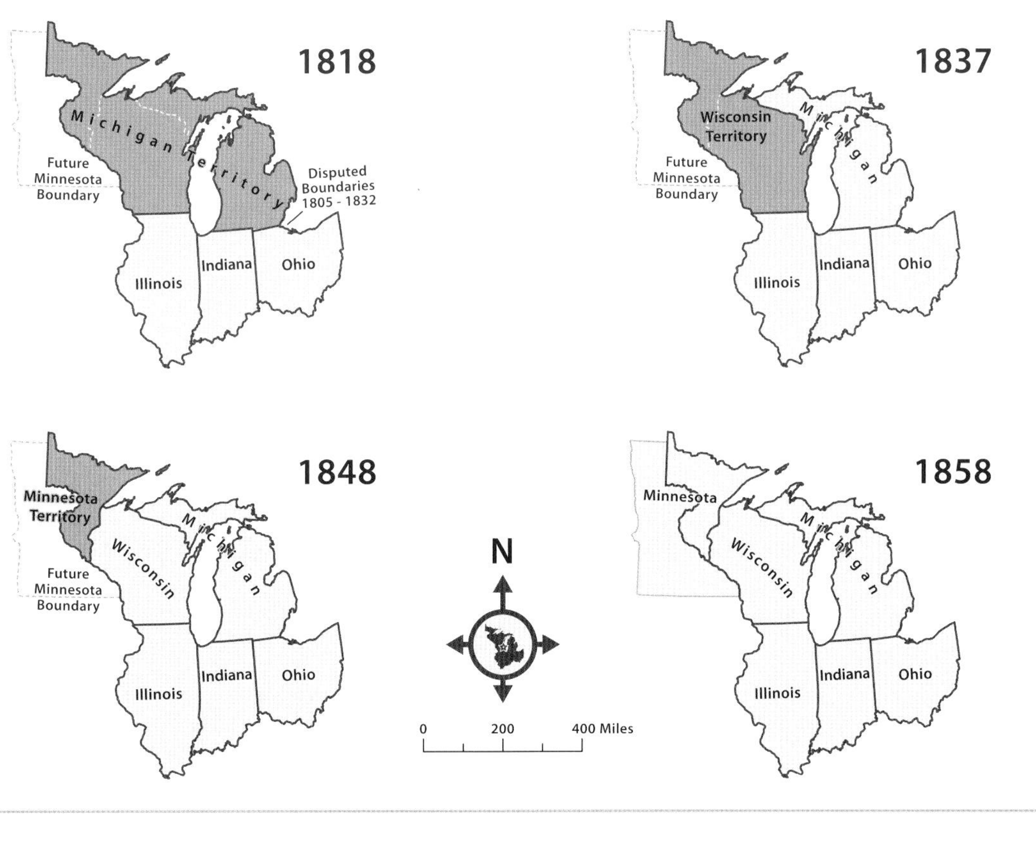

miles. Illinois leaders wanted to develop a port at Chicago to connect Illinois to businesses in New York and New England.

Thus the Wisconsin Territory had lost its southern border and the city of Chicago to Illinois as well as the Upper Peninsula to Michigan. European and American settlers wanted to hold on to whatever was left. They claimed that the Mississippi River should be Wisconsin's western border. That way, the Wisconsin Territory would have included the northeastern corner of Minnesota, called the Arrowhead region because of its pointed shape. But the lumberjacks and fur traders of the Arrowhead saw themselves as different from the farmers and lead miners of Wisconsin. The proposed capital, Madison, was far from them. They feared the state government would neglect them. Additionally, some congressmen worried that the Arrowhead would give Wisconsin an odd shape.

Some northern congressmen wanted to draw Wisconsin's northwestern border east of the Chippewa River. That proposed border would have left Wisconsin without its present-day northwest corner. The congressmen hoped they could combine that area with part of Minnesota to create an additional northern state. Thus, the north would have two extra votes in the United States Senate, since every state had two senators. Those two extra votes could have been crucial in settling disputes about slavery.

As they did with Michigan, members of Congress reached a compromise. They approved a border that went from the westernmost point of Lake Superior down the St. Louis River to "the first rapids in the same, above the Indian village." It then went south to the St. Croix River. The border follows the St. Croix River all the way to the Mississippi River. This boundary was set in 1846. Two years later, in 1848, Wisconsin became a state.

City Founders

As the Wisconsin Territory developed during the 1830s, so did Milwaukee. By 1833, Milwaukee's residents had changed from a group of interconnected American Indian communities to a mixed Native and French settlement. Within thirteen years, other Europeans had settled in Milwaukee. With the help of the US government through military campaigns, the Europeans pushed American Indians out and founded three rival villages that eventually merged into a single city.

Milwaukee was ripe for growth after the opening of the Erie Canal in 1825. Milwaukee had the largest bay of any nearby city, including Chicago, Kenosha, Racine, and Port Washington. The Milwaukee River was also deeper than the rivers at any of the other communities on Lake Michigan. The bay and the river meant Milwaukee could easily float the largest ships on the Great Lakes. Four men—Solomon Juneau, Morgan Martin, Byron Kilbourn, and George Walker—recognized the area's advantages and put into motion their separate visions for Milwaukee's future.

Solomon Juneau, the former voyageur, founded a settlement called the Town of Milwaukee in 1818. Residents nicknamed it "Juneau-town." By the 1830s, the fur supply had dwindled, and Juneau needed another form of income. In 1833, he sold half his land to Morgan Martin, a lawyer originally from New York state. Martin was only twenty-eight, but he had become very successful at buying and selling land. By 1835, the two men and Juneau's brother, Pierre, were in the real estate business. They bought and sold hundreds of acres of land in what is now downtown Milwaukee and the Third Ward.

Solomon Juneau built the first log cabin in Milwaukee and later replaced it with this two-story house on East Michigan Street. | *WHI Image ID 43571*

In 1835, the governor of Wisconsin Territory, James Doty, appointed Juneau as Milwaukee's first postmaster. This meant Juneau was the head of the area's post office. Juneau and Martin built Milwaukee County's courthouse in 1836 in what is now Cathedral Square. They also built a four-story hotel, called the Bellevue House, at the corner of Wisconsin Avenue and Broadway in 1836. They started improving the streets that same year, when Juneau hired Nelson Olin to flatten Wisconsin Avenue from the river to the lake. Martin estimated that he and Juneau spent $100,000 on improvements around town, which would be about $1.5 million today.

Juneautown was soon a **boomtown** with more than a thousand white residents. Many of the settlers were Yankees, people of British descent who migrated from New York, New England, and

Pennsylvania and practiced Protestant religions. Most of the French and French Canadian settlers were Catholic. They celebrated their first mass at Solomon Juneau's house in 1835. Construction of St. Peter's Catholic Church was completed four years later.

In 1836, the Wisconsin Territory organized the county of Milwaukee. Juneautown became part of Milwaukee County. Morgan Martin left Milwaukee after 1837. Solomon and Josette Juneau continued doing business with new settlers on their own. Solomon sold them lumber to build their homes and supplies to fill those homes. Josette worked as hostess, midwife, and nurse for women in the community. By 1835, she also had eight children to raise, with more to come.

Byron Kilbourn | *WHI Image ID 9486*

In 1834, Byron Kilbourn arrived in Milwaukee to conduct a land survey. Kilbourn was a Yankee. He was born in Connecticut but raised in Ohio. He liked Milwaukee and decided to stay. The residents of Juneautown already occupied the east bank of the Milwaukee River, so Kilbourn chose a piece of land on the west side of the river. There, he built a house for his wife, Henrietta, and two young daughters near what is now Third Street and Juneau Avenue. He had no right to claim that land, which was legally owned by local Native peoples. But the US government sold him the land anyway for $1.25 per acre. Kilbourn named his community "Town of Milwaukee on the West Side of the River." This village was commonly referred to as "Kilbourntown."

Kilbourn tried to improve the part of town he had founded. He built a land office, a general store, a warehouse, and a hotel. He also began to plan streets and bridges. In 1836, he asked engineer and land surveyor Increase Lapham to come to Milwaukee to conduct a land survey. Lapham's work included drawing a map of the area and listing its physical features. Within two years, Lapham had cataloged every plant and shell in the Milwaukee area. Lapham also documented the locations of American Indian mounds (*see page* 4) and studied meteorites, the tides of Lake Michigan, and weather patterns.

The residents of Juneautown and Kilbourntown never got along with one another. Each felt the others had no right to be there. Juneau and Kilbourn competed fiercely for land sales. Kilbourn's map of Milwaukee was completely blank on the east side of the river, where Juneautown was located. He wanted new settlers to think

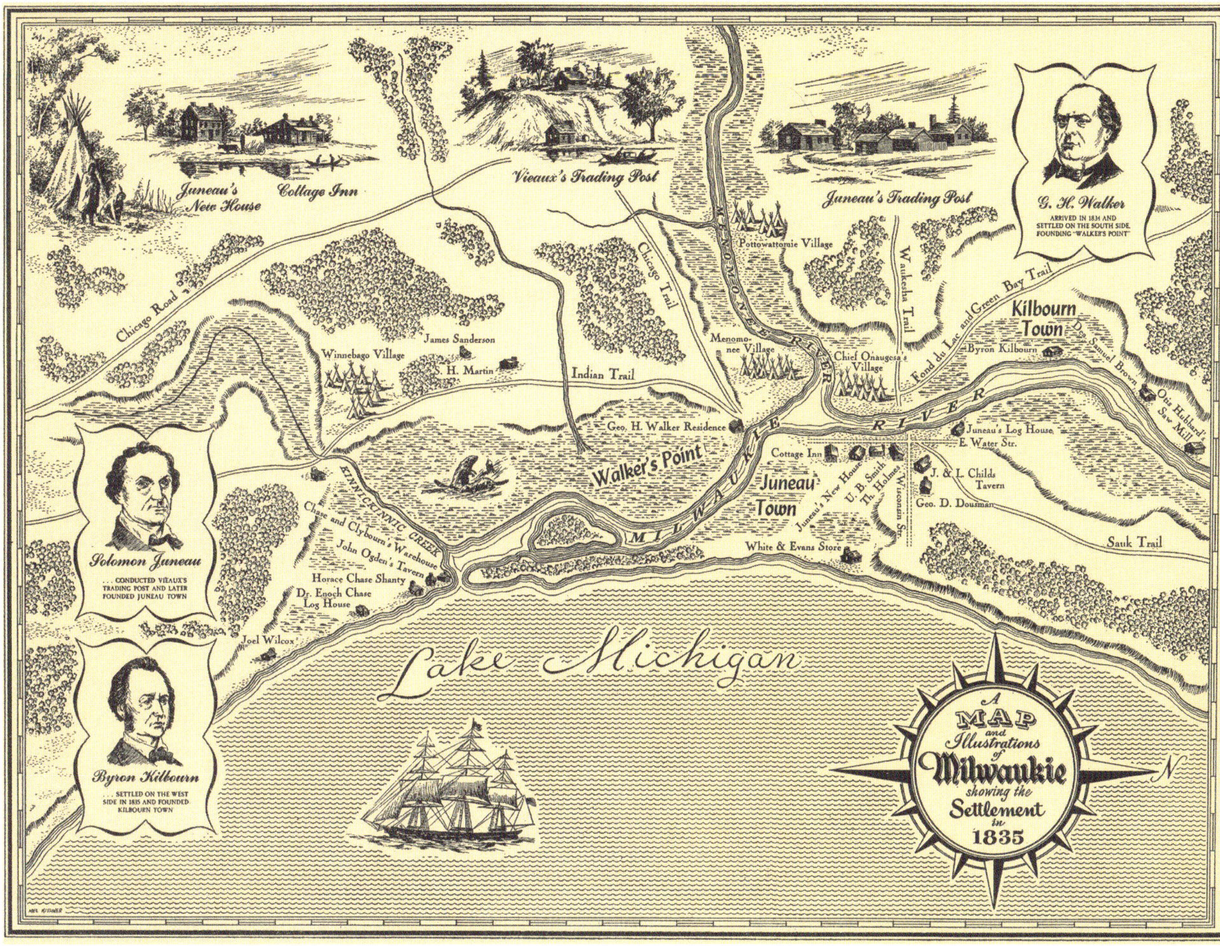

This map of Milwaukee drawn in the 1900s shows Walker's Point, Juneautown, and Kilbourntown, including buildings, trails, and American Indian villages.
| WHI Image ID 98810

that no one lived there and that Juneau had no land for sale. If either Juneau or Kilbourn made an offer to an individual, the other often followed with a more attractive offer.

Colonel George Walker can be considered another founder of the developing city. Known for his jolly personality, he was said to be an excellent dancer and ice skater. Walker was originally from Virginia and later lived in Illinois. In 1834, he settled south of the meeting of the Menomonee and Milwaukee Rivers, near Lake Michigan. This area became known (and is still known today) as Walker's Point.

Walker's Point should have been an ideal location for a village, but Walker had a lot of problems. He was much younger than Solomon Juneau and Byron Kilbourn. He lacked the experience, powerful friends, and relationships with investors that the older men had. He also made several bad business deals, buying land for more than it was worth and selling it for little profit. Worse yet, he claimed the land illegally. It was still the property of local Native peoples. The US government found out and invalidated Walker's sales. After that, few people wanted to take a chance on settling in Walker's Point.

Early Businesses

Life in early Milwaukee was hard. Summers were hot and humid. Winters were cold and snowy. Downtown, where most people lived, was a swamp. People had to live primarily off the land. However, Milwaukee did have some taverns and hotels, and a few consumer goods were sold at trading posts.

Taverns and brewing companies were some of the community's first businesses. Jacques Vieau Jr. opened Milwaukee's first tavern in 1835 at what is now the corner of Water and Clybourn Streets. He called it the Triangle Inn and hammered on a large iron triangle to call patrons to meals. Milwaukeeans also got a second tavern, the Shanty Inn, at the present-day site of the Milwaukee County Historical Society. It had a dirt floor in the back half of the barroom and lasted only a few years.

Hotels were another growing business in Milwaukee. Caleb Wall came to Milwaukee from Springfield, Illinois, in 1842. He wanted to start a "**temperance** hotel," where alcohol was not served. He purchased the Milwaukee House (formerly Juneau's and Martin's Bellevue House). He banned alcohol and locked the door at ten o'clock every night to discourage guests from leaving to go drinking. Guests snuck out through the windows, and Wall realized his plan was hopeless. Therefore, he opened a bar, hired a two-piece band, and promoted his hotel as the center of Milwaukee's growing social scene.

Real estate was a third important economic sector. Uriel Smith was an early real estate developer in the city. He arrived in Milwaukee in 1835. He and his wife, Lucy, spent their first few months living in a tent near Bay and Beecher Streets in what is now Bay View. Smith started out as a tailor. He quickly sold all the cloth he had brought from the east and started buying blanket cloth made by American Indians from Juneau's trading post. He sewed the cloth into men's overcoats and men's and women's pantaloons. Lucy died around 1837. Smith stayed until 1850, then went to California during the gold rush with his second wife. He returned one year later and opened a real estate office in Walker's Point. In 1868, he bought a significant amount of land south of Lincoln Avenue in Bay View. He divided the land into lots, which he sold to other settlers so they could build homes. Leaders of St. Augustine of Hippo Catholic Church

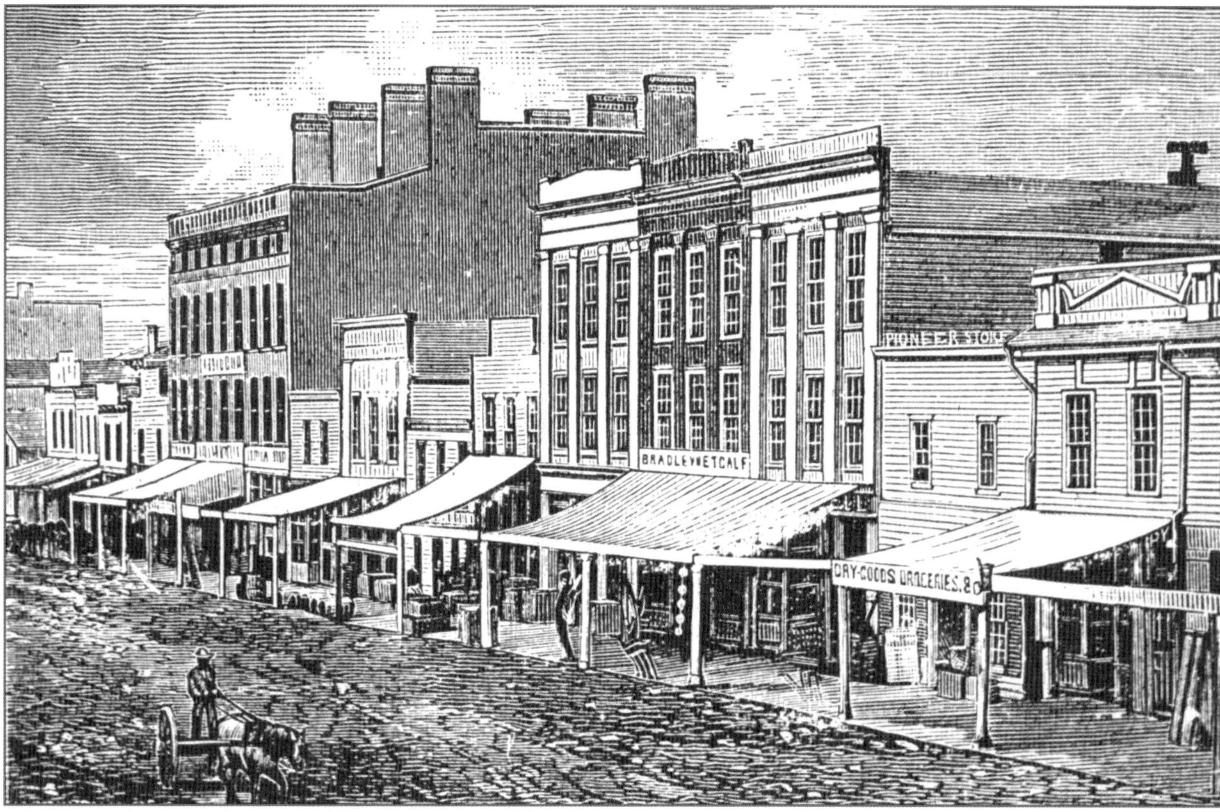

This illustration shows a row of businesses along East Water Street in 1844, including one selling dry goods and groceries. | *WHI Image ID 5226*

purchased nine of Smith's lots in 1889. Smith built a home for his family in 1890 at 2418 S. Howell Avenue. It still stands today.

Consumer goods were another important part of the city's growing economy. As more and more people came to the city to live and work, people brought in more products for sale. Some set up trading posts. Beginning in 1836, residents could buy milk for twenty cents per quart and potatoes for between $3.50 and $6.00 per bushel. Other entrepreneurs made goods for sale. For example, Miss S. E. Chamberlain opened a dressmaking shop in 1837. Along with dresses, she sold stockings, ribbons, cosmetics, and artificial flowers.

The Bridge War

For five years, the villages of Juneautown, Kilbourntown, and Walker's Point remained separate. But maintaining separate local governments was expensive, so the territorial government merged Juneautown and Kilbourntown into a single village in 1839. Walker's Point was added in 1845. The new community was divided into five wards. The First Ward was east of the Milwaukee River (Juneautown). The Second and Fourth

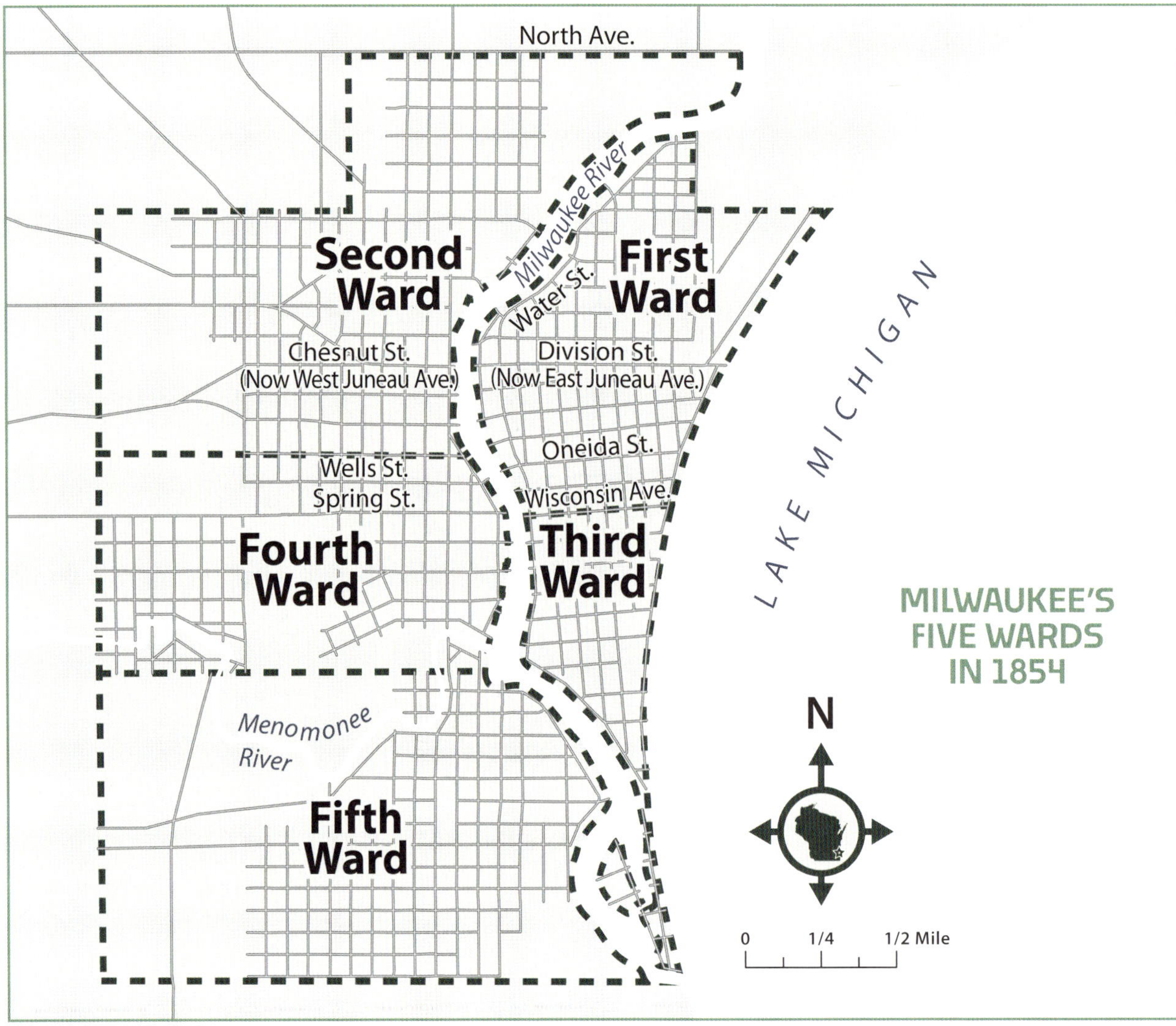

Map by Colter Sikora

Wards were west of the Milwaukee River (Kilbourntown). The Third and Fifth Wards were south of what is now downtown. However, their union did not put an end to the original villages' rivalries. Each ward still competed for residents, and they were still physically separated by the rivers. **Ordinances** varied from ward to ward. Each ward had taxing and spending powers. These differences led to a conflict that has become known as the Bridge War.

Roads did not line up across the east and west banks of the rivers. Therefore, it was hard to build bridges. Byron Kilbourn was happy about the situation. The Chicago Road led straight into Kilbourntown. Therefore, when people came north on the road, they stopped in his town first. They purchased land from him because they could not cross the Milwaukee River to Juneautown. Nonetheless, Juneautown still held the bulk of Milwaukee's population, since it was much older. In 1840, leaders of Juneautown convinced the territorial legislature to authorize bridge construction. Construction took four years, in part because the people of Kilbourntown refused to contribute their share of the money. Finally, Milwaukee County stepped in and built a bridge at an angle to connect Chesnut and Division Streets. The county had built three other bridges by 1844. One connected Spring Street to Wisconsin Avenue. Another spanned Wells Street to Oneida Street. The fourth bridge connected Juneautown to Walker's Point.

The conflict continued in the spring of 1845. A **schooner** rammed into the Spring-Wisconsin bridge, and the western end of the bridge sank. The residents of Kilbourntown thought Walker's Point residents had paid the schooner's captain to damage the bridge. They armed themselves with axes and crowbars one night and destroyed the west end of the Chesnut Bridge. They were preparing to move on to Wells Street when the alarm rang out in Juneautown. The east siders took up rifles and shotguns. They also wheeled out the village's only cannon and pointed it at Byron Kilbourn's house. They had no cannon balls, but a jeweler donated some clock weights. However, Jonathan Arnold, a prominent resident of Juneautown, talked the angry mob into going home. He pointed out that Kilbourn's daughter had died the night before and that her body was still in the house. Shelling the home with ammunition would have been disrespectful.

While cooler heads prevailed that night, the conflict wasn't over. Within a few weeks, an angry mob from Juneautown tore down their end of the one remaining Milwaukee River bridge. They also destroyed the bridge to Walker's Point for good measure. The next year, city leaders got the territorial legislature's approval to improve and rebuild several bridges. The Bridge War ended without any lives lost, although a few people were seriously injured, and there is still physical evidence of the old rivalries. Anyone who has driven through downtown Milwaukee knows that the streets still do not line up and some bridges were built on angles.

Despite the conflicts and clashes that arose among Milwaukee's residents in the first half of the 1800s, the village drafted a city charter in December 1845. It was approved by the territorial legislature on January 31, 1846, two years before Wisconsin became a state. Becoming a city improved the community's status. It helped attract more businesses and residents. It also meant that local government could provide more services to the people.

Primary Sources

First Impressions

Some of Milwaukee's earliest white residents recorded their observations in letters, journals, newspapers, and other publications. From these documents, we can learn about life in Milwaukee as the city began to take shape. Read the following letter, poem, and newspaper excerpt and then answer the questions that follow.

LETTER, 1835

Green Bay, August 30, 1835

Friend Kimball:

The land about Milwaukee is the best in the Territory, and as Milwaukee is the only harbor for some distance, either way on the lake, it must of necessity become a place of great importance. It is now laid out in lots, for two miles north and south, and one and a half miles east and west, which lots will, I think, sell immediately for from $100 to $1000, and much money has been made, speculating in lots already.

I think money can be made here in the lumbering business, if one had capital, as all kinds of lumber sell readily, and for high figures. The winter is the same here, as in New England, or nearly the same.

The settlers will all get their claims for $1.25 per acre, as it is considered very mean to bid against them; some of them have already sold their claims at high figures, in one case, for $8,000. I have also entered a few lots of land at ten shillings per acre.

There is a mill at the mouth of the Menomonee, owned by Farnsworth & Brush, which they wish to sell, together with a large quantity of pine land of the best quality, for $40,000; have been offered $30,000. But I must close this letter, as the mail is about leaving.

Respectfully yours,
D. Wells, Sr.

Source: James S. Buck, *Pioneer History of Milwaukee: From the First American Settlement in 1833, to 1841, with a Topographical Description as It Appeared in the State of Nature, Illustrated, with a Map* (Milwaukee: Milwaukee News Company, 1876).

POEM, CIRCA 1876

The white man came with pick and spade,
And soon our hills were brought to grade;
  Those hills, so round and pretty—
Our river front was lined with docks,
Canals were built, with gates and locks,
And soon we had a city.

Source: James S. Buck, *Pioneer History of Milwaukee*.

EXCERPT FROM THE *MILWAUKEE ADVERTISER*, 1836

It is called by the Indians, the Beautiful Land, and, by the early French, "La Belle Terre." The river is the largest upon the western shore of the lake, joining with the Menomonee two miles above its mouth, and although nothing has as yet been done to improve its harbor, the largest vessels can enter the river, and have, at different times, discharged their cargoes at the various wharves in the city, and when a harbor is built, it will be one of the safest on the Lake.

A year ago, Milwaukee had no existence, the land being owned by the government; but there are now from five to six hundred inhabitants. A year ago, there was not a frame building in the place. Now there are from fifty to sixty finished, and double that number would have been built if material could have been procured.

Clay, of the finest quality for brick, has been found in great abundance, along the Menomonee and Milwaukee rivers, from which a kiln has been burnt. Lime is also abundant.

Success to La Belle Terre, soon to become La Belle City.

Source: James S. Buck, *Pioneer History of Milwaukee.*

- **According to the letter from D. Wells Sr., what were two sure ways of making money in Milwaukee during this period?**
- **How does the poem show positive change in Milwaukee? How might it show negative change?**
- **According to the newspaper excerpt, how was Milwaukee's economy changing? How was its population changing?**
- **How might the newspaper excerpt represent a biased perspective? Whose point of view is dominant, and whose is left out? What specific language in the excerpt illustrates this?**
- **What do these documents tell you about Milwaukee in the 1830s? What do you think it would have been like to live there during that time?**

CHAPTER 3

CHAPTER QUESTIONS

- Why did early immigrants and migrants leave their homes? Why did they choose Milwaukee?
- How have schools and other city services changed since the 1800s?
- How was Milwaukee connected to the rest of the state and the country?
- Who held power in early Milwaukee, and why?
- How did the Civil War affect Milwaukee's residents?

A New City
1845–1865

Milwaukee was still a small frontier town when it officially became a city in 1846. Within twenty years, it became an important American city as its population grew from 10,000 in 1846 to 71,440 in 1870. By 1860, it was the twentieth-largest city in the United States. (It was bigger than Cleveland but smaller than Detroit.) City government began to provide services such as schools, sanitation, and police. During these decades, Milwaukee connected to the rest of the United States by trading goods and sending soldiers to fight in the Civil War.

An 1853 bird's-eye-view map of Milwaukee looking east toward Lake Michigan at about Sixth Street between Wisconsin Avenue and Michigan Street | *WHI Image ID 6554*

A City of Immigrants

In the mid-1800s, most new Milwaukee residents were European immigrants. Nearly two-thirds of these early immigrants were German. The first Germans arrived in the late 1830s, and thousands more came in the 1840s. They left Europe to escape crop failures, unemployment, and political unrest. They read letters from relatives and friends who lived in Milwaukee. The letters described Milwaukee as a great place to make a living. Most of the Germans who moved to Wisconsin were skilled workers such as carpenters, masons, painters, shoemakers, smiths, or tailors. Others were farmers with dreams of someday buying land to farm. Most of them settled north and west of the original Kilbourntown. Milwaukee was soon the most German city in the United States.

A painting of one of Milwaukee's first houses. It was built near the Milwaukee River. The owner of the house, Mathias Stein, moved to the region in the late 1830s. | *WHI Image ID 28083*

Beginning in 1845, large numbers of Irish immigrants arrived. Most left home because of the Irish Potato Famine, a time when many people in Ireland were starving due to failed potato crops and political strife. Most of the Irish settled in the Third Ward, a swampy area south of downtown. They frequently took jobs that involved hard physical work. They dug canals, filled in swampland, flattened streets, laid railroad tracks, and worked as servants in homes. These jobs paid less than the skilled jobs many Germans had. The Irish wanted better jobs, but many did not have the right training. Additionally, some employers were prejudiced and refused to hire Irish workers.

Smaller numbers of northern European immigrants came from Britain, Holland, Norway, Sweden, and Denmark. Central Europeans, including Bohemians (Czechs), Austrians, Poles, and Swiss, also came to Milwaukee. So did Slavs and Jews from eastern Europe. Although Milwaukee was becoming a diverse city, for the most part each new group settled in its own neighborhood.

By 1850, almost one hundred Black Americans had settled in Milwaukee. Some were formerly enslaved people who moved north in search of opportunities. In Milwaukee they took up various

History in Focus

Population Growth

Approximate Population of Selected US Cities			
	1850	**1860**	**1870**
Boston	137,000	178,000	251,000
Chicago	30,000	109,000	299,000
Milwaukee	20,000	45,000	71,000
New York	696,000	1,175,000	1,478,000

Source: "U.S. Population History from 1850," *Demographia*, accessed June 26, 2022, http://www.demographia.com/db-uscity1850.htm

This chart shows the approximate population of Milwaukee and other large US cities from 1850 to 1870. How did Milwaukee compare to the other cities shown? When did Milwaukee's population grow the most?

professions. Records show that early Black Milwaukee residents included fourteen barbers, seven cooks, six whitewashers, three masons, and one farmer. Ezekiel Gillespie, a formerly enslaved man who moved to Milwaukee from Tennessee, opened a produce shop in 1852 at the corner of Mason and Main Streets. (Gillespie would later become well known for winning an important court case that gave Black men the right to vote in Wisconsin.)

Most of the first white settlers in Milwaukee were Yankees who had moved to Milwaukee from Pennsylvania, New York, and New England. Yankees spoke English and belonged to Protestant churches. Most lived in the Yankee Hill neighborhood just north of downtown. Many Yankees did not like immigrants from other countries because they saw the immigrants as different from them. European immigrants spoke a variety of languages, and many were Catholic. Some immigrant groups drank more alcohol than the Yankees did. They even drank on Sundays. Germans built beer gardens that Yankees criticized for encouraging drinking and gambling.

Milwaukee had a strong temperance movement. People in favor of temperance wanted to limit or ban the drinking of alcohol. John B. Smith, a state senator from Milwaukee, voted for the state legislature to ban the sale of alcohol on Sundays. German and Irish immigrants learned of the proposal, formed a mob, and started a bonfire at Milwaukee's city hall. Some men went to Smith's house with rocks and clubs. One threw a rock through his window. Smith was not home, so some of the men went inside, smashed his lamps, and poured kerosene over his furniture.

Religious differences also led to violence in the 1850s. One Sunday night, a speaker at a Methodist church gave a lecture on what he saw as the evils of Catholicism. A group of Catholics showed up and threatened him. Catholics and Methodists started tearing up the pews and clubbing one another.

Some residents of the newly chartered city were not religious at all. The Forty-Eighters were German intellectuals who had fled a series of revolutions in 1848. They included professors, students, judges, and journalists. They rejected traditional religious beliefs. Some were atheists. The Forty-Eighters started the Milwaukee Musical Society. It had a one-hundred-voice chorus and an orchestra. The society performed pieces by German composers. Many considered them one of the best choruses in the United States. But the Forty-Eighters ridiculed Catholics. Therefore, Milwaukee's Catholic bishop forbade the Milwaukee Musical Society from performing at St. John's Cathedral.

Mathilde Anneke
| *WHI Image ID 3701*

The Forty-Eighters were also involved in Milwaukee's feminist movement. In 1852, Mathilde Anneke arrived in Milwaukee. In Germany, Mathilde and her husband had published a newspaper about workers' rights. After arriving in Milwaukee, she founded the city's first feminist newspaper, *Frauen Zeitung* (Women's Times). She hired German-speaking women to set the type. Male printers organized to keep the women out of their trade. Due to the men's actions, Anneke published only seven issues. Undeterred, she continued to work with national figures such as Susan B. Anthony and Elizabeth Cady Stanton in their campaign for women's suffrage, or women's right to vote. Like other Forty-Eighters, Anneke also opposed slavery. When the Civil War broke out in 1861, she wrote articles supporting the Union for German publications. After the war, Anneke founded a school for girls in Milwaukee. She ran it until her death in 1884.

Early Government and Services

Milwaukee County in the 1840s consisted of the city of Milwaukee and seven towns. The original city was a little more than seven square miles in 1846. The seven towns existed outside the city of Milwaukee. Towns are a form of government in rural areas. They provide basic levels of public services, including road maintenance and polling places for elections. (Today, towns also provide fire protection.) The county provided towns with law enforcement and schools. Milwaukee County was divided in half along Twenty-Seventh Street. There were four towns in the western half and three in the eastern half.

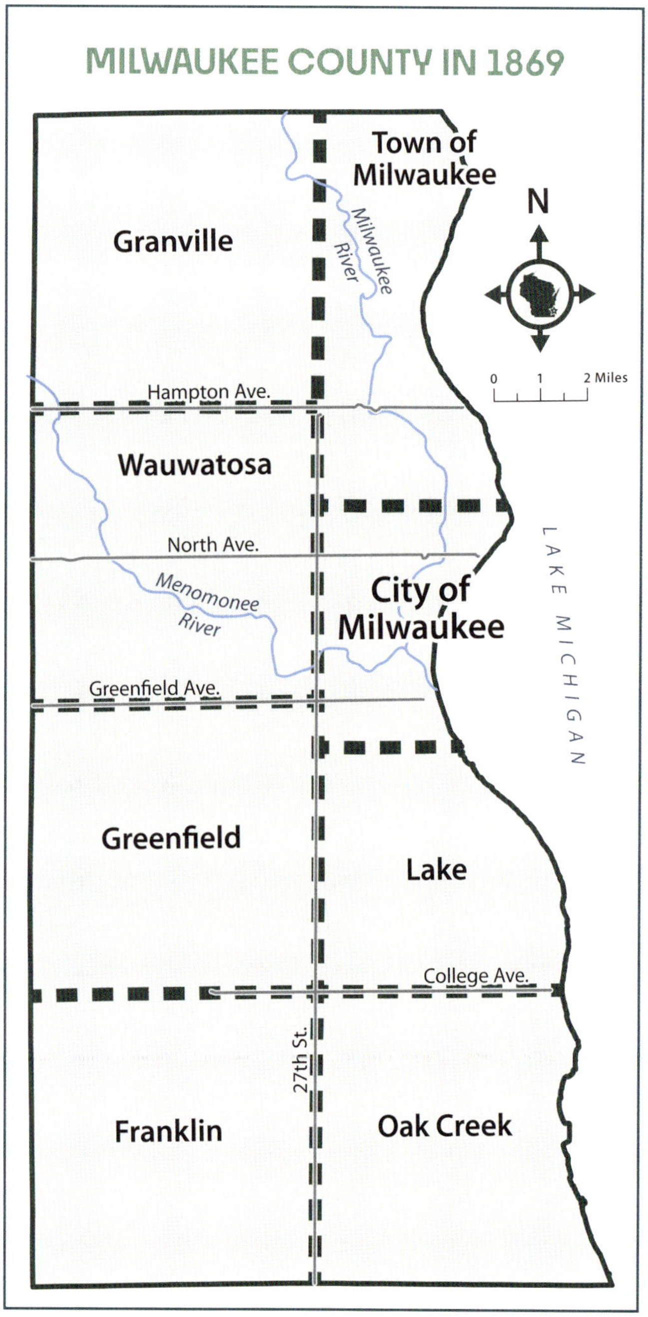

Map by Colter Sikora

The city's two main political parties in the 1840s were the Whigs and the Democrats. By the start of the Civil War in 1861, most of the Whigs had joined the new Republican Party. In general, the Democrats supported workers, while the Whigs advocated for businesses. Most Yankees supported the Whigs. Many immigrant workers liked the Democrats.

At this time, only white men could vote, according to the state constitution passed in 1848. To vote, a man either had to have been born in the United States or declare his intention to become a US citizen. Although Native men had been born in the US, most Native people were not considered US citizens until 1924, and so most Native men were not allowed to vote during this time. The American-born male children of immigrants could vote when they became adults. With so many immigrants living in the city, the Democrats won most of Milwaukee's elections in the 1840s and 1850s.

The Democrats nominated Solomon Juneau for mayor in 1846. He did not want the job. It paid no salary, and he preferred to stay in business instead of politics. But Juneau also wanted what was good for the city, so he reluctantly accepted the nomination. He easily defeated the Whig candidate. Voters also elected a city council that they called the Common Council, which would make decisions for the city along with the mayor. Juneau turned much of his authority over to John B. Smith, a member of the council who was later elected to the state legislature.

Milwaukee did not have a city hall in its early years, so the Common Council moved around a lot. From 1846 until 1847, it met in the basement of the First Methodist Church. Then it moved to a horse stable. The stable caught fire in 1850, and many of the city's records were destroyed. The council could not go back to the church because it had also burned down. (Fires were a big problem at that time because many buildings were made of wood.) After a couple more moves, the Common Council settled into Milwaukee's first city hall in 1861. During these early years, the council established schools, improved sanitation, tried to limit alcohol consumption, and hired a police chief.

Milwaukee did not have any public schools until 1846. Prior to that year, children attended private schools if their families could afford tuition. *Milwaukee Sentinel* editor Rufus King encouraged the Common Council to start public schools. The Common Council appointed a fifteen-member school board in 1846. King was the board president and later became the city's first school superintendent.

Milwaukee had only five public schools at first. The First Ward School was in the basement of St. Peter's Church. Two schools were in old private school buildings, and two were held in the basements of rented houses. Much of the land surrounding Milwaukee was still farmland, and students attended school from June until August before taking a four-week break for harvest time. Then they returned to their lessons from October to early April, when planting began. The school day lasted from 6:00 a.m. until 4:30 p.m. Students had an hour and a half to walk home, eat lunch, and return to school. In the 1800s, most children left school long before graduating so they could start working.

The Common Council did not give the schools much money. The initial annual budget was only $7.61 per student (about $250 in today's money). Nowadays, schools spend more than $10,000 per student each year. Back then, the budget covered rent for the schools, heat by wood or coal, teacher salaries, and a few classroom supplies. Each school had one teacher. The teacher often had more than one hundred students. Teachers covered every subject

This list of rules for Milwaukee public school students was created in 1846. Which of these rules are you expected to follow today? | *WHI Image ID 2205*

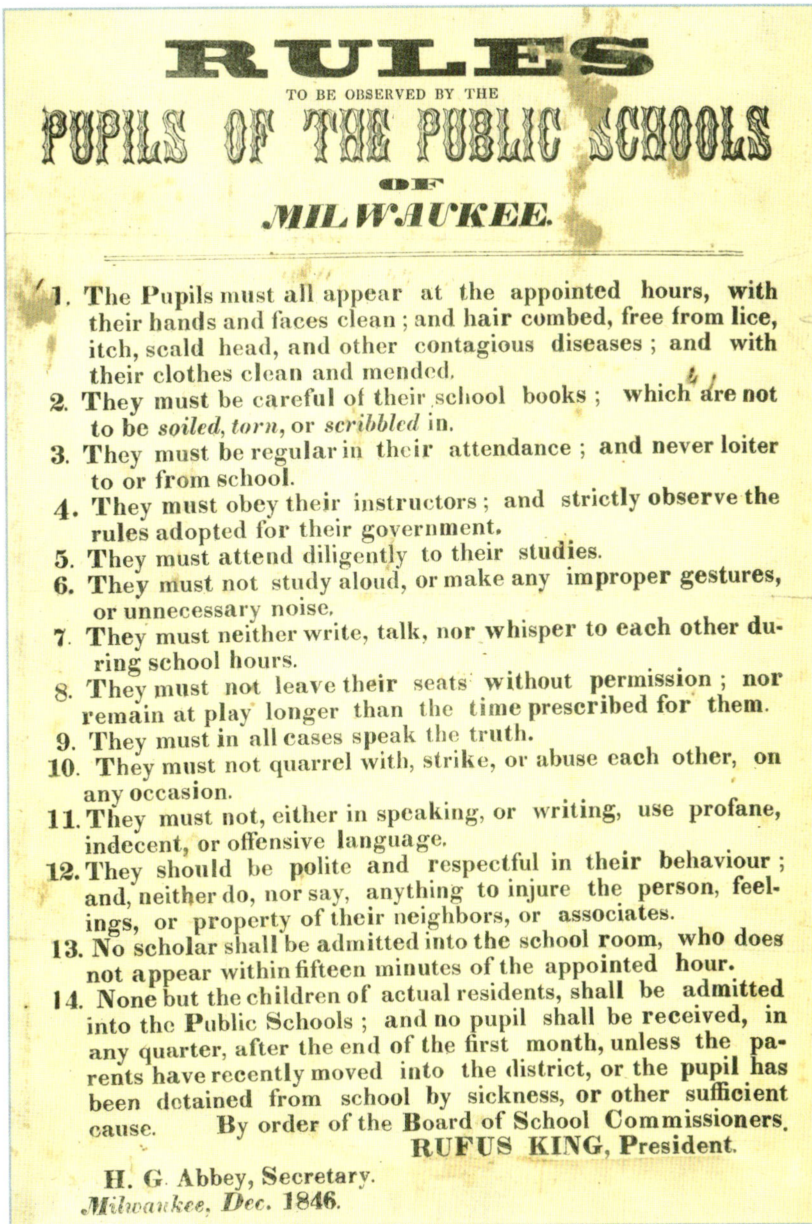

RULES

TO BE OBSERVED BY THE

PUPILS OF THE PUBLIC SCHOOLS

OF

MILWAUKEE.

1. The Pupils must all appear at the appointed hours, with their hands and faces clean; and hair combed, free from lice, itch, scald head, and other contagious diseases; and with their clothes clean and mended.
2. They must be careful of their school books; which are not to be *soiled, torn*, or *scribbled* in.
3. They must be regular in their attendance; and never loiter to or from school.
4. They must obey their instructors; and strictly observe the rules adopted for their government.
5. They must attend diligently to their studies.
6. They must not study aloud, or make any improper gestures, or unnecessary noise.
7. They must neither write, talk, nor whisper to each other during school hours.
8. They must not leave their seats without permission; nor remain at play longer than the time prescribed for them.
9. They must in all cases speak the truth.
10. They must not quarrel with, strike, or abuse each other, on any occasion.
11. They must not, either in speaking, or writing, use profane, indecent, or offensive language.
12. They should be polite and respectful in their behaviour; and, neither do, nor say, anything to injure the person, feelings, or property of their neighbors, or associates.
13. No scholar shall be admitted into the school room, who does not appear within fifteen minutes of the appointed hour.
14. None but the children of actual residents, shall be admitted into the Public Schools; and no pupil shall be received, in any quarter, after the end of the first month, unless the parents have recently moved into the district, or the pupil has been detained from school by sickness, or other sufficient cause.

By order of the Board of School Commissioners.

RUFUS KING, President.

H. G. Abbey, Secretary.

Milwaukee, Dec. 1846.

and grade. They taught reading, writing, spelling, grammar, arithmetic, history, geography, science, music, and German. Teachers taught students to recite lessons from memory. Discipline was very strict and included corporal punishment. This was physical punishment that usually involved a teacher hitting the student with a cane.

Five permanent school buildings opened in 1851 and 1852. The school board approved three high schools in 1857, but they closed in 1860 due to financial problems. Children could stay in school until age sixteen, but most dropped out sooner to work and help support their families. School attendance was not required.

Lack of funds also made sanitation difficult. All over the city, people threw garbage into their yards for hogs to eat. They emptied chamber pots into the streets. Human and animal waste ran down the road, trickled into the rivers, and infected the drinking water. Milwaukee did not get its first sewer line until 1850. It ran only down Wisconsin Avenue.

The infected water caused cholera outbreaks. (Cholera is a dangerous illness that is caused by drinking water or eating food that contains a certain kind of harmful bacteria.) Milwaukee's first cholera outbreak lasted from 1849 until 1850. Six or seven residents died each day. Burials had to happen quickly. Four or five corpses might be thrown into a cart at a time and rushed off to the burial ground. One day, City Marshal Tim O'Brien arrived at a cemetery and found eighteen bodies waiting for him. In one especially tragic incident, a day or two later he went to help a family and found that the mother and father were dead, and a young child was sick. The older daughter had planned to get married that day.

City workers hauled away a thousand cartloads of solid waste from the streets to try to combat the outbreak. It was about one-fifth of the total. The Common Council was not willing to spend the $3,000 required to clean up the rest. At least three hundred Milwaukeeans died by the time the cholera outbreak ended. The actual number may have been higher. City officials tried to cover up the number of deaths to keep the city from looking bad.

Women played active roles in public health causes. The Sisters of Charity of St. Vincent de Paul founded St. John's Infirmary in 1848. It became St. Mary's Hospital ten years later. They also started the city's first orphanage. In 1857, Dr. Laura J. Ross Wolcott began practicing medicine in Milwaukee. She was the third female physician in the United States. (Even though she was an accomplished doctor, she was denied admission to the Medical Society of Milwaukee County until she married its president.) Milwaukee women also led the temperance movement and helped low-income residents.

Milwaukee got its first police chief in 1855. William Beck had been a police officer in New York. He was also the sheriff department's first detective. As a detective, Beck achieved fame by breaking up a burglary ring. He had tracked the burglars down to the Red Sun saloon and hid under a bed while the men divided their loot. Thus, Beck was the obvious choice for Milwaukee's first police chief.

Wheat, Beer, and Transportation

Milwaukee's early economy was built on two things: wheat and beer. The city government and private businesses developed a transportation network to facilitate the sale of both these goods.

By 1860, two-thirds of county land was owned by farmers. Wheat was the biggest crop. In fact, Wisconsin produced more wheat than all but one other state in 1860. Milwaukee, with its large harbor, shipped wheat all over the world.

Beer was Milwaukee's other chief export. Jacob Best was one of the city's most famous brewers. He opened the Empire Brewery in 1844. His son Philip took over the company in 1860 and renamed it Best and Company. Philip's daughter Maria later married Frederick Pabst, a Great Lakes ship captain. Pabst took over the company in 1865. He was only twenty-nine years old. He renamed the brewery after himself in 1889. Within three years, he was brewing more than one million barrels of beer annually.

Frederick Pabst | *WHI Image ID 60077*

Pabst made a lot of money. He built a resort in Whitefish Bay (a village north of the city) and opened it in 1889. The resort included a hotel, restaurant, band shell, and amusement park. As many as ten thousand people visited the resort each summer in the 1890s. They traveled by horse and buggy, railroad, trolley, or

A photograph of Pabst's Whitefish Bay Resort, around 1914 | *WHI Image ID 47963*

steamship. The resort closed in 1914. By then, the city offered more things to do. People no longer needed to travel to Whitefish Bay to find entertainment. Pabst also built a mansion for his family on Grand Avenue (now Wisconsin Avenue) in the 1890s. No one lives there today, and the house is open for tours. Additionally, Pabst opened the Pabst Theater in 1895 as an opera house. It still holds concerts and other performances.

Pabst was one of four men known as Milwaukee's beer barons. Valentin Blatz, Frederick Miller, and Joseph Schlitz were the other three. All four brought their brewing know-how with them when they immigrated from Germany. Blatz started as foreman at Joseph Braun's Cedar Brewery. After Braun died in 1851, Blatz married Braun's widow, Louise, and bought the company from her for $500. Blatz grew the operation into Blatz Brewing Company. He was the first Milwaukee brewer to put beer in bottles instead of selling it exclusively in barrels.

Frederick Miller arrived in Milwaukee in 1855 with $9,000. He spent $8,000 of that sum buying the Plank Road Brewery from Charles and Lorenz Best, sons of Jacob Best. The brewery was in the Menomonee Valley. The nearby Menomonee River provided water for the brewing of the beer. Miller shipped beer down the river and through the Great Lakes.

Miller opened a boardinghouse next to the brewery for his unmarried male employees so they would not have to walk several miles to and from work each day. Workers woke up at 4:00 a.m. and worked until 6:00 p.m. Miller gave them four meals per day. At breakfast, served at 6:00 a.m., the men were offered meat, potatoes, eggs, bread and butter, and coffee. Lunch was at 9:00 a.m. It included meat, cheese, bread, and pickles. Dinner was at noon. The workers ate soup, a choice of two meats, vegetables, and cake, though the cake was not sweet like it is today. Finally, supper was at 6:00 p.m. It consisted of meat, salad, eggs, tea, and cake.

Joseph Schlitz
| WHI Image ID 46621

Schlitz was the last of the major breweries to be founded, and it became one of the largest. Joseph Schlitz worked as a bookkeeper in August Krug's tavern brewery. After Krug died in 1856, Schlitz took over the business and married Krug's widow, Anna Marie. He changed the name of the brewery to the Jos. Schlitz Brewing Co. In 1871, Schlitz donated thousands of barrels of beer to the people of Chicago after the Great Chicago Fire of 1871 destroyed most of the city's breweries. Schlitz soon became the most popular beer in Chicago. Chicago was the railroad capital of the United States. Schlitz used the city's railroads to expand his business into the rest of the country.

History in Focus

Plank Roads and Railroads

Milwaukee farms and breweries shipped wheat and beer all over the United States and the world. Starting in the 1840s, wagons transported smaller quantities of goods on roads built from wooden planks. The plank roads replaced old wagon trails, which were difficult to drive on when muddy. Watertown Plank Road opened in 1853. It ran fifty-eight miles from Watertown to Milwaukee. It cut transportation time between those cities from three days in wet weather to a day and a half in any weather. The road attracted farmers, peddlers, and settlers. They paid one cent per mile to use the road or two cents if pulling a freight wagon. The company that built the road made as much as $1,300 per week from tolls. Other roads connected Milwaukee to Appleton, Fond du Lac, Green Bay, Lisbon, Janesville, Mukwonago, and Waukesha. Many of these roads are still in use, though the wooden planks were replaced by concrete and asphalt years ago. They were also converted from private to public use.

Railroads transported goods even faster. Byron Kilbourn was elected mayor in 1848 and made railroad construction a priority. By 1850, a two-car train carried fifty passengers from the Menomonee Valley to Wauwatosa in only twelve minutes. The train, named the *Wisconsin*, traveled at the amazing speed of thirty miles per hour. The speed astonished its most famous passenger, city founder Solomon Juneau. The route extended to Waukesha in 1851, where the train was greeted by hundreds of farm families and a brass band. Soon, there were railroads connecting Milwaukee to towns as far west as La Crosse.

Kilbourn was the primary owner of the La Crosse & Milwaukee Railroad. He wanted to expand his business. In 1856, men who worked for him bribed the governor and seventy-two of the state's seventy-eight legislators to give him land. They also paid newspaper editor Rufus King and other local opinion leaders to ignore the bribery. Eventually, the bribery was exposed, and the railroad went bankrupt. Milwaukeeans were angry. Many of them had invested money in Kilbourn's company and had lost their life's savings. Kilbourn eventually left town and later died in Florida.

This drawing was made sometime around 1850. The locomotive pictured ran on the Milwaukee & Mississippi Railroad, which later became part of the Chicago, Milwaukee, & St. Paul Railroad. | *WHI Image ID 25353*

His product became known as "the beer that made Milwaukee famous." In 1875, Schlitz was returning from a trip to Germany when his ship hit a rock and sank near England. He did not survive. Krug's nephews, the Uihleins, assumed control of the brewery.

The Civil War

When Wisconsin became a state in 1848, it entered the Union as a free state. Slavery was never legal in Wisconsin, even when it was a territory. Still, people's opinions about slavery differed throughout the state. Some white citizens supported the owning of slaves in other states. Some were against slavery but did nothing to stop it. Others, called **abolitionists**, fought actively to end slavery in the United States. Milwaukee had a strong abolitionist tradition. The city and nearby areas had abolitionist newspapers, such as the *Waukesha Freeman*. Many of its residents were active in political parties that supported abolition, including the Liberty Party and the Free Soil Party. Many Milwaukeeans campaigned to end slavery.

Politically, Milwaukee was a divided city. Traditionally, Milwaukeeans had voted Democratic. But former Democrats and former Whigs were actively forming a different political party around this time, and the name "Republican Party" was first used in 1854 in nearby Ripon, Wisconsin. Republicans, like many Milwaukeeans, opposed slavery. Milwaukee voted against Abraham Lincoln, a Republican, in the presidential election of 1860, but by only 901 votes.

The US Civil War began in 1861 when Southern states **seceded** from the country over the issue of slavery. When war broke out, recruiters came to Milwaukee to enlist men for the Union army. Enough men volunteered to fill an entire regiment (about one thousand men). Most Americans thought the Civil War would be a quick war. They were wrong. As news about the brutalities of the war spread, the number of volunteer soldiers declined.

Congress implemented a draft in 1862. The draft commissioners placed the names of Wisconsin's 10,888 eligible young men in a wooden box. They blindfolded a boy and told him to pull names out one at a time. A commissioner read the names aloud. Of the 4,537 Wisconsin men drafted that year, 1,662 failed to report. Another 19 deserted, and 988 were discharged for one reason or another. Married men who were older than age thirty-five were exempt, so many men rushed to get married. In 1863, the federal government drafted 4,172 men in Milwaukee County and four surrounding counties. Only 34 went into service. Almost half of the rest were declared medically unfit. Other draftees paid money to get out of the war. Others simply failed to show up.

Immigrants' reaction to the war was mixed. The German editor of the *Milwaukee Herald* closed his newspaper in 1862 to lead a group of his employees into the war. Other immigrants were more skeptical. As newcomers, they did not see it as their war. Some of the immigrants had fled wars in their home countries and resisted joining one in the United States. However, most immigrants could not afford to buy their way out of the draft. Therefore, they were more likely to have to serve than men who had been born in the country.

When the war began, there were 122 Black men recorded as living in Milwaukee. At that time, Black people were not accepted into the army. Later in the war, as the need for soldiers grew, rules were changed and Black men were added to the draft. Alfred Carroll, who grew up in Milwaukee, enlisted in 1864. He served in the 29th United States Colored Infantry Regiment.

HISTORY IN PERSON

Joshua Glover, Freedom Seeker

This mural depicting the freeing of Joshua Glover appears on the Interstate 43 overpass at Fond du Lac Avenue. | *John Nondorf*

Some of Milwaukee's abolitionists famously helped a freedom seeker break out of jail in the city. Joshua Glover had escaped slavery in St. Louis, Missouri. In 1852, he arrived in Racine, Wisconsin, and took a job in a sawmill. Two years later, his former enslaver came looking for him. The Fugitive Slave Act required federal marshals to capture Glover and return him to slavery. Concerned about the security of the Racine jail, the marshals took Glover to Milwaukee. The jail was located at what is now Cathedral Square Park. There, abolitionist Sherman Booth rallied a crowd to protest Glover's arrest. Inflamed by Booth's words, five thousand people descended upon the jail. They broke down the door and freed Glover. He then escaped to Canada through the Underground Railroad. Today, a historic marker in Cathedral Square Park and a mural on the Interstate 43 overpass commemorate these events.

The war closed the Mississippi River to commercial shipping. Goods had to be shipped through the Great Lakes instead. Milwaukee's location on the shore of Lake Michigan was, once again, a great benefit to the city. Milwaukee shipping increased from 40,000 pounds of freight in 1860 to almost 250,000 pounds in 1865. As the war increased demand for products made in Milwaukee, railroads also profited. They carried wheat, which was made into bread to feed Union soldiers. Milwaukee soon surpassed Chicago as the world's largest shipper of wheat. Alexander Mitchell was Milwaukee's leading banker and railroad operator in the 1860s. He and other businessmen consolidated operations by buying small railroads and forcing others out of business.

General Rufus King | *WHI Image ID 25585*

Soldiers also needed meat. Milwaukee and other Wisconsin communities packed a lot of pork and beef during the war. Meat-packers more than doubled their number of hogs slaughtered. The animal hides were used to make leather boots, belts, and harnesses. The number of **tanneries** in the city jumped from thirteen in 1860 to thirty in 1870. John Plankinton, a meat-packer, had the largest income in Milwaukee at this time. He made $104,400 that year (about $3.2 million today). The average worker made less than $600 annually (about $18,000 today).

Rufus King, a newspaper editor who opposed slavery, became the city's most famous Civil War officer. He led the Iron Brigade at several key battles. But his military career did not last long. In 1862, Union forces fought Confederate troops led by General Thomas "Stonewall" Jackson at the Second Battle of Bull Run. Jackson retreated. King was experiencing medical problems and failed to call in reinforcements to halt Jackson. Jackson got away, and King was widely criticized. He resigned his commission.

Milwaukee women contributed to the war in several ways. Many took over jobs for their husbands, fathers, and brothers. They worked on farms and in factories. The North was cut off from Southern cotton, so Wisconsin women tended sheep and wove wool into cloth. Other women became teachers, which at the time was still a largely male profession.

Henrietta Kilbourn (married to Byron), Martha Mitchell (married to Alexander), and Caroline Walker (married to George) raised money and support to open the Milwaukee Soldiers Home in 1864. It provided care for more than 2,500 injured veterans during its first year. The women held a special state fair in 1865 that raised more than

An 1876 illustration of the National Home for Disabled Volunteer Soldiers, also known as the Milwaukee Soldiers Home | *WHI Image ID 23678*

$100,000 for the home. They opened a new set of buildings in 1867 near South Forty-Third Street and West National Avenue. The buildings are still there today, near the Clement J. Zablocki Veterans Administration Medical Center. In 2019–2021, six of the Soldiers Home buildings were restored and renovated. Housing was added for veterans who are homeless or at risk of becoming homeless.

The Civil War began to turn in favor of the North in 1863 with the battles of Gettysburg and Vicksburg. By the time the war ended in April 1865, Wisconsin had lost 3,602 men in combat. An additional 7,627 died of disease or accidents. When news of the peace reached Milwaukee, thousands of people ran into the streets and rang bells in celebration. But the cries of joy turned to sadness a few days later when they learned of President Lincoln's assassination. Four thousand Milwaukeeans walked in a funeral march to the courthouse while forty thousand watched. Another chapter of history had closed.

Martha Mitchell | *WHI Image ID 106346*

Primary Sources

Coming of Age

The following sources provide insight into Milwaukee's early growth spurt. Think about what these newspaper excerpts and the poem tell you about this time period and then answer the questions that follow.

MILWAUKEE SENTINEL ARTICLE, 1849

Directly in front of the residence of George H. Walker . . . there is no road, but a slough hole, through, over, or under which is *impossible* for a loaded team to pass, and in which, for the last week, at least six teams per day are engulphed, sometimes six at a time.

Source: *Milwaukee Sentinel*, April 2, 1849

MILWAUKEE SENTINEL INTERVIEW, 1857

Chicago has always looked upon our prosperity and progress, with a sinister eye, and she cannot bear to see us hold such equal success with her in the contest for supremacy. She therefore devised a well-planned scheme through means of a grant of land to prostrate us at one blow, and give her supreme control of all those resources, which of right belong to us and which if succeeded would have had the desired effect. . . . The emergency was upon us, and required the most prompt and energetic [action] to meet, and for one I was not disposed to shirk or shrink from any effort or responsibility in my power to secure a favorable result.

—Byron Kilbourn

Source: *Milwaukee Sentinel*, June 30, 1857

POEM, 1874

Now in this fair State, our joy and our pride,
There stands a young City both large and wide:
Of her I will speak Milwaukee the fair
And of some of the men who placed her where
  She stands in her pride and beauty
Who came here in their youth and prime
The landmarks of that early time,
  And true to every duty

Surely we'll ne'er forget the time
In thirty-seven, eight and nine
When first we saw Milwaukee Bay.
From off the steamer that wended its way
  To this far off land of the "Nitch'ee"
Eager were we to grapple our fate
As we came from almost every State
  To found this queenly city

Source: Two stanzas from a poem read before the Old Settlers Club in 1874. Reprinted in James S. Buck, *Pioneer History of Milwaukee: From the First American Settlement in 1833, to 1841, with a Topographical Description as It Appeared in the State of Nature, Illustrated, with a Map*, rev. ed. (Milwaukee: Swain & Tate, Book and Job Printer, 1890), 324.

- **What does the first newspaper article excerpt tell you about Milwaukee in 1849?**
- **What prediction did Byron Kilbourn make about Chicago? Did his prediction come true?**
- **Give three examples of surprising descriptions of Milwaukee in these sources. Do any of the descriptions of Milwaukee in the poem surprise you? Why?**
- **Which document(s) refer to horse transport? Which refer to shipping?**
- **Pretend you were alive in the 1850s but had knowledge of the twenty-first century. What advice would you give to Kilbourn about a plan for the city?**

CHAPTER 4

An Industrial City
1865–1886

CHAPTER QUESTIONS

- How did workers' lives change during this time? How did labor unions affect their lives?
- How did workers' lives differ from the lives of the wealthy?
- What were women's lives like compared to today?
- How were urban environmental problems similar to or different from today?

The Civil War ended in 1865. Southern states returned to the Union, and the practice of slavery ended. The American economy began to depend more on industry than agriculture. Milwaukee played an important part in the new industrial economy. Immigrants continued coming to the city, looking for jobs. They found work, but factory owners grew rich while paying their laborers very little. Low wages and dangerous working conditions inspired workers to form **labor unions**. Although union members had some success in improving work conditions and pay, they often came into conflict with employers. Some of those conflicts turned deadly.

Drawing of the Milwaukee River made in 1874 | *WHI Image ID 28379*

Old and New Industries

Milwaukee exported a large amount of goods during and after the Civil War. Thousands of ships left Milwaukee's harbor every year. Docks along the Milwaukee River were full for miles. Old industries, such as wheat and beer, continued to expand. New industries, such as iron and manufacturing, boomed. The city's industrial production increased from $18 million in 1869 to $93 million in 1889.

Wheat, flour milling, tanning, and brewing remained important. Milwaukee shipped half a million to 1.3 million barrels of wheat every year from 1868 to 1882. Milwaukee's twelve flour mills produced more than one million barrels of flour in 1884. Only Minneapolis and St. Louis made more flour that year. The city's fifteen tanneries turned more than half a million animal hides into leather in 1886. They shipped leather goods all over the United States and to Europe. Additionally, beer production increased from 58,666 barrels in 1865 to 1,117,256 in 1885. Milwaukee's brewers had almost $9 million in sales in 1885.

A two-masted schooner on the Milwaukee River in 1870 | *WHI Image ID 24994*

Milwaukee was usually ranked as one of the top four meatpacking cities in the United States throughout the 1870s and 1880s. In 1879, meat was the city's most valuable export. The packers used every part of the hog. They used the meat for food. They cleaned the intestines and used them as sausage casings. They made the hair into brushes or stuffed it into mattresses. They turned the rest of the animal into fertilizer for farmers.

John Plankinton soon became the city's most important packer. He came to Milwaukee from Delaware in 1844. He had nine dollars with him, and he used that money to buy a cow. Within a year, he had the largest butcher shop in Milwaukee County. Soon, Plankinton was one of the richest men in Milwaukee. Plankinton partnered with another butcher, John Layton, in 1852. Layton owned a hog farm near Lincoln and Forest Home Avenues. The two men opened a packinghouse downtown. They sold meat all over the United States. After a few years, they built a much larger packinghouse in the Menomonee Valley. Layton left the business in 1863. Plankinton next partnered with Philip Armour from 1864 until 1885. When Armour left the company for Chicago, Patrick Cudahy became Plankinton's new partner. Plankinton and the other packers in Milwaukee slaughtered 553,077 hogs in 1886. The hogs arrived by train from across Wisconsin and the surrounding states.

Alexander Mitchell's wealth rivaled that of Plankinton. Mitchell had made his money in banking. But in 1865, he became president of the Chicago, Milwaukee & St. Paul Railroad, commonly known as the Milwaukee Road. He increased the railway's tracks from 270 miles to more than 5,000 miles over the next twenty-two years. In 1869, he started an insurance company. His offices were in the Mitchell Building at Water and Michigan Streets. He paid Edward Townsend Mix, Milwaukee's most famous architect at the time, to construct both buildings. They are still there today.

Mitchell married Martha Reed in 1841. Reed had been raised and educated on the East Coast and was interested in art, historic preservation, and feminist causes. She was also the first president of the Woman's Club of Wisconsin.

The Mitchells built a mansion at Ninth Street and Wisconsin Avenue in 1870. Martha decorated their home with the finest furniture and art. The lawn featured a gazebo and a fountain stocked with two hundred trout. The Mitchells kept more than nine thousand plants in a conservatory. Martha helped organize a weeklong Festival of Nations in 1884. It featured a ball and dinner at their estate. It was the city's biggest celebration in several years. The mansion is owned today by the Wisconsin Club and is used for member events.

Alexander Mitchell got involved with a businessman named Eber Ward from Michigan. With Mitchell's support, Ward opened an iron mill south of Milwaukee in 1866. Mitchell's railroad hauled the iron to the mill. The Milwaukee Iron Company employed more than one thousand workers after four years. Bay View, Milwaukee's first **suburb**, grew up around the mill.

Milwaukee's manufacturing industry grew after the Civil War. By the 1880s, only Pittsburgh and Cincinnati had larger percentages of people working in manufacturing. Most cities specialized in one type of manufacturing, but Milwaukee made many things. For example, in 1880, the city's fifty-two clothing manufacturers sold $3.7 million in clothing. In 1885, Milwaukee factories produced $5 million in iron products and $4.5 million in leather goods. They also made $2 million in tobacco products, including cigars, cigarettes, chewing tobacco, and snuff.

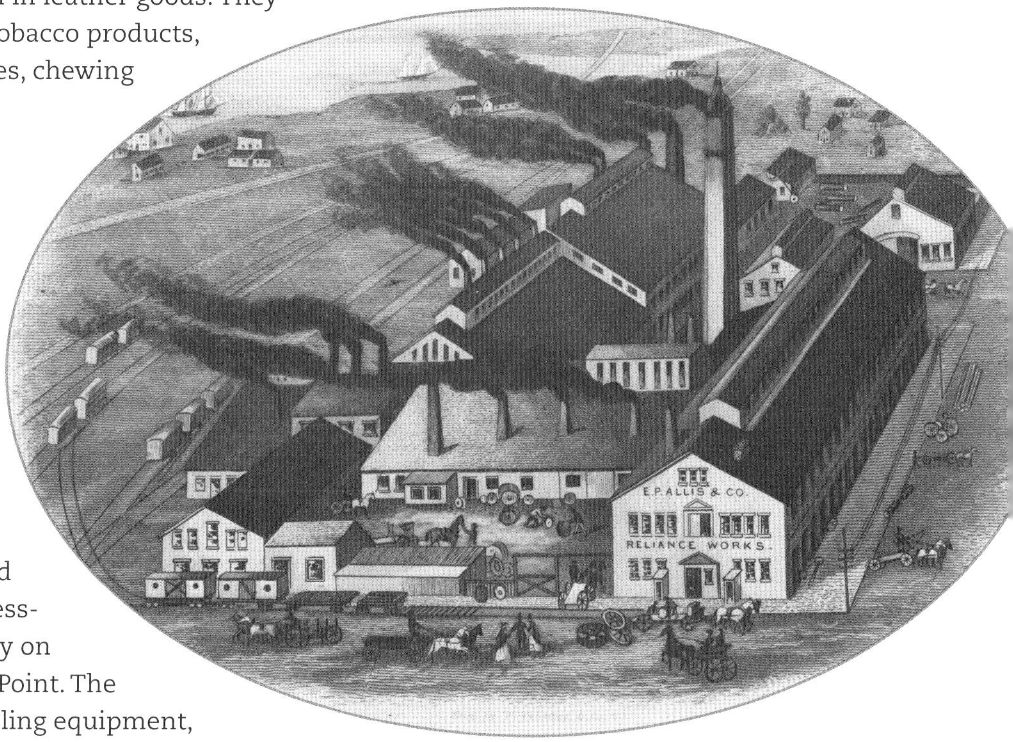

Edward P. Allis Company's Reliance Works | *WHI Image ID 52847*

Edward P. Allis was a leader in manufacturing. Allis came west from New York in 1846. He worked in tanning for several years before buying the bankrupt Reliance Works in 1861. Reliance Works was a foundry and small manufacturer. Within six years, Allis had made the company successful and built a new facility on twenty acres in Walker's Point. The new shop made flour-milling equipment, small steam engines, and heating elements for mechanical devices. In 1871, Allis won the contract to manufacture all the pipes and pumps for the city's new water system. He also started making sawmill equipment and steam engines. By 1889, Reliance Works employed almost 1,500 workers, which was as many as the Bay View iron mill.

The city needed more land for factories. A group of businessmen started to fill in the swampy Menomonee Valley in 1869. They hired workers to fill it with dirt and gravel and as much garbage as Milwaukeeans could haul. By 1886, the valley stank of rotting food, decaying animal parts, and ash. Nonetheless, the valley soon had lumber yards and coal yards, a Pfister & Vogel tannery, and a Pabst bottling plant. George Burnham's brickyard made millions of light-yellow bricks. The bricks came from a type of clay that is almost unique to the Menomonee Valley. Many buildings were constructed with these cream-colored bricks, and Milwaukee became known as the Cream City. The city's stockyards were also in the valley. They supplied meat to Plankinton, Layton, and other meat-packers.

Most significantly, the Milwaukee Road's shops were on 160 acres of the Menomonee Valley. The shops made and repaired all of the Milwaukee Road's railroad cars. General manager Sherburn S. Merrill led nearly 1,800 workers by the mid-1880s.

History in Focus

Pfister & Vogel Leather Company

Many immigrants in the nineteenth century moved west to cities like Milwaukee in search of opportunities. German immigrants Guido Pfister and Frederick Vogel moved from New York state to Milwaukee in 1847. They had both worked for a leather tannery in New York and wanted to break out on their own. They founded G. Pfister & Co. (later named Pfister & Vogel Leather Company) in 1848. Like other tanneries, the company sold leather to manufacturers that made shoes, boots, and gloves. As railroads linked US cities, Pfister & Vogel shipped leather throughout the country. It quickly grew to be the largest tanning company in Milwaukee. In the early 1900s, it was one of the biggest tanneries in the world, employing 3,500 workers.

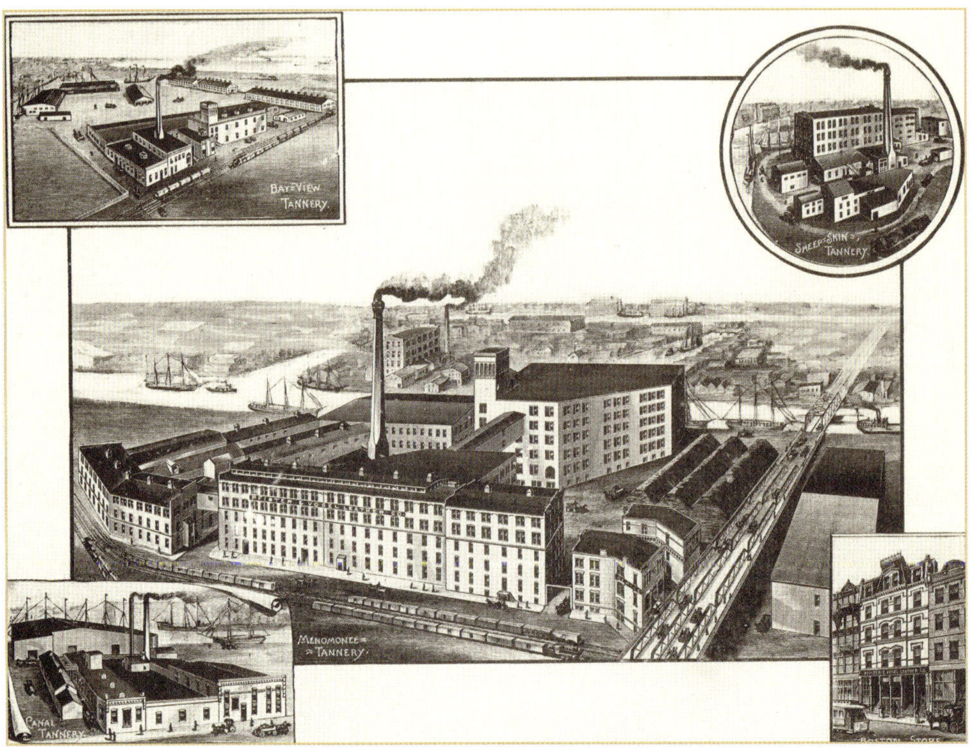

The Pfister & Vogel Leather Company eventually had several tanneries in Milwaukee and other cities. | *WHI Image ID 137681*

Men like Plankinton, Mitchell, Ward, and Allis made hundreds of thousands of dollars per year. Average people did not do as well. Brewery workers, for example, made only $40 or $50 per month in the 1870s (roughly $800 to $1,000 in today's money). By the 1870s, machines were doing many of the factory jobs that skilled workers used to do. Unskilled laborers could operate the machines, but they were paid little. There were fewer jobs for skilled laborers that paid enough to support a family. Still, some professions did well. Plumbers made about $4.00 per day in the 1870s. Cabinetmakers earned $2.25, and carpenters made as much as $3.00 per day. Supervisors were paid more. Brewery foremen, for instance, made as much as $3,000 per year (about $60,000 today).

Although their income was limited, Milwaukee's workers in the 1870s and 1880s had a wider variety of items to choose from when shopping than ever before. The railroads brought in goods from the eastern United States. Low-cost items could be purchased at dime stores. Milwaukee had more than two hundred grocery stores by the 1880s. Coffee, tea, butter, molasses, raisins, salt, spices, vinegar, codfish, and sardines arrived in Milwaukee every day. There were also new, exotic foods like olive oil and ketchup. Fruits and vegetables were available in cans. Iceboxes kept food cold and fresh.

Traffic along Grand Avenue and the bridge over the Milwaukee River. Notice the streetcar and the horse-drawn carriages in the street. | *WHI Image ID 7438*

Department stores sold clothing and a variety of household goods. T.A. Chapman and Company was Milwaukee's first department store. It opened in 1872. By 1888, the store had almost three hundred employees, most of them women. Other retailers included Schuster's (opened in 1884), Gimbels (1888), Goldmann's (1892), and Boston Store (1897). Chapman's, Boston Store, and Gimbels were downtown. Schuster's anchored the North Third Street shopping district. Goldmann's was in the Mitchell Street shopping district. All but Goldmann's opened additional locations as the city grew.

Many goods were now made in factories, instead of by hand, and could be mass-produced. Supply increased, and prices decreased. Shoppers could buy low-cost clothing and kitchenware. Milwaukeeans no longer had to build their own furniture, as cabinetmakers now supplied tables, chairs, bed frames, cradles, and coffins.

A Second Wave of Immigrants

Thousands of immigrants continued to settle in Milwaukee each year. In fact, 47 percent of Milwaukeeans in 1870 were foreign born. Most arrived seeking jobs, even though jobs were unskilled and low paying. Any job was a chance at a better life. Milwaukee's population increased from 45,246 in 1860 to 204,468 in 1890. It went from being the twentieth-largest city in the United States to the sixteenth.

Germans were still the largest group of immigrants, and Milwaukee was still a city with a strong German heritage. The German language was taught in schools. Even non-Germans learned the German language so they could do business more easily with German speakers. German restaurants, beer gardens, theaters, bands, orchestras, choirs, and newspapers remained popular.

Poles, from Poland, were the second-biggest immigrant group in Milwaukee. Like most other immigrants, the Poles came to Milwaukee to find jobs. Most of them settled on the south side of the city. A second, smaller community developed on both banks of the

Bird's-eye view of Milwaukee looking south down Eighth Street from Schlitz's Park in 1882 | *WHI Image ID 23133*

HISTORY IN PERSON

Kaszube's Park

Measuring just 40 by 100 feet, Kaszube's Park is the smallest public park in Milwaukee County. It contains a picnic table, a few trees, and an old anchor on display. The park commemorates the Kaszub people who once occupied Jones Island. A plaque states that the site was designated a historic landmark in 1974 "in recognition of a unique multi-ethnic fishing village that flourished on this peninsula and played a significant role in the city's history." The small green patch is surrounded by railroad tracks, storage buildings, and shipping containers, evidence of another important part of Milwaukee's past.

Kaszube's Park in 2004 | *Iulus Ascanius via Wikimedia Commons*

Milwaukee River between Brady and Locust Streets. Most Poles who settled in these two places performed unskilled labor in factories or tanneries. A third group of Polish immigrants, the Kaszubs (pronounced "ca-shoobs"), established a fishing village on Jones Island, once home to a Potawatomi summer village. At its height, Jones Island had eleven saloons, two grocery stores, two meat markets, two bakeries, a general store, and a post office. Between 1,600 and 2,000 people lived there. But the Kaszubs had not purchased the land and did not hold a deed to it. The city of Milwaukee evicted most of them in the 1910s and 1920s, turning the island into an industrial park. One retired couple refused to leave and held out until 1943.

More than 90 percent of all Polish immigrants were Catholic. They worshiped in German or Irish churches until there were enough of them to make Polish parishes possible. Poles purchased a Lutheran church in 1866 and renamed it St. Stanislaus. Six years later, they began building a new church at South Fifth and West Mitchell Streets.

The church opened a school in 1889. It was the first Polish parochial school in the United States. Soon, St. Stanislaus Church was so overcrowded that other parishes spun off from it.

Mathilda Hughes (right) and her husband, Louis Hughes, were founding members of First African Methodist Episcopal Church. | *WHI Image ID 11756*

Jewish and Black people continued to arrive in the city as well. Like other immigrant and migrant groups, they wanted to continue their religious practices. Milwaukee's earliest Jewish residents held services in their homes, later establishing synagogues as their numbers grew. Two of Milwaukee's oldest Jewish congregations were Emanu-El (established in 1869) and B'ne Jeshurun (established in 1858). They merged in the 1920s, becoming Milwaukee's oldest and largest Jewish temple. Black Americans started their own churches as well, including First African Methodist Episcopal Church of Milwaukee (later renamed St. Mark African Methodist Episcopal, or AME, Church) in 1869.

St. Mark AME Church's congregation first met in a rented space. They later built this church at the corner of Fourth Street and Cedar Street (now Kilbourn Avenue). | *WHI Image ID 54538*

Many European immigrants struggled to adjust to life in the United States. Most of them did not speak English. Few had been to school. They arrived with little money or resources. Beulah Brinton helped immigrants who settled in Bay View. Her house was a few blocks from her cousin Eber Ward's iron mill. Working out of her home, Brinton taught women English, cooking, sewing, and child care. Brinton also gave food to hungry workers at the mill. Her personal collection of three hundred books became Bay View's first library. Brinton also published the *Bay View Herald* newspaper with her son Warren. Her house is now the home of the Bay View Historical Society.

The city established new neighborhoods to accommodate the growing population. For example, three neighborhoods grew up around the west end of the Menomonee Valley, between Twenty-Seventh and Forty-Third Streets. The Merrill Park neighborhood was named after Sherburn S. Merrill of the Milwaukee Road. It was settled primarily by Irish Americans who left the Third Ward. Many German and Slavic laborers settled in Piggsville (or Pigsville), which was named

Painting made around 1858 of a Milwaukee synagogue | *WHI Image ID 28117*

after either early Milwaukeean George Pigg or a nearby pig farm. A mix of northern and central European groups lived in Silver City. Most of them worked in the nearby railroad shops. The workers were paid in silver dollars, which is how the neighborhood got its name.

Building Milwaukee

The city expanded to accommodate its growing population. As the city grew, it laid more roads. Roads required street lighting. The lights burned natural gas beginning in 1852. But the gas lights were not very bright, and they required a team of lamplighters to light them. Milwaukee's first two electric lights were turned on at the Newhall House on April 5, 1880. (The Newhall House was considered the most beautiful hotel in Milwaukee.) According to the next day's *Milwaukee Sentinel*, a crowd gathered to see "a brilliancy equal to one thousand candles." The light above the main entrance was "surrounded by a glass globe [that] lighted the street, so much so, as to admit of reading finely printed material without difficulty." Before long, the city had installed hundreds of electric streetlights around Milwaukee.

As more people crowded into the city, new buildings went up. These structures were made of wood and were heated by stoves that burned coal or wood. Houses were built close together. If one caught fire, an entire neighborhood could go up in flames. On January 10, 1883, the six-story Newhall House caught fire. The fire department arrived with horse-drawn wagons but could not keep up with the massive fire. They tried to rescue people with ladders, but a few ladders collapsed, and none were long enough to reach the top floors. The firefighters yelled for the guests to jump out the windows and into nets. But there weren't enough people to hold the nets taut, and those who jumped perished. Sources differ on the total number who died, but most estimates say around seventy bodies were found

An artist's depiction of firefighters rescuing a woman from the Newhall House fire | *WHI Image ID 128524*

An artist's depiction of the Newhall House fire | *WHI Image ID 128519*

among the ashes the next day. The fire was so hot that forty-three people were burned beyond recognition. There was no way to guess who they were because the hotel register had gone up in flames. The Newhall House fire was the most destructive fire in Milwaukee's history at the time.

Urbanization created more problems than just fires. Diseases spread quickly because people lived so close together. Many people rejected vaccines because of fear or distrust. Coal smoke hung in the air and blackened the beautiful Cream City brick buildings. Builders cut down trees to make room for homes, which meant there were fewer trees to block runoff rainwater. Thus, the Milwaukee and Menomonee Rivers flooded more often. Human, animal, and industrial waste drained into the river system. According to one estimate from 1907, the people and horses of Milwaukee made 133 tons of manure per day. The waste ran down the streets every time it rained. It spread disease and caused a horrible odor.

The city tried to fix these problems by building a sewer system. City officials also switched the source of drinking water from the rivers to Lake Michigan. Reliance Works built the biggest pump in the world at the east end of North Avenue a mile west of the lake. It drew lake water into the Kilbourn Park reservoir. From there the water flowed through pipes to homes and businesses.

HISTORY IN PERSON

North Point Water Tower

The North Point Water Tower at the east end of North Avenue regulated the pressure of water that came from the Kilbourn Park reservoir. The pump, reservoir, and water tower are no longer in use, but the buildings still stand today. In 1968, the North Point Water Tower was made a Milwaukee County Landmark. Visitors are not allowed to climb the 213-step steel staircase to the top of the tower. However, anyone can take in its ornate exterior, made of Cream City brick.

North Point Water Tower | *Carol M. Highsmith Archive, Library of Congress, Prints and Photographs Division*

The growing population also required new government buildings and educational institutions. Milwaukee County built a new courthouse in 1873 at Cathedral Square. It housed the county and federal courtrooms, the Common Council chamber, the county offices, and most of the city offices. The city built several new police and fire stations. The Milwaukee Public Library moved into its present location at Eighth and Wisconsin in 1895. Milwaukee Public Schools (MPS) expanded from twenty-two schools in 1871 to thirty-seven schools in 1888. Schools began to offer kindergarten classes in 1878. High schools offered job training in the evenings from 1880 until 1897. In the early 1900s, MPS began to operate two vocational high schools to prepare teens for different kinds of jobs.

Milwaukee County Court House around 1885 | *WHI Image ID 68184*

Higher education took place at private schools, not public schools. Wealthy women could attend the Milwaukee Female Seminary (soon renamed Milwaukee College) beginning in 1848. It offered training in teaching, nursing, child care, and managing a home. By 1884, it had ten resident teachers and fifty boarding students. In 1895,

The first building of Milwaukee College in 1852 | *WHI Image ID 54036*

it merged with Downer College to form Milwaukee-Downer College at the present site of the University of Wisconsin–Milwaukee. It merged with Lawrence University of Appleton, Wisconsin, a coeducational institution, in 1964. Other women's colleges in the city were Alverno College, founded in 1887 as St. Joseph's Normal School, and St. Mary's College (later called Mount Mary College and today known as Mount Mary University), established in 1929.

Men could attend Marquette College or the Lutheran Concordia College. The latter, now Concordia University, was established in 1881. Jesuit Catholic priests established Marquette, also in 1881, with five professors and thirty-five students. Marquette moved to Wisconsin Avenue in 1907, added schools of law and medicine, and became a university. In 1909, it became the first Catholic university in the United States to admit both men and women.

These private institutions charged tuition, which kept the average Milwaukeean from enrolling. In 1880, the state legislature passed a law requiring a school for teachers, called a "normal school." The school opened five years later on Wells Street between Eighteenth and Nineteenth Streets. It offered a two-year co-ed program to certify teachers. It was one of the forerunners of the University of Wisconsin–Milwaukee. Women who graduated from the normal school or one of the women's colleges could pursue careers and earn their own money, at least until they married. Many employers, including the public schools, refused to employ married women.

The Beginning of Labor Unions

The period of history from 1865 to about 1900 is often called the Gilded Age. Mark Twain, author of *The Adventures of Tom Sawyer* and *The Adventures of Huckleberry Finn*, gave the period its name. He thought wealthy Americans were engaged in wasteful and ridiculous excess. Men such as John D. Rockefeller, Cornelius Vanderbilt, Andrew Carnegie, and J. P. Morgan made vast amounts of money because they had nearly complete control over entire industries. Rockefeller was in oil, Vanderbilt in shipping and railroads, Carnegie in steel, and Morgan in banking. Critics called them "robber barons" because they made millions of dollars and paid their workers very little. But other people pointed out their great acts of philanthropy. For example, Andrew Carnegie donated more than 90 percent of his wealth to charities and cultural institutions, including colleges, libraries, hospitals, and opera houses. Rockefeller gave away about half his

Alexander Mitchell's home and gardens in 1872 | *WHI Image ID 80840*

wealth. Carnegie and Rockefeller believed in the "Gospel of Wealth," or the duty to give away their money. In Milwaukee, John Plankinton, Frederick Layton (son of meat-packer John Layton), Alexander Mitchell, Eber Ward, and Edward Allis made a lot of money, some would say at the expense of their workers. Layton, like Carnegie and Rockefeller, gave away a lot of his money.

The average worker's wages improved during the Gilded Age. But workers still made much less than their employers. From 1860 to 1900, the wealthiest 2 percent of American households owned more than one-third of the nation's wealth. The top 10 percent owned roughly three-fourths of it. Nationally, the typical factory worker made less than $1.75 per day in 1880 (less than $40 per day in modern money). In Milwaukee, factory jobs paid less than $1.25 per day.

Many jobs were unsafe. Workers in flour mills breathed in grain dust and coughed it up for hours at home. Brewery workers did a lot of heavy lifting. Meat-packers slipped and fell in pools of blood. They could be cut or maimed. Tannery workers got chemicals on their skin, under their fingernails, and in their eyes. Ironworkers had to endure temperatures of more than 160 degrees.

Workers organized labor unions to try to improve pay and working conditions. Skilled craftsmen organized some of the first labor unions. Milwaukee craft unions of the 1840s and 1850s included carpenters, coopers (barrel makers), masons, mechanics, and typographers. They limited the number of people who could join their craft in order to keep wages high. These unions generally blocked women, Black people, and Asian people from joining.

The shoemakers formed one of Milwaukee's successful unions. They organized the Order of the Knights of Saint Crispin in 1867 to protest the mechanization of their trade. Machines were replacing some workers, and workers wanted to protect their jobs. The union spread to shoemakers in other cities. Membership peaked at fifty thousand. It was briefly the largest union in the United States. The Panic of 1873—a **stock market** crash—nearly ended the organization because so many of its members were put out of work.

Workers (and some children) at the Willms cigar factory in Milwaukee in 1896. The cigar factory was in the back of the Willms house. | *WHI Image ID 86338*

Other Milwaukee labor unions managed to survive the financial crisis. Ironworkers established a local office of the national Sons of Vulcan labor union at the Milwaukee Iron Company in Bay View in 1869. They built their headquarters, Puddler's Hall, in 1872. (A puddler is a specific type of worker in the steel-making process.) They opened a tavern inside the building one year later. The mill is long gone today, but the tavern is still there. It is the second oldest in the city.

Labor unions began to change in the 1870s and 1880s. As unskilled factory jobs became more common, new unions organized for unskilled workers. Members of these unions wanted better pay, an eight-hour work day instead of ten or more, a five-day week instead of six, and safer working conditions. They organized **strikes** and **boycotts** to force management to negotiate with them. Several strikes broke out in Milwaukee in 1872. Strikers included brewery workers, cigar makers, coal heavers, coopers, pipelayers, printers, sailors, ship carpenters, trunk makers, and the bellboys at the Newhall House hotel.

Employers opposed unionization. Some refused to hire workers with a history of union activity, adding those workers' names to something called a blacklist. They hired nonunion workers during strikes instead of negotiating with striking employees. Some employers hired spies to report on union activity or security forces to violently break up union gatherings. But unions refused to give up. Strikes continued into the 1880s. In one strike, twelve hundred iron and steel workers walked off their jobs to demand better wages. Usually, the unions with the most members and the most activities received wage increases.

Some Milwaukee unions joined the Knights of Labor. Founded in 1869 in Philadelphia, Pennsylvania, the Knights worked to organize workers on a national scale. The Knights advocated for an eight-hour workday and an end to child labor. The group organized several successful strikes and managed to convince employers to give in to some of its demands. As the Knights won victories, membership soared. Unlike most early unions, the Knights of Labor admitted women and Black Americans after 1878. The Knights operated in almost every major US city by the mid-1880s. They had seven hundred thousand members by 1886, including sixteen thousand Milwaukee workers.

Foundry workers at the Edward P. Allis Reliance Works participated in the May 1886 strike for an eight-hour workday. | *WHI Image ID 1990*

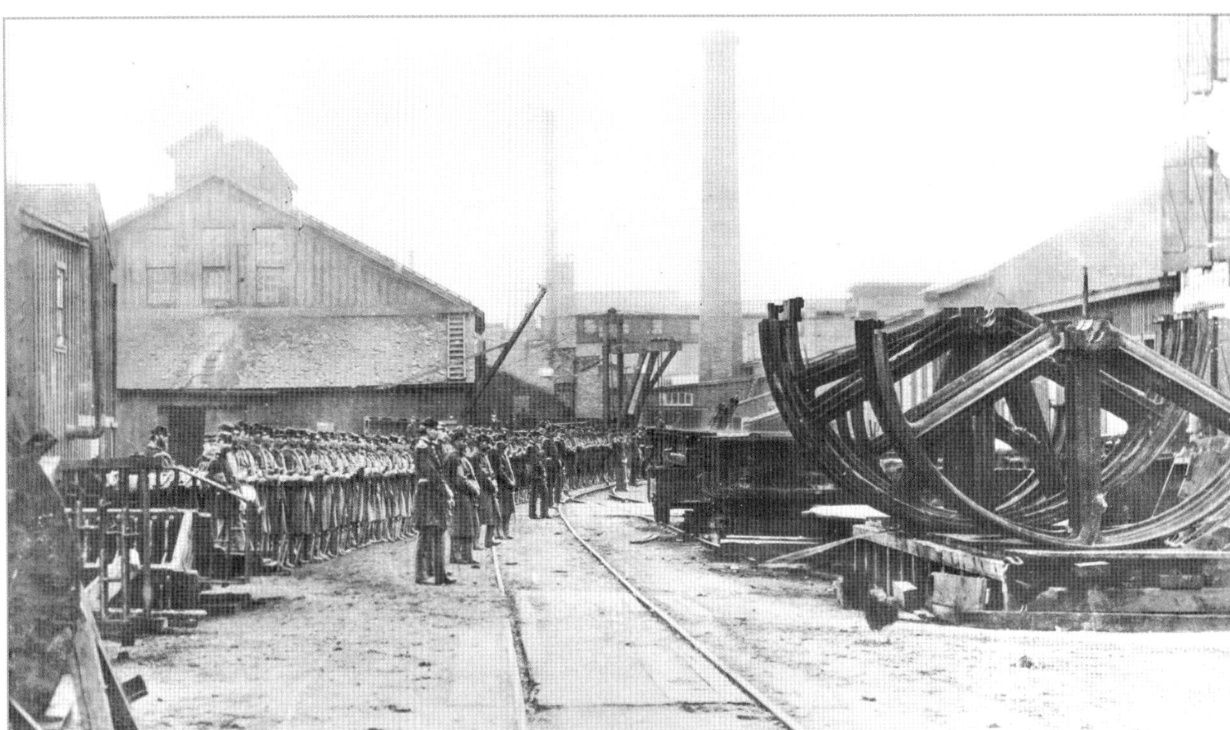

Labor unions gave employers an ultimatum in 1886. If they did not agree to an eight-hour day by Saturday, May 1, then workers at private businesses across the city would strike. The city had already given municipal workers an eight-hour day in March. Some private employers followed the city's lead and agreed to the eight-hour day, but most resisted. May 1 arrived, and strikes and lockouts followed. At least six thousand laborers in Milwaukee did not work that day. They organized a parade the next day with three thousand marchers, twenty thousand spectators, and every band they could find. They carried banners stating their demands, including one that said "Eight hours for work, Eight hours for rest, Eight hours for what we will."

The next day, workers in Chicago organized a rally and strike for an eight-hour day. It was peaceful until some of the workers confronted a group of strikebreakers. The police retaliated by firing on the crowd, killing two people. A group of **anarchists** organized a major rally the next day in Chicago's Haymarket Square. This rally was also peaceful until the police ordered the crowd to disperse around 10:30 p.m. One of the anarchists allegedly threw a bomb at the police, who then fired into the crowd. Seven police officers and at least four workers were killed in the Haymarket Riot.

The Bay View Massacre

The Milwaukee labor parade in 1886 was the most-attended event in the history of the city at that point. Several days before, more than twelve thousand workers attended a picnic in support of labor rights, where several speakers demanded an eight-hour day. Soon, everyone in the crowd was chanting for it. Some men in the Knights of Labor went back to their headquarters at St. Stanislaus Church and talked to their members. On May 3, about eight hundred workers marched from the church calling for an eight-hour day and a strike. Polish workers and tradesmen left their jobs and joined the march. They first stopped at the CM&StP Car Company, which built railroad cars. They gained more followers there and moved on to Reliance Works. Company management turned high-pressure water hoses on the marchers. But when the employees at work heard the chanting outside, they left their workstations and joined the march.

Wisconsin Governor Jeremiah Rusk arrived in Milwaukee in a special train car provided to him by the owners of CM&StP Car Company. He set up his office at the Plankinton Hotel. Manufacturers twice asked him to call out the Wisconsin National Guard, but Rusk decided to let Milwaukee police handle it.

Monday, the first day of the workweek, came. A general strike ensued. About fifteen thousand workers did not work on May 3. The city's industry nearly ground to a halt. Only the Bay View iron mill stayed open. About fifteen hundred men marched to Bay View to shut down the mill. Rusk finally called out the Wisconsin National Guard.

The strikers asked to be admitted to the Bay View mill, but the manager would not let them in. The crowd then refused to let the manager back into the mill. The Lincoln Guard, a branch of the Wisconsin National Guard, arrived by special train and got him back inside. Then the Lincoln Guard formed a line in front of the mill to protect it from the strikers, who were throwing rocks. More than 250 guardsmen were on-site by midnight. Workers inside the mill argued about whether they should join the strike.

The Kosciuszko Guard, a branch of the Wisconsin National Guard made up mostly of Polish grocers, clerks, and saloonkeepers, arrived on foot early in the morning on May 4 to try to stop the strike. The strikers felt betrayed. They lived in the same neighborhoods and went to the same churches as the guardsmen. The strikers called them names and blocked them from joining the Lincoln Guard. Some strikers threw rocks at the Kosciuszko Guard.

By then, word of Chicago's Haymarket massacre had reached Governor Rusk. Under pressure from local employers, he called the leader of the Sheridan Guard, a heavily Irish branch of the National Guard, on the telephone (a new technology at the time). Rusk reportedly told him that if the strikers tried to enter the mill, the guardsmen should shoot to kill. The strikers, unaware of what had happened in Chicago or the governor's order, began to march on the mill around nine o'clock on the morning of May 5. They were told to halt. When they refused, guardsmen followed their orders and started firing. Massive chaos ensued. People ran everywhere. At least six men were shot and killed; so was a thirteen-year-old boy who had joined the crowd. A retired worker, who lived in Bay View but was not a part of the strike, was struck and killed by a stray bullet. Two other bodies were found near the railroad tracks, but they were never identified. Police and the National Guard broke up a second strike of about two thousand Germans on the north side of the city. Shots were also fired in that strike, but no one was killed. Labor leaders asked the governor to call off the National Guard, but he refused unless the strikers disbanded. The organizers agreed to go back to work at ten hours per day.

Funerals at St. Stanislaus were packed with mourners. Fifty strike leaders were later tried in court for organizing an unlawful assembly.

Most were convicted and sentenced to six to nine months of hard labor. Other workers, including those at Reliance Works, were fired and blacklisted, meaning no other factories would hire them. According to the *Milwaukee Journal*, some businesses paid cash to members of the Kosciuszko Guard as a reward for their actions at the mill. Area residents boycotted the guard members' businesses, some of which were forced to close.

Every year, usually on the first Sunday in May, the Wisconsin Labor History Society sponsors a reenactment of the Bay View massacre on the site of the mill, which has long since been torn down. More than two hundred people attend each year, either as participants or spectators. A memorial service is held afterward in honor of those who died in the tragedy.

Primary Sources

Becoming American

Americans born in the United States could be hostile to immigrants. Even some earlier immigrants discriminated against newer arrivals. Others welcomed immigrants but wanted them to speak English and adopt American customs. *McGuffey Readers* were a series of reading and spelling books edited by William Holmes McGuffey, a teacher from Ohio. Each book contained stories, poems, essays, and speeches that taught reading and spelling. They also taught values and moral lessons. *McGuffey Readers* were widely used in US schools from the mid-1800s to early 1900s. The Milwaukee school board adopted *McGuffey Readers* in 1867, after McGuffey visited Milwaukee. They were used in Milwaukee until 1878. Read the following stories published in an 1866 edition of *McGuffey Readers* and answer the questions that follow.

WHERE THERE IS A WILL THERE IS A WAY

Henry Bond was about ten years old when his father died. His mother found it difficult to provide for the support of a large family, thus left entirely in her care. By good management, however, she contrived to do so, and also to send Henry, the oldest, to school, and to supply him, for the most part, with such books as he needed.

At one time, however, Henry wanted a grammar [book], in order to join a class in that study, and his mother could not furnish him with the money to buy it. He was very much troubled about it and went to bed with a heavy heart, thinking what could be done.

On waking in the morning, he found that a deep snow had fallen, and the cold wind was blowing furiously. "Ah," said he, "it is an ill wind that blows nobody good."

He rose, ran to the house of a neighbor, and offered his service to clear a path around his premises. The offer was accepted. Having completed this work, and received his pay, he went to another place for the same purpose, and then to another, until he had earned enough to buy a grammar [book].

When school commenced Henry was in his seat, the happiest boy there, ready to begin the lesson in his new book.

From that time, Henry was always the first in all his classes. He knew no such word as *fail*, but always succeeded in all he attempted. Having the *will*, he always found the *way*.

Source: William Holmes McGuffey, *McGuffey's New Fourth Eclectic Reader: Instructive Lessons for the Young* (Cincinnati: Wilson, Hinkle & Co, 1866).

THE IDLE SCHOOL-BOY

I will tell you about the laziest boy you ever heard of. He was indolent about every thing. When he played, the boys said he played as if the teacher told him to. And when he went to school, he went creeping along like a snail. The boy had sense enough; but he was too lazy to learn any thing.

When he spelled a word he drawled out one syllable after another as if he were afraid the syllables would quarrel, if he did not keep them a great ways apart.

Once, when he was reciting, the teacher asked him, "What is said of Hartford?" He answered, "Hartford is a flourishing *comical* town." He meant it was a "flourishing commercial town"; but he was such a drone, that he never knew what he was about.

When asked how far the Kennebec was navigable, he said, "It was navigable for boots as far as Waterville." The boys all laughed, and the teacher could not help laughing, too. The idle boy colored like scarlet.

"I say it is so in my book," said he. When one of the boys showed him the book, and pointed to the place where it was said, that the Kennebec was navigable for *boats* as far as Waterville, he stood with his hands in his pockets, and his mouth open as if he could not understand what they were all laughing at.

Another day, when his class were reciting a lesson in defining, he made a mistake worse than most of the rest. The word A-ceph-a-lous was printed with syllables divided as you see. The meaning of the word was, "without a head."

The idle boy had often been laughed at for being so slow in saying his lessons. This time, he thought he would be very quick and smart. So he spelled the word before the master had a chance to put it out. And how do you think he spelled it?

"A-c-e-p-h, Aceph," said he, "a louse without a head." The boys laughed at him so much about this, that he was obliged to leave school. The teacher said, "He was a drone, and the working bees stung him out of the hive."

You can easily guess what luck this idle boy had. With all his father's care to have him learn, he *would* be a dunce; not because he was a fool, but because he was too lazy to give his thoughts to any thing.

He had some fortune left him. But he was too lazy to take care of it, and now he goes about the streets, begging his bread. He often wishes that he had been more attentive to his books when young. But he can not live over again the time he has spent so badly, and he must be a poor ignorant fellow for the rest of his life.

Source: William Holmes McGuffey, *McGuffey's New Fourth Eclectic Reader*.

- **What are two things in the first story that could have prevented Henry from doing well in school? What did Henry do to solve his problems?**
- **Why did the boy in the second story do poorly in school? How did others treat him?**
- **What do you think the author intended to be the moral of the second story? Do you agree or disagree with the author's interpretation of events? What else might have been causing the boy's difficulties?**
- **How did these stories reflect so-called American values at the time they were written? How might you describe "American values" today?**

CHAPTER 5

Moving onto a World Stage
1886–1910

CHAPTER QUESTIONS

- What shaped Milwaukee's political movements during the late nineteenth and early twentieth centuries?
- What were some of the factors that led to suburbanization?
- What influenced the emerging American and Milwaukee cultures? How did those cultures compare to the cultures that immigrants brought from their home countries?
- How has Milwaukee's culture changed or stayed the same since the early twentieth century?
- How were Milwaukee's largest immigrant populations the same? How did they differ? How did differences lead to cultural divides?

Milwaukee experienced new twists on familiar themes in the period between 1886 and 1910. The city grew into a global industrial power. More immigrants arrived, mostly from Europe. The city expanded. Suburbs sprang up. New cultural institutions developed. Voters elected reformers who wanted to change city government and improve life for everyone. Some improvements were made—the city became safer, healthier, and cleaner. At the same time, many government officials were corrupt. A new political group burst onto the scene, earning the nickname "sewer socialists."

View of Milwaukee from city hall in 1904 | *WHI Image ID 54784*

Reform Movements

During the late 1800s and early 1900s, labor unions continued to organize across the United States. They were part of a larger movement called populism. Populists wanted to create a more humane society. They thought wealthy people should pay more in taxes. They also wanted to limit child labor. They supported giving voters the power to pass **referendums** and to **recall** elected officials. A referendum is a question that appears on an election ballot. It gives voters a chance to vote on a particular issue. A recall election happens when voters are unhappy with an elected official and decide whether to remove them from office. Both reforms would give people a greater voice in government.

Populist farmers and labor leaders organized the People's Party of Wisconsin in 1886. By this time, many Milwaukee workers were angry. They did not like how elected officials had handled the Bay View massacre. To them, neither of the major political parties met their needs. The Republicans supported business. Democrats supported labor, but the Milwaukee branch was dishonest. They took bribes. The People's Party looked like a good alternative.

The People's Party ran several candidates for city and county offices in 1886. They won only 7.5 percent of the state vote. However, Milwaukee's workers voted overwhelmingly for them. The party won most of the Milwaukee County offices. It also won two Wisconsin state assembly seats and a seat in the US House of Representatives. Populists won several seats on the Milwaukee Common Council the following spring as well. Victory, however, did not last long. The Republicans and Democrats set their differences aside and ran joint candidates in the next series of elections. The People's Party lost. Some aldermen (members of the city council) returned to trading favors for bribes.

Henry Payne, a Republican, was involved in the city's worst case of corruption in the 1890s. He ran the Milwaukee Electric Railway and Light Company (TMER&L, or "timmeral"). He bribed city, county, and state officials to award TMER&L a **monopoly** on streetcars. Without any competition, Payne could charge riders whatever he wanted. He charged five cents per ride. Streetcar riders, who made only a few dollars per day, considered that fare too expensive. Payne made a lot of money but did not pay his workers much. His employees formed a labor union. They went on strike in 1896 for better wages. Payne refused to negotiate. He brought in 1,200 replacement workers.

The public sided with the union. Some wore pins that said, "To Ride Gives Me a Payne." They refused to ride the streetcar. Hotels refused to rent rooms to replacement workers. Local stores would not sell to TMER&L, so Payne had to buy supplies in Chicago. The strike lasted two months, until someone fired shots at two TMER&L streetcars. Public opinion turned against the strike, and workers returned to their jobs.

David Rose | *WHI Image ID 61755*

The strike showed that Milwaukeeans wanted reform. In 1898, David Rose, a Democrat, campaigned for mayor. Rose was a master campaigner. He dressed in fine clothes when trying to impress big donors, but he would wear work clothes to shake hands with ordinary workers. He gave stirring speeches and marched in parades. He was not religious until the end of his life, but he visited churches across the city to appeal to churchgoers.

Rose promised to end TMER&L's hold over the city. Once in office, however, he changed his position. Rose negotiated a thirty-five-year city contract with TMER&L in 1899. TMER&L agreed to reduce fares to four cents per ride, and the Common Council approved the contract. The public was outraged that TMER&L received a long-term monopoly on streetcar services. As it turned out, however, a four-cent fair was a pretty good deal by the 1930s.

Voters reelected Rose in 1900. They did it again in 1902, 1904, and 1908. He won a majority only once. But these were three-way races, and he only needed more votes than the other two candidates. Rose appointed friends and supporters to city offices. In return, they organized voters for Rose's reelection campaigns.

Rumors swirled that Rose was taking bribes. District Attorney Francis McGovern started an investigation in 1901. By 1905, McGovern had charged eighty-three city and county officials with crimes. He found that several aldermen had sold saloon licenses and exemptions to building codes for cash. They also stole city supplies of coal, hay, oats, and horses. Rose was not prosecuted, but his reputation suffered even further.

But City government made progress in other areas. Milwaukee transformed its fire department from a volunteer force to a professional one. It also spent more money on the police department. The city was safe. In 1906, there were only six burglaries and one murder in Milwaukee. Chicago, by comparison, had 840 burglaries and twenty-two murders that year.

The city set up a park commission in 1889. It purchased land for Humboldt, Kosciuszko, Mitchell, Lake, Riverside, and Washington Parks. Famous landscape architect Frederick Olmsted, designer of New York's Central Park, designed the latter three. These public parks offered residents new opportunities for recreation. Lake Park offered boat rentals at park lagoons. Riverside had tree-lined carriage roads. Washington Park had a zoo.

Milwaukee also had one of the best public health programs in the United States. The city formed one of the first boards of health in 1867. The board isolated people with contagious diseases from the rest of the population. These diseases included cholera, diphtheria, typhoid, and yellow fever. The board encouraged smallpox vaccinations. The city was also one of the first in the United States to regulate the distribution and sale of milk. These rules reduced the spread of diseases.

Milwaukee fixed its garbage problem. People used to throw garbage in the streets. The city had also buried trash in the suburbs or dumped it into Lake Michigan. But in 1902, the city opened a garbage-burning facility called a crematorium on Jones Island to burn garbage. The new crematorium helped reduce disease and bad odors.

A horse-drawn milk wagon in Milwaukee | *WHI Image ID 3241*

Students and teachers from the Milwaukee Day School for the Oral Instruction of the Deaf. This was Wisconsin's first public day school for deaf students, established in 1885. | *WHI Image ID 123731*

Students in a Milwaukee classroom in 1909 | *WHI Image ID 7469*

Milwaukee Public Schools (MPS) had improved vastly by 1910. The district added classes for deaf students, blind students, and students with speech disorders. In 1904, MPS started selling school lunches. Students no longer had to walk home for their midday meal.

MPS had three high schools until 1907. Milwaukee High School opened in 1867. It was later called East Side, East Division, and Riverside High School. South Side (South Division) High School opened in 1893. West Side (West Division) High School opened in 1894.

Students at work in the carpentry and woodworking shop at the Milwaukee School of Trades around 1910 | *WHI Image ID 88475*

The city's population grew. Therefore, MPS added more high schools. Milwaukee School of Trades joined MPS in 1907. It later became Milwaukee Trade and Technical High School. It is now the Lynde and Harry Bradley Technology and Trade School. The original North Division opened in 1907. The Milwaukee Normal School became the Milwaukee Girls' Trade and Technical High School in 1909. Its students studied home economics and secretarial skills.

All these improvements required more tax money, but the public services provided had widespread support in Milwaukee.

The Sewer Socialists

After members of the People's Party were voted out of office in the early 1900s, the socialists took up their issues. Socialist groups were active all over the world. They wanted to increase equality between people. They wanted better wages, benefits, and working conditions for all workers. Some also wanted racial and gender equality. Socialists thought wealthy people should pay more in taxes to provide services such as pensions for the elderly and health care for all people.

Some socialists wanted to replace existing governments. They were willing to use violence. Most socialists, however, wanted peaceful change. Milwaukee's socialists were the peaceful kind. Many of them came from Germany, where socialism was popular. In Milwaukee, they wanted more funding for city services. These services included fire and police protection, parks, public health, and public schools.

Victor Berger was Milwaukee's leading socialist. He had immigrated to Milwaukee from Austria-Hungary. In 1892, he bought a newspaper and renamed it *Vorwärts* (meaning "Forward"). He turned it into the city's leading socialist newspaper. He used it to advocate for labor unions. Berger urged factory owners to shorten the workday and improve safety. He wanted to make school required for all children. He thought government should give people old-age and health insurance. He also wanted city government to take over transportation, communication, utilities, and mines. Then, more people would have access to the things they needed.

In 1895, Berger visited Eugene Debs. Debs was a nationally known union leader. He was in jail in Illinois for leading a railroad strike. Strikes were illegal at that time. Berger introduced Debs to socialist ideas. In 1897, the two men founded a group called Social Democracy of America. It became the Socialist Party in 1901. Its first local chapter was in Milwaukee. That chapter called itself the Social Democrats. They recruited members block by block. They published their ideas in newspapers, pamphlets, and posters. They wrote these materials in different languages so that more immigrants could read them.

Women played an active role in the party. They organized some of their own branches. Those branches encouraged women to join strikes. Socialist women lobbied for an end to child labor. They also wanted to end nighttime labor for women. That way, women could be home to care for their families. Socialist women campaigned for women's suffrage. In 1919, Wisconsin became the first state to ratify the Nineteenth Amendment to the US Constitution, which gave women the right to vote.

Meta Schlichting Berger was one of Milwaukee's best-known socialists. She graduated from the Wisconsin State Normal School and taught elementary school for three years. In 1897, she married Victor Berger. Meta advised Victor on how to achieve his goals. She also helped him publish his newspapers. Voters elected Meta Berger to the Milwaukee school board in 1909. She wanted MPS to provide playgrounds, low-cost lunches, and medical exams to children. She thought teachers should receive annual pay raises and pensions. Voters reelected her several times. She served on the school board for thirty years, including some terms as board president. Later, she served on the Wisconsin State Board of Education. She also served on the boards of regents for the state normal schools and the University of Wisconsin. She was opposed to war and active in the women's suffrage movement. After Victor died, Meta was elected to fill his position on the Socialist Party's National Executive Committee. That achievement was extremely rare for a woman at the time.

Victor and Meta Berger and their children, Doris, Jack, and Elsa, around 1910 | *WHI Image ID 123890*

In 1898, the Social Democrats in Milwaukee ran a full slate of candidates for city offices. They campaigned on a platform of expanded city services. They said the city should take control of all public utilities. They also said it should provide jobs to the unemployed. They argued for free legal and medical services for people in need. They also wanted free schoolbooks for children. They said there should be more public swimming pools. They wanted the city to sponsor low-cost symphony concerts. Most famously, the Social Democrats planned to remove human waste by extending the sewer lines throughout the county. This plank of their platform earned them the nickname "sewer socialists."

The Social Democrats received only 5 percent of the vote in the mayoral election. (Democrat David Rose won that year.) Undeterred, they kept running candidates every two years. Social Democrat candidates received more votes every time. Victor Berger ran for mayor in 1904. He finished in third place with 25 percent of the vote. The Social Democrats won nine of the forty-six seats on the Common

Robert La Follette | *WHI Image ID 10650*

Emil Seidel and Victor Berger | *WHI Image ID 56202*

Council that year. They also won several less important elections. Once in office, they earned a reputation for being hardworking and honest.

At the state level, voters elected Robert M. La Follette governor in 1900. He was a Republican. He was also a progressive. Like the socialists, progressives wanted clean, uncorrupt government. For example, La Follette thought railroads gave too much money to political campaigns. He proposed limits on what they could spend. He also wanted to limit the amounts they could charge their customers. La Follette established the direct primary election in Wisconsin. In this system, people, not political parties, choose nominees for elected office. He also supported the recall and the referendum. He joined the fight for women's suffrage. He established the country's first workers' compensation system. He also supported minimum wage laws. Voters reelected Governor La Follette in 1902 and 1904. In 1906, they elected him to the US Senate.

Clearly, socialism and progressivism had become popular in Wisconsin. In 1908, the Social Democrats ran Emil Seidel for mayor of Milwaukee. He was a self-made man, meaning he achieved success through his own hard work rather than through powerful friends or family. People liked that about him. Seidel became a wood carver at age thirteen. He started a woodworkers' union at age nineteen. He became a socialist when he was in his twenties. He was also a small-business owner. He had served on the Milwaukee Common Council since 1904. Seidel finished in second place in the mayoral election of 1908, losing to David Rose.

Seidel ran again in 1910. This time, the Social Democrats triumphed. Seidel won with 46 percent of the vote. The party also captured twenty-one of thirty-five seats on the Common Council. They won ten of sixteen county board seats. They also won two judgeships. Voters elected Charles Whitnall as city treasurer and Daniel Hoan as city attorney. Both men were Social Democrats. Voters chose Victor Berger for US Congress. By 1910, Milwaukee was the most socialist city in the United States.

History in Focus

Machine Shop of the World

Milwaukee businesses made a lot of money after 1886. Wheat and beer were still big exports. However, manufacturing made much more money. The Walker's Point neighborhood led the way. Pawling and Harnischfeger made cranes. Nordberg Manufacturing Company made mining equipment. A. O. Smith built world-famous automobile frames. Edward Allis's company became Allis-Chalmers in 1901. It led the world in industrial engines. Allen-Bradley made industrial controls. It became part of Rockwell Automation in 1985. Its headquarters are still in Walker's Point.

Inside the Allis Chalmers factory around 1911 | *WHI Image ID 85363*

Many other factories were outside of Walker's Point. Most were small and sold items in the Milwaukee area. Others were larger and exported to the world. The Falk Corporation was one of the bigger ones. It made gears in the Menomonee Valley. Ladish Company forged machine parts in Cudahy. William Harley and Arthur Davidson built their first Harley-Davidson motorcycle in Davidson's father's backyard in 1903. They moved into a factory at Thirty-Fifth Street and Juneau Avenue in 1917. Thanks to these industries, Milwaukee earned the nickname "Machine Shop of the World."

Early Suburbs Spring Up

Milwaukee's population continued to increase. By 1910, there were 373,857 people in the city. The city expanded for the growing population. Several new suburbs **incorporated**. Milwaukeeans spread out. A third wave of immigrants moved to Milwaukee, and the new immigrants filled in older areas of the city.

By 1902, Milwaukee had more people per square mile than any other city in the United States except Boston and Baltimore. The city wanted to reduce its **population density**. It **annexed** land from surrounding towns. By 1900, the city extended west to roughly Thirty-Fifth Street. It went north to Keefe Avenue and south to Cleveland Avenue.

Map by Colter Sikora

Bay View and North Milwaukee were two suburbs that joined the city. Bay View, home to the iron mill and some factories, incorporated as a village in 1879. As the city annexed more land, it eventually reached Bay View's northern border. Bay View's residents wanted city services, such as water and sewer lines, better roads, and streetlights. They voted to join the city in 1887. North Milwaukee was at the crossroads of two railroad lines. They were near Thirty-Fifth Street and Villard Avenue. North Milwaukee incorporated as a village in 1897. By 1902, it had two major factories: one made bridges and the other made bicycles. It also had dozens of smaller factories, a newspaper, three hotels, and a village hall. North Milwaukee's residents voted for annexation in 1929 so they could begin to receive city services.

Two suburbs incorporated on the city's North Shore, on Lake Michigan, as well. Whitefish Bay started out as a farming and fishing community. Beer baron Frederick Pabst opened his resort there in 1889. The resort attracted tourists and new residents. The village incorporated three years later. East Milwaukee (now Shorewood) has a similar history. In the mid-nineteenth century, it was a farm community. It also had a couple of sawmills, a paper mill, a flour mill, and a limestone mill. Then, in 1872, a resort opened at what is now Hubbard Park. Amusement parks followed. The railroad brought new residents after 1886. They wanted better services than the Town of Milwaukee could provide. Therefore, East Milwaukee incorporated as a village in 1900. The village changed its name to Shorewood in 1917.

The four southern suburbs were based on industry. European farmers settled in West Allis in 1837. They called the community Honey Creek after the creek that runs through it. In the 1880s, the Chicago & North Western Railway laid tracks and built a station there. It renamed the community North Greenfield. In 1891, the Wisconsin State Fair moved to North Greenfield. The railroad and the fair brought additional residents. Finally, in 1900, the Edward P. Allis Company built its factory complex at Seventieth Street and Greenfield Avenue. It was west of their old factory in Walker's Point. Thus, the community acquired its current name, West Allis. Thousands of people moved there from all parts of the state. They took jobs with Allis or in other factories that opened nearby. West Allis incorporated as a village in 1902. It became a city in 1906. West Allis annexed land from the towns of Greenfield and Wauwatosa. It is now 11.5 square miles.

West Milwaukee, South Milwaukee, and Cudahy also used low taxes to attract factories. West Milwaukee grew out of the towns of Greenfield and Wauwatosa. Pawling and Harnischfeger, a company that made motors and cranes, moved there in 1905. West Milwaukee incorporated as a village the following year. South Milwaukee was part of the Town of Oak Creek. Farmers of European descent settled there between 1838 and 1846. The Bucyrus Steam Shovel and Dredge Company (later Bucyrus-Erie) moved there from Ohio in 1892. Other manufacturers followed. South Milwaukee incorporated as a village in 1892 and as a city in 1897. Cudahy was in the Town of Lake. It was named after Patrick Cudahy's meatpacking business. It relocated there in 1892. The community became a village in 1895 and a city in 1906.

The Changing Face of the City

As suburbs continued to form around it, the city of Milwaukee was changing. According to the 1890 census, 86.4 percent of all people in the city were foreign born. The national average was only 33 percent. In fact, Milwaukee was the most European city in the United States. Germans and Poles were still the biggest ethnic groups, but immigrants from several other European countries had also arrived.

Many German Americans made enough money to move to newer sections of the city. Those who had lived in Yankee Hill, for example, moved up to the east side. Some went as far as Shorewood. Germans who had lived near downtown moved north and northwest. They built thousands of duplexes. They lived in one unit and rented out the other.

The Poles were still Milwaukee's second-largest ethnic group. Most of them had settled on the south side, near St. Stanislaus Church. The new arrivals outgrew that church and started St. Josaphat, a new parish. Eventually, they outgrew that church too. They then constructed a larger building. Because they had little money, the

Construction workers in front of the partially built St. Josaphat's Church | *WHI Image ID 39438*

residents did much of the construction work themselves. Neighborhood women ran picnics, plays, and other events to raise money. Families took out second mortgages on their houses to help pay for construction costs. Parish members saved money by using recycled building materials from the federal post office in Chicago. They completed construction in 1901. However, they could not afford to finish decorating it until 1929. St. Josaphat became the largest church in Milwaukee. It was so big and so beautiful that the pope declared it a basilica, which is a Catholic church building that is given special ceremonial privileges.

The Poles who built St. Josaphat could afford only small plots of land for their houses. As the Poles saved money and were able to make improvements, many jacked up their houses and built a second living unit in the basement. People nicknamed the houses "Polish flats." The family typically rented out the basement unit. It had its own entrance on the side of the house or through the porch. Some residents built a third floor with an additional living unit. Some added a unit to the side of the house. And some built a "back house." It was literally a rental house in the backyard. They could jack that house up too. It was not uncommon for one family to rent to four others on its property. Building new back houses is illegal today. However, people can still buy and sell them. Some are still occupied. Others have been turned into garages.

The Third Ward was an Irish neighborhood until 1892, when a fire swept through it. Having lost their homes and jobs, the Irish residents eventually vacated the area. Most moved to Yankee Hill or the Merrill Park neighborhood. Many new arrivals from Italy then settled in the Third Ward. A second, smaller group of Italians settled in Bay View. The Italians were Catholic, like most of the Irish and Poles. They established Our Lady of Pompeii Church in 1905. Because of its color, people called it the Little Pink Church. The county tore it down in 1967 to make room for a freeway. However, Our Lady of Pompeii is still recognized every year at Festa Italiana, which is the oldest of Milwaukee's lakefront ethnic festivals.

Many Greek immigrants settled north of downtown. Unlike other groups, most Greek immigrants were young men without families. Some got jobs in nearby tanneries. They wanted to make money and return home. Others started small businesses, such as restaurants, saloons, grocery stores, and candy stores. The Greeks were Orthodox Christian. They organized Annunciation Greek Orthodox Church in 1906. They used rented space until they could afford to build their own church building in 1914. In 1961, they opened a new church near Wauwatosa. Frank Lloyd Wright, Wisconsin's most famous architect, designed it.

A Greek American parade in Milwaukee around 1910 | *WHI Image ID 55617*

Serbs established St. Sava Serbian Orthodox Church in 1912 in Walker's Point. They held services in a house until they could open a church building. They moved to their current site, a cathedral at Fifty-First Street and Oklahoma Avenue, in 1956. Likewise, Slovenian immigrants built St. John the Evangelist in Walker's Point. The current parish is located in Greenfield. Croatians established the Sacred Heart Parish Church near the Schlitz brewery in 1917. The congregation moved to its site at Forty-Ninth and Wells Streets in 1949. Czechs, Hungarians, Norwegians, Slovaks, and Ukrainians also had their own churches in the city.

By 1915, St. Mark AME Church had more than one hundred members, and there were three other large Black churches in the city. Calvary Baptist was the city's first Black Baptist church. It moved several times before parishioners bought a building on North Fourth Street for their church. It later moved to Teutonia Avenue. St. Benedict the Moor parish was founded as a Catholic mission in 1908 to serve the city's growing Black population. St. Benedict built a church and boarding school for elementary through high school students on State Street in 1923.

There were about ten thousand Jews in Milwaukee by 1910. They came from all over eastern Europe. Many lived in a formerly German neighborhood north of downtown. Jewish residents established synagogues. Some performed skilled labor. Some opened stores. They received little help from Christians, but they could still help one another. They opened the Milwaukee Jewish Settlement House in 1900. The Settlement, as it was called, provided services to the Jewish community. It hosted athletic clubs and social clubs. It also

Lizzie Black Kander
| *WHI Image ID 38113*

offered classes on the English language, sewing, and cooking. Lizzie Black Kander, a Jewish woman born in Milwaukee in 1858, taught the cooking classes. She published her favorite recipes in *The Settlement Cookbook* in 1901. It is still considered an American classic.

Milwaukee celebrated its many heritages with a Bazaar of All Nations that lasted for a week in 1896. People dressed in their traditional clothing. They operated booths and filled whole buildings with offerings of their food, music, and ethnic dances. This event was the beginning of Milwaukee's ethnic festivals.

Immigrant and American Culture

Milwaukee was a culturally diverse city. Each ethnic group was distinct. Sometimes they came into conflict. At other times, they enjoyed Milwaukee life together.

By 1910, Milwaukee's foreign-born population had slipped to 78.6 percent, but it still had the highest percentage of European immigrants in the United States. And Milwaukee was still very German.

History in Focus

Golda Meir

Golda Meir was one of the eastern European Jews who found a new home in Milwaukee. She was born Goldie Mabovitch in Russia in 1898. Russians openly persecuted Jews at that time. Her father left for New York in 1903, then moved to Milwaukee in 1905. By 1906, he could afford to bring Golda, her two siblings, and her mother to Milwaukee. The family lived in an apartment on Walnut Street.

Golda attended Fourth Street School from 1906 until 1912. She went on to North Division High School. From there, she went to Milwaukee State Normal School (now the University of Wisconsin–Milwaukee). She earned a teaching certificate after one year. Golda then taught in Milwaukee Public Schools and in a Jewish folk school.

Golda married Morris Meyerson, and they moved to Palestine, a state in the Middle East, in 1921. At that time Palestine was under British control. Arabs occupied most of the state. The Meyersons joined the movement to transform Palestine into the Jewish state of Israel. Golda took on several roles in Israel's government, including prime minister. She changed her name to Golda Meir in 1956. The name means "to illuminate" or "to burn brightly" in Hebrew. Fourth Street School was renamed Golda Meir Gifted and Talented School in 1979 and later the Golda Meir School.

About 53.5 percent of city residents identified as German American. More people read newspapers in German than in English. German art, opera, and theater were still popular. In 1891, German businessmen started a new social club. It was called the Deutscher (German) Club. The club purchased banker and politician Alexander Mitchell's home in 1898. They used it to host parties.

Milwaukee schools taught the German language. However, in 1889, the state government passed the Bennett Law. The law required all children between ages seven and fourteen to attend school. It also required that all core classes be taught in English. Core classes included mathematics, science, and social studies. The law applied to both public and private schools. Republican governor William Dempster Hoard signed it into law.

German Milwaukeeans saw the Bennett Law as an attack on their culture. Catholic and Lutheran schools denounced the law. The Democrats seized the opportunity to take over the state government. They condemned the law during the next election. They won the governorship and enough seats in the legislature to **repeal** the law. Public and parochial schools in Milwaukee went back to teaching German at all grade levels.

Meanwhile, on the south side, the Poles also faced discrimination. Walter Kempster was the city's health commissioner. He did not have any Polish doctors on his staff. He forced Polish children out of their homes to vaccinate them. He also required people to live in hospitals where they were isolated from others while his staff fumigated their homes during disease outbreaks. The Poles hated him so much that they stoned his ambulances. Poles also reported being mistreated by Milwaukee police officers.

Like other groups, Milwaukee's Poles chose to help themselves. They started fraternal organizations. The fraternal clubs sold low-cost life insurance to members. They also offered social activities like picnics, concerts, and plays. They sponsored boy and girl scout troops independent from national scout organizations. Fraternal clubs promoted American and Polish patriotism. They also directed consumers to Polish-owned businesses.

The Polish Roman Catholic Union of America (PRCUA) and the Polish National Alliance (PNA) were two of the biggest fraternal organizations for Poles. They had a bitter rivalry. PRCUA required its members to be Catholic. PNA let everyone in. Many of its members sent their children to public schools. Milwaukee's Archbishop Sebastian Messmer criticized them. He thought their children should go to Catholic schools. The two organizations founded rival newspapers.

The PNA newspaper attacked Messmer. Messmer was Swiss. PNA wanted a Polish bishop instead. Messmer retaliated. He forbade Catholics from reading the PNA's newspaper. The feud lasted until 1913, when Messmer received a Polish assistant.

Some new recreation options in the city appealed to people from many ethnicities. Amusement parks dotted the city and suburbs. Beer gardens offered food, beer, and bands. Miller's outdoor beer garden attracted a lot of working-class people. The Schlitz Palm Garden was indoors at Third Street and Wisconsin Avenue. It attracted people who were upper-middle class. It had a two-story atrium with lots of glass and marble. It featured exotic plants, artificial ponds, and fountains.

A hand-colored postcard of the Schlitz Palm Garden | *WHI Image ID 43001*

Baseball was popular with people across cultures and ethnicities. Milwaukee had some amateur teams in the 1860s. Its first professional team started playing in 1877. It was called the West End Club. In 1878, the team joined the National League as the Milwaukee Grays. The team finished in last place and shut down that year. The city hosted minor league baseball teams from 1884 until 1900. Some teams played under the name Milwaukee Brewers. Others called themselves the Milwaukee Creams or Cream Citys. They played most of their home games at Borchert Field. The stadium covered one square block at Eighth and Burleigh Streets. Connie Mack managed the team from 1897 until 1900. He is considered one of the greatest baseball managers in history. In 1900, the Milwaukee Brewers and seven other teams formed the American League. The owners of the league's eight teams had their first meeting in a tavern on Third Street and Kilbourn Avenue. The Brewers finished in second place in the league in 1900. Mack left to manage the Philadelphia Athletics, and the Brewers finished in last place in 1901 without him. The team moved to St. Louis in 1902 and became the Browns. Milwaukee then hosted a minor league team, also known as the Brewers. That team left for Ohio in 1953, the same year the Boston Braves moved to Milwaukee, bringing major league baseball back to the city.

Primary Sources

A Monster Factory Town

During the 1800s and 1900s, Milwaukee earned its reputation as an industrial city. In the following primary sources, two charts show the increase in production in two of Milwaukee's major industries: beer and leather. Two book excerpts delve into other products that Milwaukee factories cranked out. Look closely at these sources, and then answer the questions that follow.

Annual Production of Beer by Milwaukee Breweries, Select Years	
Year	Output (in barrels)
1866	68,658
1870	108,845
1874	292,141
1878	426,340
1882	1,052,436
1886	1,060,227
1890	1,928,082
1894	2,297,614
1898	2,184,428
1902	3,005,315
1906	3,677,095
1910	3,724,937

Hides Processed in Milwaukee Tanneries, Select Years	
Year	Output (in hides)
1866	176,217
1870	117,255
1874	203,410
1878	261,600
1882	484,674
1886	662,408
1890	662,456
1894	835,518
1898	1,015,022
1902	1,143,483
1906	2,082,186
1910	1,765,840

Source: *Fifty-Ninth Annual Report of the Chamber of Commerce of the City of Milwaukee* (Milwaukee: Radtke Bros. & Kortsch Co., 1917), 152, 170.

BOOK EXCERPT, 1922

[Christopher] Latham Sholes was the inventor of the typewriter. . . . Arthur L. Morsell a leading Milwaukee patent attorney tells the story of this remarkable invention as follows: "While the Sholeses, father and son, were not the first inventors of the broad idea, they developed the same a really practical and commercial machine. . . . The typewriter is one of the important inventions of modern times. As a substitute for handwriting, it is a great labor saver, not only for the individual who would himself write, but enables him to divide the work with another. In giving opportunity for wider business transactions with more accurate results and in providing employment for young women it is the chiefest instrument of the age, and Milwaukee, as will be seen has contributed largely to the development of this wonderful invention and has had and is entitled to an important and honorable part."

Source: William George Bruce, ed., *History of Milwaukee City and County*, vol. 1 (Chicago and Milwaukee: S.J. Clarke Publishing, 1922), 239, 241.

BOOK EXCERPT, 1922

As already stated, the industries of the city enjoy both stability and momentum in that they deal with a diversified list of articles which go in useful channels of life and must be regarded as necessities rather than luxuries. It is equally interesting to point out wherein or in what branches the production is notable or excels. The following provides instructive reading in this direction.

Iron and Steel—Milwaukee is one of the largest steel casting centers and has turned out some of the largest steel and grey iron castings made in the United States.

Machinery—Has some of the largest machinery construction shops in the world. Is a large producer of water pumping, ice making and refrigeration machinery. Has exported more excavating machinery than any other city in the country.

Engines—Has turned out large Diesel engines, the largest gas engines, Uniflow engine and a majority of the gas engines built in the United States.

Traveling Cranes—Has the largest and best equipped plant for the manufacture of electric traveling cranes and hoists in the United States. . . .

Gears and Controls—Milwaukee leads the country in the manufacture of herring bone gears for power transmission and gasoline locomotives for mining and plantation use. Furnished the electric firing controls for many battleships in the United States Navy and most of the automobile electric controls used in the country. . . .

Motorcycles—Milwaukee leads the world in the manufacture of highest quality motorcycles. . . .

Leather and Shoes—Milwaukee manufactures a more varied line of leathers than any other city in the United States. Is one of the leading shoe manufacturing cities in America. Its tanneries are among the greatest in the world. . . .

In bringing to a close this chapter, which must be regarded as the most important in noting material progress, the reader is brought to the inevitable conclusion that Milwaukee is primarily a monster factory town. Moreover, its future must be found in industrial production. It cannot in the nature of things become a successful rival to the world metropolis to the south [Chicago] either as a great financial or commercial center. Its operations in commerce and finance will always be important and will continue to grow but Milwaukee's future clearly lies in the industrial field.

Source: Bruce, *History of Milwaukee City and County*, 243, 245.

- **How did beer production and hide processing change between 1866 and 1910?**
- **In what way was the typewriter a labor-saving device? How did the production of typewriters benefit women?**
- **The author of the second book excerpt refers to "stability and momentum." What did he mean, and what evidence did he provide?**
- **How do you think different immigrant groups affected what industries grew in Milwaukee?**
- **How did the growth of these industries change the city from the mid-1800s to the early 1900s?**

CHAPTER 6

CHAPTER QUESTIONS

- What role did Milwaukee play in national events during this era?
- What are some ways that immigrants were **assimilated** or rejected? What effect did this have on society?
- How were Black American and Mexican American migrant experiences similar to the European immigrant experience? How were they different?
- How did World War I affect people's lives in Milwaukee? How did those lives change during the Roaring Twenties?

Socialism in an Age of War and Peace

1910–1929

Socialists continued their work in the period after 1910. However, their progress was interrupted by a world war. The war that would come to be known as World War I changed life in Milwaukee. It created prejudice against the German population and encouraged a culture of **conformity**. After the war, Americans enjoyed a period of economic growth. Milwaukee's exports increased, as did the number of people working in factories. Many more women joined the workforce. Black Americans and Mexican Americans came to Milwaukee to find jobs, and the city and suburbs expanded.

Boys of Riverside High School, in Milwaukee, with reading matter to send to the soldiers in France | ***WHI Image ID 132128***

Socialist Reforms

The socialists won the city and county elections in April 1910. They got to work right away. They improved daily life with better and more efficient services. They helped workers by increasing pay for city employees. Wages rose from $1.75 per day to $2.00 per day. Socialists awarded printing, horseshoeing, and other city contracts to union shops. They increased property taxes and cut costs to pay for these benefits.

The socialists were government reformers too. They conducted the city's first property inventory to see what the city actually owned. They took the names of dead people off the voting lists. The health department increased inspections of factories, milk plants, and schools.

Most people liked what the socialists did for the city. Many business owners did not, however. They complained about tax increases and union contracts. Democrats and Republicans ran joint candidates for office in 1912. They said the socialists were anti-American and anti-business. They claimed the socialists wanted a revolution. After that, the socialists lost most of their elections, including the mayor's office and Victor Berger's seat in Congress.

City Attorney Daniel Hoan was one of the exceptions. He won a lot of cases. He collected enough fees to pay for his entire department. He used no tax money. Even though he was a socialist, people thought of Hoan as a fiscal conservative, meaning he wanted to cut government spending and reduce people's taxes. He ran for mayor in 1916. He won by about 1,600 votes. Meanwhile, the Democrats and Republicans maintained control of the Common Council. This balance between socialists and non-socialists lasted for most of the next fifty years.

Poster urging Milwaukee men to enlist in the US Marines, created around 1917 | *WHI Image ID 130546*

The Era of World War I

Milwaukee was active in world affairs in the 1910s. It played an important part in the presidential election of 1912. It also participated in World War I, which began overseas in 1914. (The US entered the war in 1917.)

The presidential election of 1912 was unique. It was a four-way race. All four candidates were progressive in some way. Theodore Roosevelt was a former president. While in office, he set aside millions of acres of land to create the National Park Service. He also broke up companies that had grown too large through unfair business practices. Roosevelt had chosen not to run for a third term in 1908. He picked Secretary of War William Howard Taft as his successor. But Roosevelt disagreed with some of Taft's policies. He tried to win the Republican presidential nomination in 1912, but the party chose Taft instead. Roosevelt then started his own party called the Progressive Party. Woodrow Wilson was the third candidate in the 1912 presidential election. He was the Democratic governor of New Jersey. Finally, Eugene Debs ran as the Socialist Party candidate.

Roosevelt campaigned in Milwaukee on October 14, 1912. He walked out of his hotel on Third Street and Kilbourn Avenue. He was going to get into a car to ride up the street to the Milwaukee Auditorium (now the Miller High Life Theatre) to give a campaign speech when an unemployed saloonkeeper shot him from a distance of only five feet. Under normal circumstances, the wound would have been fatal. But the bullet passed through the breast pocket of Roosevelt's overcoat. The pocket contained his fifty-page folded speech and his steel-reinforced glasses. Roosevelt reached under his coat and

President Theodore Roosevelt leaving the Chicago and North Western Depot after arriving in Milwaukee on his October 14, 1912, visit, during which he was shot and wounded | *WHI Image ID 2096*

felt a bullet hole in his chest. He coughed and determined that his lung had not been punctured. A doctor told him to go to a hospital, but Roosevelt ordered his driver to take him to the auditorium. He informed the crowd that he had been shot and then declared, "It takes more than that to kill a bull moose." From that point on, the bull moose was used as a symbol of the Progressive Party. Roosevelt gave a shortened (but still ninety-minute) version of his speech and then went to the hospital. Doctors determined it was riskier to operate than it was to leave the bullet in his chest. He carried the bullet with him for the rest of his life.

Roosevelt came in second place with 27 percent of the vote. He drew enough votes away from Taft, the Republican, to allow Wilson to finish in first place and be elected president. Debs finished a distant fourth.

President Wilson promised to stay out of European affairs. However, World War I was hard to stay out of. The war had four long-term causes:

- **The alliance system:** Austria-Hungary, Germany, and Italy formed an alliance known as the Central Powers. Britain, France, and Russia were on the other side. They became known as the Allies. Each country had pledged to support the other countries in its alliance.
- **Nationalism:** Each country wanted to defend its national honor.
- **Militarism:** The countries increased the sizes of their armed forces. Britain, for example, had a policy of maintaining a navy that was larger than the next two navies (Germany and France) combined.
- **Imperialism:** The great powers of Europe competed to establish more colonies in Africa and Asia. They took natural resources out of the colonies and sold goods to the local peoples. This competition was also a matter of national pride.

These tensions came to a head in 1914. The Archduke Franz Ferdinand was heir to the Austro-Hungarian throne. He was visiting Bosnia, which was part of the Austro-Hungarian empire. Many Serbs lived in Bosnia, and some of them wanted to free Bosnia from Austrian rule. Then, they could combine Bosnia and Serbia into one country. Gavrilo Princip, a Serbian nationalist, shot and killed the archduke on June 28. Germany encouraged Austria to invade Serbia, which it did. Russia then attacked Austria to defend Serbia. (Russians and Serbs have a common ancestor—the Slavs.) Germany then attacked both Russia and France. Germany went through Belgium to get to France, even though Belgium was neutral. Britain then declared war on Germany and Austria-Hungary. Although Italy was allied to these countries, it chose to remain neutral. These events happened within two months of the assassination. Nearly all the other European countries took sides. Japan joined the Allies.

The United States was officially neutral. However, it sold weapons and supplies to Britain and France. American banks loaned money to them too. Several factors pushed the United States into the war. They included:

- In 1915, Germany sank the *Lusitania*, a British passenger ship that was secretly carrying weapons. Britain and the United States denied that there were weapons onboard. One hundred twenty-eight Americans were killed.
- The German foreign minister sent a secret telegram to the Mexican government in January 1917. He urged Mexico to invade the United States. He told Mexico to take back territory it had lost seventy years earlier in the Mexican War. The British intercepted the telegram. They published it in newspapers. Americans were outraged.
- Some Americans wanted to defeat the empires of Germany and Austria-Hungary to help spread democracy around the world.

General William "Billy" Mitchell in the cockpit of his airplane | *WHI Image ID 10623*

President Wilson asked Congress to declare war against Germany in April 1917. The vote was 82 in favor and 6 against in the Senate and 373 in favor and 50 against in the House of Representatives. Nine of the 50 votes against the war came from Wisconsin representatives. Initially, Milwaukee's Germans had divided opinions about the war. Some wanted to stay neutral. Others supported Germany. But once war was declared, most people supported it. The US War Department implemented a draft, but many men volunteered for military service.

Billy Mitchell was the most famous Milwaukeean in World War I. He was a grandson of Alexander Mitchell, the banker and railroad operator. Billy Mitchell realized that airplanes would be the future of war. He developed an early version of the air force within the US Army. Mitchell led several daring missions. After the war, he commanded the US Army Air Service. Milwaukee's General Mitchell International Airport is named after him.

History in Focus

The War at Home

Milwaukeeans supported the war in a number of ways besides serving in the armed forces. The US government sold bonds to pay for the war. Milwaukeeans bought $145 million of them. Unlike other socialists, Mayor Daniel Hoan supported the war. He organized the Milwaukee County Council of Defense. The council coordinated nearly 1,500 volunteers who served in bond drives, ran victory garden promotions, and contributed to defense work in local industries. The council also published the names of people who had not given much money to the bond drive, shaming them into donating. Milwaukee was one of the first cities to meet its sales goal.

Members of Milwaukee's Motor Corps of the National League for Women's Service, photographed in 1918. The corps performed errands and other services to support the war effort. | *WHI Image ID 1952*

Milwaukeeans supported the war with more than just money. They converted more than one thousand vacant lots into victory gardens to produce extra food. Eleven thousand schoolchildren took gardening classes. Bakers baked "war bread" using 25 to 50 percent less wheat. The wheat they saved went to the war effort. Women took classes on how to conserve food and clothing. Milwaukeeans did such a good job that they produced a surplus of food. True to the socialist tradition, Mayor Hoan sold the extra food to low-income residents at low prices.

Cultural Conflicts

With the declaration of war against Germany came a flood of anti-German feelings across the country. A presidential proclamation declared that German males over age thirteen who hadn't become US citizens were "alien enemies." These "alien enemies" had to abide by strict rules limiting their use of firearms, wireless radios, and aircraft. They could not "write, print, or publish" anything that would be considered a threat against the government or members of the military. Starting in November 1917, the "alien enemies" were required to register with local officials. Women were added to this requirement in April 1918.

Anti-German feelings and suspicions were devastating in Milwaukee. Some Milwaukeeans tried to purge the city of German culture. The *Milwaukee Journal* condemned German social clubs and the teaching of the German language in schools. It proclaimed, "Every effort will be made to separate the loyal from the disloyal." The public pressured city and school employees to take loyalty oaths. The Wisconsin Loyalty Legion threw yellow paint on the houses of families that did not buy war bonds. It also started a boycott of Milwaukee's German newspapers.

The pressure was very effective. People stopped speaking German in public. Schools virtually stopped teaching the language. More than two hundred German Milwaukeeans "Americanized" their names. For example, "Schmidt" became "Smith." The Deutscher Club renamed itself the Wisconsin Club. People even stopped eating the German dish sauerkraut—or they called it "liberty cabbage" instead of its German name. The city temporarily renamed streets. For example, Meinecke Street became Lee Street. Performances of German plays and concerts stopped.

Germans and Austrians had ruled the Poles, Croats, Czechs, Serbs, Slovaks, and Slovenes for centuries. The Slavs rejoiced that their

A group of women gathered at Second (now Seventh) Street in Milwaukee in 1918. The woman on the far right holds a sign that reads "Friends of the Polish Companies in the U.S. Army." | *WHI Image ID 87099*

homelands might be liberated. On June 9, 1918, twenty thousand Slavs paraded to the Milwaukee Auditorium for a demonstration. They waved American flags, sang patriotic songs, and pledged allegiance to President Wilson.

The war was over five months later. Poland became an independent country for the first time since 1795. The victors created the new nation of Czechoslovakia for the Czechs and Slovaks. They also created Yugoslavia for the Croats, Serbs, and Slovenes.

As a socialist, Victor Berger believed that greed had caused the war. Britain and Germany both wanted to control the world economy. American bankers wanted their loans repaid. Berger published editorials against the war in the *Milwaukee Leader*, his socialist newspaper. Subscriptions declined. The federal government would not allow the paper to send or receive mail. In 1918, the government arrested and charged Berger and four other national socialist leaders with **sedition**, a crime of rebellion against the government. Despite the charges, voters elected Berger to the House of Representatives that same year. However, when he arrived in Washington, DC, Congress disqualified him from serving. The seat stayed vacant. During his trial, Berger argued that free speech was on trial, but the jury convicted all five defendants anyway. Judge Kenesaw Mountain Landis sentenced them to twenty years in prison. Berger appealed. He claimed that Landis had already made up his mind before the trial. The US Supreme Court overturned the verdict in 1921.

People posing in front of the office of Victor Berger's *Milwaukee Leader* newspaper. Berger is in the second row, tenth from right. | *WHI Image ID 86894*

Socialism did not do as well in other parts of the United States as it did in Milwaukee. Russia had experienced a communist revolution in 1917. Some Americans began to fear that voting for a socialist was the same as voting for a communist. (Communism is an extreme form of government that eliminates private businesses and ownership. In communism, the state owns all property and wealth, and everyone is supposed to share in the labor and benefits. But that has not been the reality in communist countries, where dictators control citizens' lives.) To many workers, voting for socialists no longer seemed necessary. Democrats had won important rights for workers, including an eight-hour workday. National membership in the Socialist Party declined by 75 percent. It had less than twenty-seven thousand registered members by 1920.

Berger allied himself with progressive Republican senator Robert M. La Follette. The two men agreed on reforming government and business. They both wanted to keep the United States out of European wars. In 1924, La Follette ran for president of the United States as the Progressive Party candidate. He won just one state—Wisconsin. He died the following year.

Voters kept electing Berger to Congress until 1928, when a Republican defeated him. Berger returned to Milwaukee as a newspaper editor. In 1929, a streetcar hit him while he was crossing Third Street. It fractured his skull, and he later died. With two great leaders gone, socialism and progressivism became less powerful movements in Wisconsin and Milwaukee.

A New Conformity

After World War I ended in 1918, some Milwaukeeans tried to revive European traditions. They soon found out that it was almost impossible to do so. There was still too much anger toward Europeans.

Schools were one tool used to assimilate immigrants. In school, students learned the English language and so-called American values. The state of Wisconsin passed laws that required teenagers to attend school. Milwaukee Public Schools (MPS) built new senior high schools for the growing number of students. By 1931, MPS had ten senior high schools, including two technical schools. It also had nine junior high schools, including four technical schools. There were eighty-six elementary schools. MPS started night classes for adults, and thousands of immigrants enrolled.

Adults who did well in school might take the citizenship test. Those who passed became citizens. Groups of new citizens had a big celebration at the Milwaukee Auditorium. They performed ethnic songs and dances. They placed images of their national heroes on the "altar of citizenship" and sang patriotic songs. People dressed as George Washington, Thomas Jefferson, and Abraham Lincoln handed them their citizenship certificates. Symbolically, the immigrants gave up their heritages to become American.

Not all Americans welcomed immigrants, however. Some of the least tolerant were members of the Ku Klux Klan. The original Klan existed in the South after the Civil War. It largely died out in the 1870s. The new Klan organized in 1915, and its membership grew for a time after World War I. Milwaukee's chapter started in 1921. Madison, Racine, Kenosha, and Oshkosh also had chapters. Members of the Klan hated Black Americans, Jews, Catholics, and immigrants. They held rallies and intimidated people. Mayor Hoan condemned the Klan. Most people did not participate in or endorse its activities. The Klan was active in Wisconsin until about 1928.

A poster advertising an event held in Milwaukee County in 1924 by the Ku Klux Klan | *WHI Image ID 34508*

Laws passed in this era also reflected anti-immigrant feelings. In 1924, Congress passed the Immigration Act, which strictly limited the number of immigrants from southern and eastern Europe. It also banned immigration from Asia. Congress did not revise the act until 1952, when it allowed more non-Europeans to enter the United States.

In the 1920s, some Americans criticized European immigrants for drinking too much alcohol. They wanted Congress to pass a law called Prohibition that would ban the production and sale of alcohol. Some who favored Prohibition thought it would force immigrants to assimilate. Many also believed Prohibition would reduce crime, unemployment, and domestic violence. Opponents of Prohibition argued that city and state governments would lose important tax revenue from the sale of alcohol and that many people employed by the industry would have to find other work. They argued that some people would break the law and drink homemade alcohol, which could be unsafe. Despite these protests, Prohibition became part of the US Constitution in 1920 when Congress and the states passed the Eighteenth Amendment. Police arrested thirty Milwaukeeans for public drunkenness the night before it took effect. They were trying to get one last drink while they still could. Someone played "Taps," the bugle call that the US military traditionally uses at funerals and memorials, at the Schlitz Palm Garden that evening.

Brewing was one of Milwaukee's most important industries, so Prohibition hurt the city's economy. Milwaukee's nine breweries tried to find other things to make. Schlitz switched to candy bars. Pabst made cheese. Blatz and Miller bottled soda. However, no amount of alternate goods could keep all of the brewery workers employed. Many tried to find other work. The city had almost two thousand saloons in 1918. Most of them closed. Some saloons switched to serving soft drinks, but they were not very successful.

People posing on a Schlitz beer train to celebrate the end of Prohibition in Milwaukee in 1933 | *WHI Image ID 1929*

Many Milwaukeeans ignored Prohibition. The police department had a hard time enforcing a law that so many people did not like. Hardware stores sold equipment to people who wanted to make their own alcohol. Soft drink parlors secretly (and sometimes openly) sold alcohol. **Speakeasies** popped up. Many of them were in the Third Ward. They attracted a mix of social classes. After getting a drink, people could dance, gamble, or listen to jazz. Some speakeasies were tied to the Italian mafia. The mafia used threats, murder, and blackmail to keep the police at bay. Eventually, in 1926 and 1927, federal agents raided the Third Ward and shut down the speakeasies. Even then, people continued to make alcohol at home or open other speakeasies beyond the city limits.

Congress and the states repealed Prohibition in 1933 with the Twenty-First Amendment. The beer flowed again. Parties broke out in the streets of Milwaukee. On the day Prohibition ended, instead of playing "Taps," a band played "Happy Days Are Here Again" at the Schlitz brewery.

Roaring Technology in the 1920s

Following World War I, Americans enjoyed a period of economic **prosperity** known as the Roaring Twenties. Brewing beer was illegal, but other industries boomed. Life at work improved too. Women had more job opportunities. More products were available to more people and were sold at lower prices. There were more entertainment options than ever before.

Milwaukee exported goods all over the world. These goods included heavy machinery, cranes and hoists, steam shovels, gears, automobile frames, motorcycles, motors, wheelbarrows, silk hosiery, and kitchen appliances. Some industries doubled their exports in the 1920s.

In some cases, machines replaced human workers. For example, as more people bought automobiles, the number of people who worked with horses declined. Blacksmiths, who made and repaired iron objects by hand, virtually disappeared. Factories made large quantities of textiles. Department stores sold them at low prices. As a result, many tailors, seamstresses, shoemakers, and hatmakers went out of business.

While more people were needed to work in factories, laws that limited the number of immigrants allowed to enter the US caused a labor shortage. Employers improved wages and benefits to attract workers. Some companies offered paid vacation time and health insurance. Allis-Chalmers built a hospital for its employees. Companies built gymnasiums and parks. Employees could join athletic leagues, bowling teams, marching bands, and choral groups. Company picnics and Christmas parties became a normal part of work. A few employers offered classes on hobbies or financial planning. Northwestern Mutual Life, an insurance company, gave free lunches to its employees. As wages and benefits improved, the number of strikes declined sharply.

Operators on a telephone switchboard around 1920 | *WHI Image ID 9217*

Many women already worked outside the home to earn money. Now, even more women joined the workforce. As office work increased, some took jobs as secretaries and bookkeepers. Others became telephone operators, hairdressers, and manicurists. There was also a greater need for teachers as more children stayed in school. Women continued to work in restaurants, hotels, nursing, and domestic service. They made up about one-quarter of Milwaukee's factory workers in the 1920s.

Many jobs required technical training. The state started a network of vocational schools for teenagers and young adults in 1911. The Milwaukee Vocational School opened in 1912 under this law. It is now the Milwaukee Area Technical College. Men took classes in business and technical work. Women took classes on running a household. The school added nursing and teacher education programs in 1923. It started a junior college in 1934.

Traditional colleges also offered job training. More students enrolled at the Milwaukee Normal School. By 1922–1923, it had 1,874 students. The school became the Wisconsin State Teachers College in 1927. Marquette University expanded, adding programs in business and journalism. Its medical and dental schools expanded as well. It had the largest dental clinic of any school in the United States.

The more money people made, the more they could spend. A shopping trip to a department store was a big event. Department stores sold goods made in factories at low prices. They sold many types of products and services that were otherwise offered in separate stores. For example, Gimbels had full lines of clothing for every occasion. It also had a delicatessen, bakery, restaurant, beauty salon, shoe store, bridal store, expensive furs, and a travel service.

People also had many more grocery options in the 1920s. The stores of the 1920s were not the same as the supermarkets of today. Most shopping was done by women, who had to carry their groceries home from the store. Therefore, the stores were small, and every neighborhood had at least one. Max Kohl opened his first Kohl's Food Store at Kinnickinnic and Lincoln Avenues in 1927. He soon had several stores across the county. National chains such as Piggly Wiggly, Kroger, and A&P also came to Milwaukee. Piggly Wiggly closed in 1932, a victim of the Great Depression. It returned to Milwaukee in the mid-1960s. Kroger closed too. It came back in 2016 when it bought Roundy's, which owned Pick 'n Save. A&P stayed in Milwaukee until 1979. It returned in 1983, when it bought out Kohl's. The company closed all its Kohl's grocery stores in 2002.

In the 1920s, people began to eat out more often. Local legend George Webb opened his first restaurant in 1927. It had a menu of soups, hamburgers, eggs, toast, and coffee. His wife, Evelyn, made the soups. The George Webb restaurant chain still uses her recipes today.

There were also a lot of entertainment options in Milwaukee in the 1920s. The city had a team in the National Football League, the Badgers, from 1922 until 1926. It also had a Negro National League baseball team, the Bears, in 1923. There were several ballrooms in

Milwaukee. Some of them had room for as many as five thousand people. Smaller dance clubs attracted young people who danced popular dances like the Charleston. More people could afford to attend the theater, the opera, and live music than in years past. There were also free events offered by churches, schools, community organizations, and the Milwaukee parks.

Movies were fun too. Tickets cost between twenty-five cents and one dollar in the 1910s. The Butterfly Theater opened on Second and Wisconsin in 1911. The east side's Downer Theater opened in 1915 with a single screen. The Modjeska opened on Mitchell Street in 1924. Other theaters included the Oriental (1927), the Avalon (1929), and the Riverside (1929). Some, like the Bijou Theater, began in the 1800s as opera houses and later became movie theaters.The first movies were silent. "Talkies" premiered in 1927 with *The Jazz Singer*.

If people wanted to stay home, they could listen to the radio. Milwaukee's first radio broadcast was in 1922 on WAAK. The studio was in Gimbels department store. The station played phonograph records. It also had performances with live actors. Only 9 percent of Milwaukee-area families owned a radio in 1924. But by 1927, 44 percent of all area households owned one.

A crowd of people wait to enter the Bijou Theater in Milwaukee around 1917. | *WHI Image ID 52980*

New Arrivals and New Communities

As the labor shortage continued, more Black, American Indian, and Mexican people came to Milwaukee looking for jobs. Milwaukee annexed more land for the growing population. New suburbs developed. Both the city and the county improved services for residents. But discrimination based on race or ethnic background continued.

Two men work as part of a road crew paving Janesville Plank Road around 1912. | *WHI Image ID 40296*

Many Black Americans had arrived in Milwaukee during World War I. They were looking for jobs, but they had a hard time getting hired. In some cases they did not have the necessary skills. And some racist employers refused to hire them. Many Black Americans had to take low-paying service-sector jobs. Very few made enough money to buy homes. Many banks refused to offer loans to Black people. They had to rent instead. And racist practices even limited where Black people could rent.

Many Black Americans settled in a neighborhood north of downtown that became known as Bronzeville. It was between Third and Twelfth Streets, from North Avenue to State Street. White families had moved out of that area around the time of World War I. Most real estate agents would not sell Black Americans homes anywhere in the city.

Wisconsin had passed a law in 1895 that banned racial discrimination in public places. But racist people and rules still excluded Black Americans from many theaters, hotels, shops, restaurants, and other businesses. So Black Americans started their own stores, newspapers, churches, and social clubs. Bronzeville had many businesses owned by and catering to Black Americans. They included hotels and restaurants, music clubs, tailors and barbershops, doctors, and lawyers. Black Americans organized a Milwaukee branch of the National Association for the Advancement of Colored People (NAACP) in 1915 and a branch of the Urban League in 1919. One of the founders of the Milwaukee NAACP, Ardie Clark Halyard, also cofounded Wisconsin's

People entering the Shrine of Our Lady of Guadalupe in 1926 | *WHI Image ID 128190*

first Black-owned bank. She and her husband, Wilbur Halyard, opened Columbia Savings and Loan in 1924. They provided banking services, including home loans, to many Black Milwaukeeans. The Halyard Park neighborhood was later named for them.

The numbers of Mexican and Mexican American people in Milwaukee also grew after World War I and the Mexican Revolution (1910–1920). In 1920, Pfister & Vogel Leather brought almost one hundred Mexican men to the city. Company leaders used them as strike breakers at their tanneries. They did not inform the men why they were there. Other Mexican workers followed. Men usually came first. They saved money and then brought their families. Many of them settled on the south side to be close to their jobs and Catholic churches. Holy Trinity (orginally founded by German Catholics in the 1850s) and Our Lady of Guadalupe (established in 1926) became the centers of their religious communities. By 1927, there were more than three thousand Mexican and Mexican American people living in Milwaukee. They worked in most of the city's major factories. They also opened grocery stores, taverns, and other businesses. In 1929 and 1930, they formed organizations called *mutualistas*, or mutual aid societies. These groups provided gathering places, hosted cultural events, and raised money to help new Mexican immigrants. They also started several Spanish-language newspapers, the first in the city.

Native peoples continued to relocate to Milwaukee during this time. Some left homes on reservations to move to the city. Like other new arrivals, most were seeking better jobs and living conditions. Also similar to other groups, Native peoples created organizations where they could feel a sense of community. By 1937, Milwaukeeans from several Native nations would form the Consolidated Tribes of American Indians. It provided services and social events for Native peoples living in the city. The Consolidated Tribes dance group became a popular feature of many Milwaukee festivals and celebrations.

The city's population grew 55 percent between 1910 and 1930. More than half a million people lived in the city. In addition to the large number of people who came looking for work, there were two reasons for the growth. First, many of the new residents were young families starting to have children. Second, people lived longer than in past decades due to advances in nutrition, medicine, and sanitation. Life expectancy was only 38.7 years in 1920. By 1940, it was 58.4 years.

The city was very crowded. In fact, only New York City had more people per square mile in 1920. During the decade, many white families left the city for the suburbs. By 1930, more than one hundred thousand people lived in Milwaukee's suburbs. Fox Point and River Hills were two new suburbs. Dutch farmers had settled in both communities in the 1840s. In Fox Point, they found a point of land that jutted into Lake Michigan. They decided it looked like the head or nose of a fox. The name stuck. They named River Hills after the Milwaukee River. Wealthy east-side Milwaukeeans built vacation homes in both communities during the late nineteenth and early twentieth centuries.

For people who could afford one, the automobile made it easier for people to live in the suburbs. Only about 1 percent of all Wisconsin

As the city and suburbs grew, Milwaukee added and improved roads.
| *WHI Image ID 40323*

families owned a car in 1910. By 1920, car ownership had risen to around 50 percent of families. And by 1930, nearly every family in the state owned a car. The Model T was the most popular model. It sold for about $260 in 1925 ($3,500 today).

The new residents of the northern suburbs wanted better services than what the Town of Milwaukee provided. Therefore, Fox Point incorporated in 1926. River Hills followed in 1930. Local governments then enacted **zoning** laws, which are local laws that determine what can be built on a certain piece of land. These laws required residents to build homes on large lots. The average person could not afford that much land. Thus, the two suburbs were basically just for wealthy people.

Mayor Hoan wanted to reduce the city's density. He continued to annex land from adjacent towns. Milwaukee was twenty-five square miles in 1919. It grew to forty-four square miles by 1932. It brought water lines, sewer lines, and streetcars. It was also part of the interurban train system. The interurban connected many communities in southeastern Wisconsin.

Real estate developers advertised the new neighborhoods as ideal places to raise families. Germans left their downtown neighborhoods and moved north and northwest. Poles moved south and southwest. East-side Yankees migrated to the North Shore suburbs. Irish west siders went to Wauwatosa. Germans, Czechs, and Jews settled in Sherman Park. As these ethnic groups moved, they copied architecture from their old neighborhoods. The north side of the city, for example, is full of German bungalows.

The city laid sewer pipes wherever it went. It opened a sewage treatment plant at Jones Island in 1925. As a result, raw sewage no longer mixed with drinking water. The plant dried the sewage to make fertilizer. The island expanded to four or five times its original size.

The city passed a number of laws in the 1920s that improved the quality of life for residents. Its zoning laws required new buildings to be designed to blend in with existing buildings. A factory could no longer be built next to a house. The police and fire departments hired more personnel. The police started using radios to coordinate their patrols and responses to crimes. The city paved roads for automobiles. It installed its first two traffic signals in 1922. It began adding medians to streets in 1923 to improve safety. The city also hired more public health nurses.

Milwaukee County improved services too. It built a new courthouse on the west end of downtown between 1929 and 1931. The

The new Milwaukee County Courthouse, built between 1929 and 1931 | ***WHI Image ID 53158***

courthouse still stands and houses many county offices. It is next to the county jail and the sheriff's office. Socialist Charles Whitnall established the county's vast park system. The county purchased 2,173 acres of land by 1930 that became Brown Deer, Estabrook, Grant, Greenfield, and Whitnall Parks. The county built parkways to connect major parks to each other. In 1929, the city built Lincoln Memorial Drive, a three-mile parkway along Lake Michigan. It is still a scenic shoreline drive today, with beautiful views of the lakefront.

Primary Sources

Perspectives on Socialism

People have always disagreed about politics, and this was true for Milwaukee in the early 1900s. Although many embraced the goals of socialism, others voiced their objections. Read on for a few of the varied perspectives on socialism during this time. Then answer the questions that follow.

MILWAUKEE JOURNAL EDITORIAL, 1910

Milwaukee has elected the Social Democratic ticket. The election, however, does not mean Milwaukee has converted to Socialism. It simply means that Milwaukee has been driven, for the time being[,] to the Social Democracy. It is a revolt against both the old parties. It is not in any way an adoption or approval of the Socialistic principles of economics. It is simply a repudiation, a punishment of the old parties, for their unfitness and their inefficiency.

When one thinks of it, the result was almost inevitable. All through the years, Milwaukee has been misruled, exploited and misrepresented in every way. . . . The street railway and other selfish interests have been in the saddle most of the time. . . . Those in charge of the government have used their power for their own selfish ends. The civil service has been outraged, the spoils system has been in full operation and the interests of the people have been willfully injured whenever they have not been merely ignored. It has been the reign of ward heelers and cheap politicians—of the powers that prey.

It was as plain as day that the spirit of protest was growing. To those who were not blind, it seemed certain that unless decent city government was established and maintained, there would come a day of reckoning, a radical change in the aspect of things.

Source: "The Milwaukee Election," *Milwaukee Journal*, April 6, 1910, 6.

MEMOIR OF EMIL SEIDEL, MILWAUKEE'S FIRST SOCIALIST MAYOR, 1944

Some Eastern smarties called ours a "Sewer Socialism." Yes, we wanted sewers in the workers' houses; but we wanted much, oh, so very much more than sewers. We wanted our workers to have pure air; we wanted them to have sunshine; we wanted planned homes; we wanted living wages; we wanted recreation for young and old; we wanted vocational education; we wanted a chance for every human being to be strong and live a life of happiness.

And we wanted everything that was necessary to give them that: playgrounds, parks, lakes, beaches, clean creeks and rivers, swimming and wading pools, social centers, reading rooms, clean fun, music, dance, song, and joy for all. That was our Milwaukee Social Democratic movement. There was but one way to get all of that—go after it and get it.

Source: Emil Seidel, "Building the Social Democratic Party," *The Kingdom Come: Sketches from My Life*, Part III (Unpublished manuscript, 1944).

SPEECH BY WALTER H. BENDER, CIRCA 1935

When a city so constantly stands at or near the head of its class in winning national health awards, that is for this reason barred from competition and given instead a special honor certificate, the situation clearly indicates a health department of outstanding excellence.

Few of us realize the service which our health department is rendering to make these records possible and to make and keep Milwaukee a safe place to live. . . . It includes departments of child hygiene to safeguard the health of children before and during school life; of communicable disease, covering both diagnosis and prevention methods; of inspection of food and beverages; of laboratories for chemical and bacteriological research.

It embraces clinics, classes and home supervision in connection with tuberculosis, and examinations and instructions in reference to venereal diseases. It supervises our large emergency hospital. It maintains a corps of nurses in three stations and 78 districts, and keeps and publishes an elaborate system of vital statistics. . . .

Whenever the name Milwaukee is mentioned, such a comment immediately comes to mind—not only to us who live here, but to those who know Milwaukee only as we in turn know other great cities. What are some of the ideas the name "Milwaukee" immediately suggests?

A clean city. Clean first in the primary meaning of the word. Again and again, as I have shown strangers about the city their comment has always been, "I like this town; it looks so clean." And clean in the secondary sense of the word as well. Repeated in my practice clients from out of town, interested in procuring action from some department or officer in our city government, have been amazed when I assured them that graft has not been a thing with which they would have to contend—that it was unknown in the city hall.

A safe city. Safe in many ways. First, because its outstanding health record makes it a safe place in which to live and work. Second, because its comparative freedom from crime gives to all a freedom of security, which is absent in so many great cities in this generation. Third . . . our development has kept us free from excesses of expenditure, which in times of stress like the present, have brought disaster to many cities.

A progressive city. There is a happy medium between hectic expansion on the one hand and a stand-pat, ultra conservative attitude which blocks progress, on the other. Milwaukee stands out among her sister cities as progressive in this sense. The Bible tells us where there is no vision the people perish. Conversely, that community which has men and women of vision guiding its affairs and pointing out the way of real progress is happy indeed.

Source: "Bender Speech at Banquet Tribute to Hoan Idealism," *Milwaukee Leader*, circa 1935.

- **Choose two documents and explain why the socialists won in 1910.**
- **Which of these documents could best be used to summarize the achievements of the socialists? Why?**
- **How could Milwaukee socialism be considered both liberal and conservative?**

Struggles through Depression and War

1929–1945

CHAPTER QUESTIONS

- What factors caused the Great Depression? What factors led to its end?
- How did people in Milwaukee fare during the Great Depression?
- How did the people of Milwaukee contribute during World War II?
- How did workers and employers view strikes differently during this time?
- How do the recreation and entertainment options of the mid-twentieth century compare to today's options?

Some people have described the children born in the 1920s as the "greatest generation" in United States history because of the number of hardships they overcame. Whether or not it makes them the "greatest," they certainly had it hard. Many people lost everything in the 1930s during the Great Depression. Somehow, many survived. Those who had been left with nothing still served their country in World War II. Just like World War I, this war changed life for Milwaukeeans in significant ways.

The Great Depression put many Wisconsinites out of work. This engraving depicts people lining up to collect unemployment compensation payments. In 1932, Wisconsin became the first state to pass an unemployment compensation law. | *WHI Image ID 54579*

The Great Depression

The Roaring Twenties ended on October 24, 1929, with a devastating stock market crash. Stock markets go through cycles of growth and decline. The 1920s was a period of very strong growth. The growth, however, was based on loans. Some Americans had purchased stocks (shares of a company) on margin, meaning they paid 10 percent or 20 percent of the price and borrowed the rest of the money. Investors panicked when the stock market declined 11 percent in one day. They wanted to get their money out of stocks right away. A massive sell-off occurred on October 29, which is now known as Black Tuesday.

People panicked. They rushed to the banks to take out all their money. But banks keep very little money on hand; they loan out almost all of it to their customers. Therefore, banks were unable to return money to the panicked savers. Many banks had to close.

The engraving at the beginning of this chapter depicts a scene much like the one in this photo. Here, people line up in Milwaukee's City Hall to register for unemployment compensation around 1936. | *WHI Image ID 80339*

The Great Depression that followed did not affect Milwaukee much at first. Factories continued to fill orders. They ended the year with a profit. But as the Depression wore on, orders declined. Factories closed or laid off employees. The number of workers in Milwaukee County declined by 44 percent between 1929 and 1933. Wages decreased by almost 65 percent. As a heavily industrial city, Milwaukee suffered more than most.

Milwaukeeans learned to live with less. Statewide, grocery sales fell 43 percent between 1929 and 1933. People bought less and cheaper food. They ate less meat, which was expensive to buy. Milwaukee Public Schools (MPS) reported that the number of underweight children more than doubled between 1929 and 1935. People wore clothes until they were worn out. Parents stitched together old clothes into new garments for their children. People stopped going to the dentist. A lot of people could not pay their mortgages. They lost their homes. As a result, they moved in with relatives or friends. Sometimes, three or more families lived in a house meant for one. In other cases, children worked part-time jobs to help their families. Common jobs for children included selling newspapers or shining shoes. Some families abandoned children they could no longer afford to keep. A few children left home so they would not be a burden to their families. Without a source of income, some people were forced to barter, or trade, for the things they needed. In 1935, a west-side auto dealer advertised that he would trade a car for a horse or a cow.

Milwaukee's socialists promised to help low-income residents. They did very well in the 1932 elections. Daniel Hoan easily won a sixth term as mayor. The socialists also won the offices of city attorney and city treasurer. They captured twelve of the twenty-seven seats on the Common Council. Two Polish Democrats on the council often voted with them. Thus, Hoan had a working majority of fourteen votes on the Common Council. This allowed him to get some significant legislation passed. Under Mayor Hoan, the city paid unemployed people to perform jobs around the city, such as cleaning city streets and parks, improving playgrounds, and digging the Jackson Park lagoon. Hoan encouraged citizens to give people odd jobs too. Hoan also provided hot meals to residents who needed them.

It was not easy for the city to pay for these programs. Many unemployed people stopped paying their property taxes, a major source of income for the city. Therefore, Hoan had to make budget cuts. Hence, the city paved almost no streets in 1933. Hoan also reduced park lighting by one-third. Librarians cut stories out of magazines and bound them together into "books." Hoan asked city workers to accept a 10 percent wage cut. The city ran out of money in 1933, so it issued **scrip** instead. A lot of other cities in the United States did the same. By 1938, Milwaukee had issued $14.6 million of scrip.

The school district had to make cuts too, even though enrollment increased. It stopped building schools. It also laid off teachers. Some teachers had as many as forty-eight students in a class. MPS shortened the school year so it could pay teachers for fewer days.

Milwaukee County was legally required to care for those living in poverty. At one point, in 1935, the county was helping one-third of its residents. It set up relief stations that provided food to tens of thousands of families. Families received cereal, oatmeal, flour, milk, potatoes, and cheap cuts of meat. The county also provided low-grade coal for people to burn for heat. It helped people pay their rent and utility bills. Men had the opportunity to work on county park improvement jobs to earn additional funds. County taxes doubled between 1928 and 1932 to pay for these expenses.

Mayor Hoan wanted to combine the city and county governments to save money. He did not see a reason to have separate law enforcement, fire protection, and parks systems. In this plan, Hoan would have been the sole leader, or chief executive. Eighty percent of county residents already lived in the city. Voters overwhelmingly passed a referendum to combine the two governments. But the referendum was nonbinding, meaning the government did not legally have to obey it. The state refused to agree to the merger. Some people in the state legislature worried that a larger city would give the socialists more power. However, the city was still able to transfer all its parks to the county by the end of 1936.

Milwaukeeans received a lot of help from the federal government. Voters elected Franklin Roosevelt president of the United States in 1932. He promised "a new deal for the American people." The New Deal put people back to work with government jobs. These jobs were supposed to be temporary until the private sector could recover and hire workers. The jobs did not pay much, but they were still jobs. New Deal programs put tens of thousands of people in the county to work. In 1936 alone, Milwaukee County residents received nearly $26 million in benefits.

Some of these government jobs were done indoors. The federal government's Works Progress Administration (WPA) hired people to catalog the police department's fingerprint file. It also hired people to create an index of *Milwaukee Sentinel* articles for the public library.

Franklin D. Roosevelt campaigning for the presidency in Milwaukee in 1932. FDR is in the car, waving his hat to the crowd. | *WHI Image ID 54380*

People cleaned public buildings that had not been thoroughly cleaned in a while. WPA workers wrote histories and guidebooks for the city and some of the suburbs. Workers collected and repaired seventy-five thousand toys and bicycles. They then loaned them out to children. The county used WPA funds to sponsor art shows and Music under the Stars, a series of concerts in the parks.

Workers on a WPA program site at the State Fair Grounds in 1939 | *WHI Image ID 33205*

The WPA also sponsored the Milwaukee Handicraft Project. It was one of the few WPA programs run by and for women. It started in 1935. It employed seven hundred women during its first year. They made scrapbooks to entertain hospital patients. They also repaired and bound books for schools. The program trained nearly five thousand people, most of them women, to make dolls, costumes, drapes, quilts, and furniture. The Handicraft Project was also significant for employing a large number of Black women in a racially integrated environment. The women could use the training they received to move on to

Milwaukee women participate in a sewing project in the 1930s, making and repairing clothing for families who could not afford to pay for new clothes. | *WHI Image ID 54580*

other WPA jobs that paid more money. The program ended in 1942, as women took war-related jobs in factories at the start of World War II.

Most New Deal programs employed people in outdoor jobs. WPA and Civil Works Administration (CWA) workers built new parks and repaired existing ones. They repaired park buildings, band shells, bridges, playgrounds, and public art displays. They completed swimming pools in Greenfield and McGovern Parks. They installed electricity, sewer systems, sprinkler systems, and underground telephone lines in several other parks. Thousands of workers repaired streets, bridges, and sidewalks. They improved parkways, sewers, and creeks. They also remodeled schools, firehouses, and the Milwaukee Public Museum. They gave guided tours of the Washington Park Zoo and tended the flowers at the county greenhouse.

Another agency, the Public Works Administration (PWA), had two major building projects in Milwaukee: the Parklawn housing project and the Linnwood Water Treatment Plant. The Parklawn housing project opened in 1937 on forty acres of land west of Sherman Boulevard at Mud Creek (now called Lincoln Creek). Most of the homes were two-story brick houses. The project had 518 housing units for low-income families. There were 1,400 families on the waiting list by 1938. The federal government turned over Parklawn to the city of Milwaukee in 1950.

HISTORY IN PERSON

Linnwood Water Treatment Plant

The Linnwood Water Treatment Plant was the Public Works Administration's second big project in Milwaukee. It put 1,700 men to work and cost $5 million. The plant opened on the east side of Milwaukee in 1939. The building was architecturally impressive, with an iconic central tower. It was built to provide clean drinking water to the city and reduce water-borne illnesses. The plant still functions today, treating water from Lake Michigan to provide millions of gallons of clean water to residents every day.

Aerial view of the water treatment plant on the shore of Lake Michigan, photographed in 2016 | *Carol M. Highsmith Archive, Library of Congress, Prints and Photographs Division*

Young men and women who needed jobs could join the National Youth Administration (NYA). One NYA program employed young women, ages eighteen to twenty-five, to make clothes for families receiving aid from the government. Another program made gym uniforms and aprons for MPS. MPS used the aprons in kindergartens and in cooking and shop classes. The NYA also made operating-room uniforms for doctors and nurses. Workers established a weaving department to produce upholstery material and woven rugs. By 1940, the NYA had trained more than two thousand young people.

Men also had the opportunity to join the Civilian Conservation Corps (CCC). The CCC was for men ages seventeen to twenty-eight. They worked in six Milwaukee parks: Estabrook Park, Grant Park, Honey Creek Parkway, Menomonee River Parkway, Sheridan Park, and Whitnall Park. The CCC required its workers to live in barracks in the parks. The program gave them free meals and five dollars per month. It also sent twenty-five dollars home to workers' families. The CCC constructed a dam in Estabrook Park to control flooding. It also started an erosion-control project for the Honey Creek Parkway. It improved other parkways by building roads and bridges and planting trees and shrubs.

HISTORY IN PERSON

Whitnall Park

Whitnall Park has been called the crown jewel of Milwaukee. CCC workers built roads and bridges for the park. They dug lagoons and a lake. They also cleared blockages from streams, built dams, and developed waterfalls. The CCC moved tons of earth, planted thousands of trees and shrubs, and created an eighteen-hole golf course. The WPA also provided workers for the project beginning in 1939. They took the interurban train to the park each day and created beautiful gardens. Today, Whitnall Park is Milwaukee County's largest public park with 606 acres of land, nine flower and plant gardens, miles of trails, and a variety of ecosystems.

Gardens at Whitnall Park in 2022 | *Lightburst via Wikimedia Commons*

A child rides his tricycle at the end of a cul-de-sac in his Greendale neighborhood around 1939.
| *WHI Image ID 32013*

The CCC's biggest building project in Milwaukee was the Village of Greendale. It was one of three federally sponsored "greenbelt communities." The others were Greenhills, Ohio, and Greenbelt, Maryland. An office of the US government called the Resettlement Administration designed them. The communities combined the advantages of city and country life. Each village was near a major city: Milwaukee, Cincinnati, or Washington, DC. The villages were surrounded by parkland, garden areas, and farms. Roads and train tracks connected them to the cities.

Nearly two thousand men from the WPA built 572 living units in 366 buildings in Greendale. The buildings had concrete foundations, cinder-block walls, and no basements. Each home had a utility room with a coal-fired furnace and laundry facilities.

The village opened in 1938. It offered housing at low rents for lower-middle-class families. A newly married couple might start out in a small "Honeymooner." They could move to a bigger unit after they had children. The homes encircled a village square with shops, offices, and a village hall. Walking paths connected the neighborhoods to each other and to the square.

Greendale was designed to be a model city for working-class residents. Yet the people who planned it used racist policies to restrict who could live there. Only white people were allowed to rent homes in Greendale.

The federal government later allowed the residents to purchase their homes. The village also grew over time. The original village became a historic landmark in 2013. The original homes are no longer affordable for lower-middle-class people.

Progress in Hard Times

As bleak as things were, not everything in the Great Depression was bad. With no jobs, Milwaukeeans had more time to further their educations and to pursue low-cost entertainment.

More teenagers chose to stay in school than in previous decades. Milwaukee used New Deal funds to build new schools, including Pulaski High School. Adults took classes in art, dance, and vocational skills at the school district's thirty-two social centers.

The city's libraries were free to use. The number of books checked out increased 24 percent between 1929 and 1932. Part of the increase was due to a new mobile delivery service. The central library also created new research departments, making it useful to more than just casual readers.

There were many other free or low-cost entertainment options as well. For about a quarter, people could see a movie or a circus performance. Children could play on free playgrounds. Church and fraternal activities were a lot of fun too. The county used more than $1 million in New Deal funds to improve the Milwaukee Public Museum. More than one million people visited the sunken gardens at Mitchell Park in 1938 to see the flowers in bloom. The county offered dance classes in the public parks. It also built band shells at Washington Park and Humboldt Park. Both parks still host free concerts today.

Sports remained popular in the 1930s. Borchert Field got electric lights in 1935. This allowed the minor league Milwaukee Brewers to play night games. Company teams, like the Milwaukee Valves and

Children at the public library in Greendale around 1938
| *WHI Image ID 63058*

the Ryczek Morticians, played sandlot games. Attendance was free. Some of those games drew more than ten thousand spectators. The Green Bay Packers football team played some of their games at Borchert Field in the late 1920s and early 1930s. They moved their Milwaukee games to State Fair Park in 1934. They beat the New York Giants there in the 1939 National Football League Championship. Both amateur and professional boxing were popular. People had more time for recreational sports, and bowling was so popular that Milwaukee was considered the bowling capital of the world during this time.

A program for a football game between the Green Bay Packers and the Chicago Cardinals, played at Milwaukee's Wisconsin State Fair Park in 1939 | *WHI Image ID 87508*

After Prohibition ended in 1933, the city's seven remaining breweries and taverns went back to doing what they did best. The city hosted a celebration party at the Milwaukee Auditorium. It admitted fifteen thousand people and turned away another five thousand. By the end of the night, the crowd had eaten 500 pounds of hot dogs, 300 pounds of potato salad, and 250 pounds of sauerkraut.

The party was so popular that Mayor Hoan made it an annual event at the lakefront. The event was known as the Midsummer Festival. It included boat races, carnival rides, theater performances, and ethnic dances. It also had concerts by accordion orchestras, high school bands, and church choirs. The city held the event every year from 1933 to 1941. It drew more than one million visitors. It was the forerunner of Summerfest and the city's ethnic festivals.

Milwaukee in the 1930s had a lot of family-friendly entertainment options. A description of the city in *Milwaukee in the 1930s: A Federal Writers Project City Guide* (which was funded by the New Deal) does not sound very different from the city today:

> It is to be sure, the rankest exaggeration, and it is resented as such, to say that "Milwaukee takes the sidewalks up at ten o'clock," for there is quite a little downtown activity right up until midnight. But "night life" to the majority of Milwaukee citizens means gathering of friends in one anothers' homes, an early movie, a fish fry in the corner saloon, study or play at the evening schools or social centers, a meeting at the club, trade union or church society, or "just the family" at home listening to the radio. Lights wink out and the city goes to bed early; if the radio blares too loud and long neighbors may call a squad car. Saturday is firmly established as "date night;" it is difficult to get a big party of Milwaukeeans together during the week, and they will readily admit their town cuts a poor figure as a siren among cities. Milwaukee-after-dark is no "glamour girl," but a comfortable matron relaxing in bedroom slippers.

Shifts in Power

Labor unions gained strength under the New Deal. Socialist ideas remained popular, though the Social Democrats lost power. In 1933, Congress passed laws to make it easier to form unions. Unions went on strike for better pay, benefits, and working conditions. There were 107 strikes in Milwaukee in 1934. Twenty-seven thousand workers participated. Almost every strike resulted in a 5 to 10 percent increase in workers' wages. Strikes were so common that the students at Dover Street School in Bay View tried one. They demanded no homework and shorter school days. They were not successful.

A strike by transit workers in 1934 turned deadly. During the Depression, fewer people rode streetcars because they did not have jobs to go to. The Milwaukee Electric Railway and Light Company (TMER&L) cut wages to make up for the loss of fares. Eight union organizers protested, and TMER&L's president, S. B. Wray, fired them. Union members walked off their jobs on June 26, and the electric streetcars ground to a halt. More than thirty thousand union supporters took to the streets of Milwaukee and West Allis. Riots broke out. Police arrested ninety-seven people. Fifty people, including seven police officers, were injured in just three days. A crowd of five thousand people stormed the Lakeside Power Plant in St. Francis. They wanted to shut down power from Port Washington to Kenosha. One person in the crowd died after being accidently electrocuted. Management and labor agreed to meet. The TMER&L president agreed to almost all union demands in just two minutes.

Franklin D. Roosevelt (in dark hat), Wisconsin governor Julius P. Heil (at far left), and other officials visit the Allis-Chalmers plant in 1942. | *WHI Image ID 2024*

The strikes were effective. Average pay for factory workers was $16.14 per week in 1932. It increased to $24.11 per week by 1936. Paid vacation time became normal. In light of these victories, even more people joined unions. There were fifteen thousand union members in Milwaukee County in 1929. By 1939, membership reached more than one hundred thousand. New unions organized too. Some people accused unions of being communist or anti-American. In reality, most union members considered themselves to be very good Americans. They celebrated patriotic holidays and pledged themselves to their country.

As a socialist, Daniel Hoan supported unions. However, fewer people voted for socialists after 1933. Franklin Roosevelt used a lot of socialist ideas in the New Deal. Voters concluded that Democrats could get them everything that socialists could. They still reelected Hoan in 1936. However, the Social Democrats kept only five of the twenty-seven seats on the Common Council. After that, Hoan had a hard time fulfilling his goals without majority support among the aldermen.

In 1912, Wisconsin had switched to nonpartisan elections for most local offices, such as alderman, county board, mayor, and state superintendent of public instruction. This system is still used today. Candidates run without party labels in a primary. The top two candidates from the primary advance to the general election. Milwaukee had very few Republicans. Therefore, most of the time, the general election came down to a Social Democrat and a Democrat.

The Democrats ran Carl Zeidler for mayor in 1940. He was a well-liked candidate. He was very outgoing and an excellent singer. He went around the city and sang *God Bless America* and popular music. He could sing in four or five languages, which helped him campaign in every ethnic neighborhood. He often brought along a brass or jazz band. Zeidler was thirty-one years old and unmarried. He stayed quiet on controversial issues. He finished in second place in the primary. Hoan finished first. The two men faced off in the general election. People liked Zeidler's personality, youth, and enthusiasm. They elected him with 56 percent of the vote.

Escorted by an honor guard of scouts, Mayor Carl Zeidler leaves city hall to participate in events at the Wisconsin State Fair in 1941. | *WHI Image ID 33331*

Zeidler proved that running for office and running the city are two different things. He did not have the knowledge or skills to make changes in city government. So he stuck with what he knew best, which was singing and speaking at public events. That would all change halfway through his term when the United States entered World War II in 1941.

Milwaukee in the War

World War II had its roots in World War I. Italy and Japan had not received much land after the first war. They felt they deserved more and wanted to expand. The victors also punished Germany severely. They took away a lot of its territory and most of its military. Germany wanted to regain power, status, and land.

Germany, Italy, and Japan all had economic problems in the 1920s. Italy had high inflation, and many workers were without jobs. Japan had few raw materials. Germany was supposed to pay very large **reparations** to Britain and France but was unable to do so. The Great Depression made things even worse for all three countries.

The leaders of the three countries promised to solve their people's problems. The king of Italy appointed Benito Mussolini, a socialist, prime minister in 1922. By 1923, Mussolini had total control of Italy. He outlawed other political parties. He seized control of the press, banks, industry, and labor. In Japan, Emperor Hirohito was the official leader. However, the military generals had the real power. They invaded China in 1931. They wanted China's oil and other natural resources. Then they could expand the military and conquer eastern Asia. Finally, the president of Germany appointed Adolf Hitler as chancellor (head of the government) in 1933. Hitler modeled his rule after Mussolini's. He won full legal control of Germany by 1934. He outlawed all political parties, other than his own Nazi Party. Hitler blamed the Jewish people for Germany's loss in World War I. Jews were an easy scapegoat because Germans saw them as outsiders. Many Jewish people lived in Germany, but they were not considered German by their countrymen.

The three countries made very aggressive moves between 1935 and 1939. Italy invaded Ethiopia and Albania. Japan was in an open war with China. Germany annexed Austria and invaded Czechoslovakia. The leaders of Italy, Japan, and Germany agreed to an alliance in May 1939. They were then known as the Axis powers. Hitler invaded Poland in September of that year. By 1940, Germany controlled most of Europe, including France. Italy was fighting in multiple parts of North Africa that same year. Japan conquered large parts of Southeast Asia and many Pacific islands by 1941. Britain was the only major power that was still fighting in Europe at that point.

The United States was officially neutral until 1941. However, it sent weapons to Britain. It also placed economic sanctions, or penalties, on Japan. For example, the US banned the sale of oil to Japan. Japan responded by bombing the American naval base at Pearl Harbor,

Hawaii, on December 7, 1941. Congress declared war on Japan the next day. Germany and Italy declared war on the United States four days later, on December 11.

World War II involved almost all Americans in one way or another. Milwaukeeans, including German immigrants, condemned Hitler. Roughly seventy thousand Milwaukee men and women joined the armed forces. Carl Zeidler was one of them. He resigned as mayor and accepted a commission aboard a US merchant vessel. He was in charge of a gun crew. The ship left New York in September 1942. A German submarine torpedoed the ship in December. Zeidler never made it back.

Milwaukee industry also contributed to the war effort. Allen-Bradley made aircraft instruments, radar sets, and walkie-talkies. Ladish Company made plane propellers. Falk Corporation made gears for ships. A. O. Smith produced torpedo casings and aircraft landing gear. It became the largest bomb maker in the United States. Harley-Davidson made military motorcycles. Most notably, Allis-Chalmers put twenty-five thousand people to work at one point during the war. It made battlefield tractors and motors and electronic components for ships. It also worked on the Manhattan Project, the US government program that developed the atomic bomb.

Welder Enola O'Connell working on a gasoline trailer tank at Milwaukee's Heil Company in 1943 | *WHI Image ID 40876*

World War II ended the Great Depression. Nearly anyone who wanted a job could have a job. Men left small towns to find work in factories in the city. The migration of Black and Native peoples to Milwaukee increased. Unfortunately, even with a labor shortage, people in minority groups often found only lower-paying jobs or jobs with poor working conditions. And many unions still accepted only white people as members at this time. Many women went to work as their husbands and brothers went off to war. In fact, women made up one-third of Allen-Bradley's workers. However, women earned less money than men and rarely served as union leaders. And many women still had children to care for at home.

History in Focus

Remarkable Women in Wartime

Many Milwaukee women made extreme sacrifices for the war. Mildred Fish-Harnack was one of them. She was born in Milwaukee in 1902 and attended West Division High School. In 1925, she earned a master's degree from the University of Wisconsin. She married Arvid Harnack, a native of Germany, in 1928. The couple moved to Germany, where Mildred earned a doctorate. The Harnacks were against Adolf Hitler and the Nazi Party, and they decided to actively work against them. The Harnacks used their connections to meet influential people. They obtained classified information about German military activities. They used secret radios to transmit the information outside of Germany. German authorities arrested them in 1942. They convicted the Harnacks of spying. They hanged Arvid on Christmas Eve. Initially, Mildred got a four-year prison sentence. However, Hitler wanted to make an example out of her. He had her executed on February 16, 1943. Mildred was the only American woman executed on Hitler's personal orders.

Another Milwaukee woman who joined the war effort was Elizabeth Richardson. Richardson graduated from Milwaukee-Downer College and worked for several years in advertising before joining the American Red Cross with several friends. They traveled to England and France, where they volunteered as part of a "Clubmobile," a group of volunteers who provided doughnuts and coffee to troops. Their visits provided a much-needed connection to home during the war. Richardson died in July 1945 in a plane crash while traveling between assignments. She was twenty-six years old.

Milwaukee residents made many adjustments to their everyday lives during wartime. They practiced blackouts to protect the city from German bombers, in case the planes ever made it that far. Every neighborhood was supposed to have an air raid warden to keep people safe and administer first aid if an attack happened. People had to ration basic items. Metal, tires, and gasoline were in short supply. So were basic food items like meat, butter, and sugar. The federal government sent many of these items to soldiers who were fighting the war. It issued **ration books** containing stamps to civilians. Shoppers needed stamps to purchase food and other household goods. This limited how much each person could buy so that more resources could be directed to the war effort. People also planted victory gardens to grow their own food. Milwaukee County opened up ninety acres of parkland to cultivation. One group of patriotic police officers grew tomatoes and cucumbers behind their precinct station.

Many Americans learned to do without items they were used to having. They ate peanut butter and jelly sandwiches when they could not get meat. To save gasoline, people stopped driving. Trolley ridership soared. Stores no longer made deliveries. High schools canceled their proms to conserve electricity in the high school gymnasium. Students at Boys' Technical High School made machine tool parts for the war effort. Other high school students made ping-pong paddles for the Red Cross and crutches for veterans.

Factories worked around the clock, seven days a week, to meet production demands. Catholic churches offered midnight masses for people who had to work Sunday mornings. Theaters showed movies and wartime newsreels late at night or early in the morning for people who worked second shift, or from late afternoon through the evening hours. The minor league Milwaukee Brewers played some early-morning baseball games so factory workers could attend. The ushers wore pajamas and passed out cereal and doughnuts to fans. A pajama-wearing band played between innings.

As professional baseball players left to serve in the military, a Midwest women's baseball league was formed. Milwaukee's team, called the Chicks, competed for only the 1944 season of the All-American Girls Professional Baseball League. They won the league championship that year but then relocated to Michigan.

Factory workers producing artillery shells in Milwaukee in 1941 | *WHI Image ID 59479*

People followed news coverage of the war closely. Milwaukee native Louis Lochner was a reporter in Berlin. He criticized German propaganda. He won a Pulitzer Prize for his coverage of *Kristallnacht* ("the night of broken glass"). On this night in 1938, Nazi troops destroyed seven thousand Jewish businesses and more than fifteen hundred synagogues across Germany and Austria. They killed hundreds of Jews that night. They also arrested more than thirty thousand men in the weeks that followed. They sent the men to concentration camps, where many of them were killed. After the declaration of war between the US and Germany, Nazis held Lochner and other American journalists prisoner for five months.

Photo taken by Dickey Chapelle of a flight nurse named Gwen Jensen standing with wounded marines awaiting takeoff near Iwo Jima, Japan, around 1945 | *WHI Image ID 85385*

Georgette "Dickey" Chapelle grew up in the Village of Shorewood, a Milwaukee suburb. | *WHI Image ID 11541*

Meanwhile, in the Pacific, Milwaukee-born Georgette "Dickey" Chapelle covered the war. She was one of just a few female combat photographers. Chapelle had earned a scholarship to the Massachusetts Institute of Technology (MIT) to study aeronautical design when she was sixteen years old. That kind of achievement was unheard of for a woman at the time. She adopted her nickname "Dickey" from Admiral Richard "Dickey" Byrd. She was fascinated by Byrd's expedition to Antarctica. Chapelle left MIT after two years because she spent too much time at the airport watching planes take off and land. She wanted to be a pilot but was nearsighted, which disqualified her. After a job taking photographs for an airline in New York City, she got work as a war correspondent. She took pictures for *Look*, *National Geographic*, and several other magazines. She photographed battles at Iwo Jima, Okinawa, and Guam. She was later killed while taking photographs during the Vietnam War.

As amazing as these stories are, the Milwaukeean who made the most headlines in World War II was neither a man nor a woman—she was Gertie the Duck. Gertie provided a welcome distraction from the war. In April 1945, Karl Schulz, a Wisconsin Avenue bridge tender, discovered a mallard duck had built a nest on a piling near the bridge. Schulz called the *Milwaukee Journal*. The *Journal* sent outdoor writer Gordon MacQuarrie to the scene. MacQuarrie gave Gertie, as she came to be known, a lot of coverage in the newspaper. Gertie laid her first egg on April 25. She had laid three more by April 28, two days before Adolf Hitler's death by suicide. John Stich, another bridge tender, announced, "If anyone harms one of those eggs, this town ain't fit to live in." Three more eggs had arrived by May 2, and so had two ships that needed the bridge raised. By now, a crowd had gathered. There was a hushed silence as the bridge opened and everyone stared. Gertie's nest went undisturbed as she guarded her eggs from the passing ships. She laid her ninth and final egg on May 4. Mother's Day arrived seven days later, and people sent her cards.

Gertie made headlines across the country and in Britain. The crowds grew with each passing day. People simply stood on the bridge and watched Gertie sit on her eggs. The first egg hatched on May 25. Boy Scout Troop 13 formed a "Gertie patrol" to protect Gertie and her duckling from the crowd. Bridge tenders went on day-and-night guard duty. Gertie hatched five more ducklings by May 31. Volunteers moved the new family to a display window at Gimbels, where they received more than two million visitors. Five of the ducklings survived infancy. The Juneau Park lagoon became their permanent home. A bronze Gertie sculpture now sits atop the bridge, adjacent to the Milwaukee Riverwalk.

The war in Europe ended on May 7, 1945; the Axis powers of Germany and Italy had lost. The United States dropped atomic bombs on Japan on August 6 and 9, then declared victory in the Pacific on August 14. Tens of thousands of people swarmed the streets of downtown Milwaukee in celebration. The next day, they began the difficult task of adjusting to their peacetime lives.

Primary Sources

The Great Migration

Six million Black Americans moved from the South to the North between 1916 and 1970. Historians call this movement the Great Migration. Most moved north to find jobs. The population of Black Americans in Milwaukee increased rapidly. In 1900, Milwaukee was home to 862 Black Americans. By 1940, that number had increased to 8,821.

In some ways, Black Americans had a similar experience to that of European and Asian immigrants who moved to Wisconsin in search of opportunities. However, they faced more racism and hostility than other groups. White-owned banks would not give them loans. White employers often refused to hire them. In Milwaukee, white real estate agents would not sell homes to Black families outside of the Bronzeville neighborhood. Some Black Americans built their own economic community. To get a sense of these tensions, read the primary sources on the next pages and answer the questions that follow. Note: Some primary sources include words that are considered insulting or harmful today.

WISCONSIN ENTERPRISE-BLADE ARTICLE, 1926

(a newspaper published by and for Black Milwaukee residents)

The beautiful and costly home of Dr. Lotz, 615 W. Galena Street, has been purchased by Mr. and Mrs. Willa Heard, through the realty company of Mr. Leon C. Pleasant and will be remodeled for a first-class tea room and hotel, consisting of 12 parlors and dining rooms. This undertaking will fill a long felt need in Milwaukee among our racial group. . . .

The lower floor of this modern building will be remodeled for dining, tea and rest rooms with one large sun parlor and an up-to-date grill; on the second floor will be guest rooms for regular patrons and transients; the third floor will be used for individual, special parties, secret orders and other organizations. The renovations and remodeling, as planned, will be second to none in the northwest. It will be combined with exquisite taste and beauty, portraying technique, French style.

Source: "Milwaukee to Have a $25,000 Tea Room and Hotel at 615 Galena Street," *Wisconsin Enterprise-Blade*, April 17, 1926.

MILWAUKEE JOURNAL ARTICLE, 1939

Between N. 6th and N. 9th Sts., businesses operated by Negroes predominate over those of whites. The number of Negro enterprises in the city has increased in recent years.

A decade ago the only Negro businesses here were a barbershop and a combination cigar factory and store. Gradually, the Negro expanded into other fields and, to a certain extent, into the professions.

Six years ago, a pharmacist came here from Chicago, where he had been working as a clerk, and opened Milwaukee's first Negro-owned drugstore. Within the last two months, he has opened his second one, at N. 8th and W. Walnut Sts. A Negro operates a sausage factory. Ten Negro physicians, five lawyers and five dentists minister to the needs of their people. . . .

The Negro professional men and entrepreneurs have formed their own "chamber of commerce," the Milwaukee Negro Businessman's league. . . .

The section in which the Negroes live is one of the oldest in the city. Many of the houses are of the Civil War era, deteriorated, crowded together. Dire poverty, sometimes approaching squalor, covers much of the area. The sixth ward, of which the district is a part, has the highest proportion of people on relief of any ward in the city. In October, it had 1,622 relief cases, compared to 981 for the next highest ward.

Source: "Milwaukee's 'Harlem' Is a Busy, Changing Community," *Milwaukee Journal*, November 26, 1939.

INDUSTRY LEADERS' WORDS, 1915–1945

"Well, we don't have a foundry in our plant, and that's the kind of work Negroes are best suited for."

—A white factory owner when asked why he did not employ Black Americans, around 1940

"We just sort of work like a family here and to bring in Negro workers would cause confusion and cause white workers to feel that their jobs had lost in dignity if being done by Negroes."

—A white industrialist, around 1940

"The first few days of the strike brought considerable violence between the Negroes who attempted to continue on the jobs and the white pickets. . . . Police had been summoned [by management] to protect those who cared to enter but in turn joined with the strikers in overturning an automobile filled with Negro workers."

—Lloyd K. Garrison, chairman of the National Labor Relations Board, writing about a strike at Wehr Steel Company, September 18, 1934

Source: Joe William Trotter Jr., *Black Milwaukee: The Making of an Industrial Proletariat, 1915–45*, 2nd ed. (Urbana: University of Illinois Press, 2007), 152, 156.

- **How did each of these documents encourage or discourage Black American settlement in Milwaukee?**
- **How did the *Wisconsin Enterprise-Blade*'s point of view differ from the other sources?**
- **What do you see as the greatest incentives or obstacles for Black Americans to live and work in Milwaukee in the 1930s and 1940s?**

CHAPTER 8

A New Metropolis

1945–1960

CHAPTER QUESTIONS

- What challenges did Black Milwaukee residents face during this time?
- How did city government's policies and actions support racial segregation?
- How would Milwaukee be different today if it had not been for the building projects of the 1950s?
- What technological advances changed people's lives most during this time?

Many people think of life in America after World War II in glowing terms. The troops returned home. Many started families. Some of those families could afford to move to the suburbs. They bought automobiles and other luxuries. But there were downsides to this period, too. Black Americans and other people of color did not receive the full benefits of postwar prosperity, and racial **segregation** was common. Conservatives who supported limited government pushed back against socialist policies. Finally, the threat of nuclear war loomed over all Americans. Throughout it all, the city of Milwaukee continued to grow, and new suburbs incorporated at a rapid pace.

Lights illuminate Wisconsin Avenue on a winter night in Milwaukee, 1955. | *WHI Image ID 10846*

The Baby Boom, the Housing Shortage, and Segregation

Most World War II veterans returned home in 1945. Their babies started being born nine months later. Births increased across the country by 20 percent in just the first year after the war's end. The Baby Boom lasted until 1964, and Milwaukee was part of it. The city also saw the arrival of many Black American families from the South after the war. Milwaukee went from being a segregated city to a segregated metropolis.

Young married people wanted to buy homes for their growing families. However, there were not enough houses available. Some couples lived with their parents or with friends. Practically any kind of shelter was acceptable. Vacant schools became temporary apartment buildings. The county set up trailers at McKinley Beach and in other county parks. The county let people stay in cabins in parks and barracks on the courthouse lawn. By 1951, there were still five thousand families in temporary housing.

Residents of Hillside Terrace, a public housing project, pose during a Christmas party in 1957. | *WHI Image ID 129806*

Black Americans continued to have more difficulty finding housing than other Milwaukee residents. Almost all of them crowded into the central city on Milwaukee's north side. Around 1960, the central city neighborhood was very small, bounded by Juneau Avenue on the south, Twentieth Street on the west, Holton Street on the east, and Keefe Avenue on the north. Many Black Americans could not afford to buy homes anywhere else. Even if they could afford it, Milwaukee real estate agents refused to sell property outside the central city to Black Americans. Banks also promoted segregation through a practice known as redlining. When looking at a map of the city, they used red ink to draw lines around the neighborhoods where Black Americans lived. They denied mortgage loans to anyone who lived inside the red lines. Without loans, Black Americans could not buy homes in other parts of the city. Some Black Americans tried to give their money to white friends so their friends could purchase

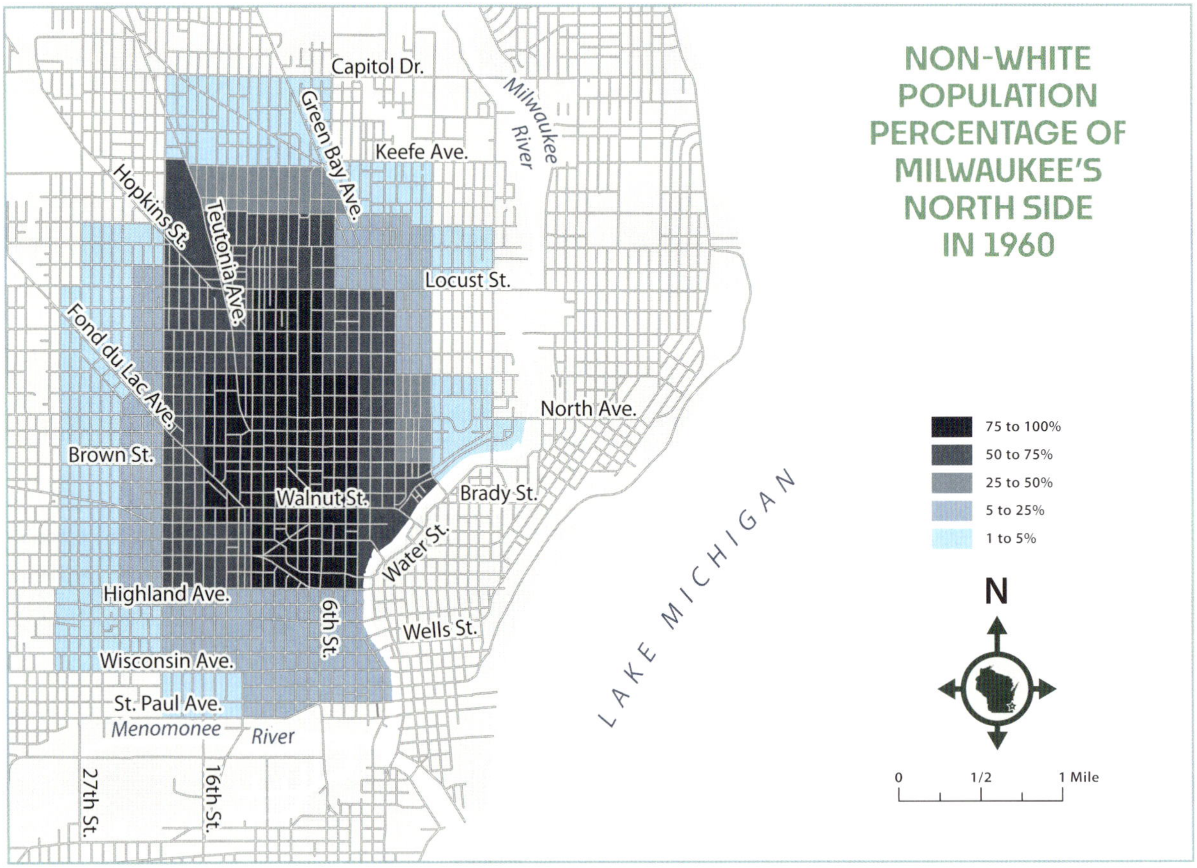

Map by Colter Sikora

homes for them. However, many white homeowners added something called **restrictive covenants** to their deeds. These covenants stated that the land their homes were built on could never be sold to a Black person. In some suburbs and city neighborhoods, as many as 90 percent of the home deeds had these restrictive covenants. The covenants were outlawed by the US Supreme Court in 1948, but the racist practices continued.

After World War II, the federal government provided veterans with home loans. Many white veterans were able to buy houses with this assistance, but Black veterans had difficulty accessing the same benefits. They faced barriers to applying. Some banks denied them loans they should have qualified for. Even when Black Americans received loans, no one would sell houses to them. Essentially, the program helped white families, but not Black families, to find better housing, and it led many white families to leave the city. Likewise, veterans were supposed to be able to go to college for free under the Servicemen's Readjustment Act (often called the "GI Bill"). A college education made it easier for white veterans to get good-paying jobs.

Then they could save up money for a down payment on a home. Although Black veterans should have benefited from this program as well, many colleges would not admit them.

The interstate highway system also promoted segregation. The federal government provided 90 percent of the funding for it. Starting in 1956, Milwaukee County built Interstate 94 from east to west through the Menonomee Valley. It also built Interstate 43 from north to south, running roughly parallel to North Third Street and South Thirteenth Street. Additional spurs connected the two main interstates to various neighborhoods, the county zoo, the airport, and Milwaukee County Stadium. Although this was convenient for some people, it was devastating for others. The county tore down thousands of homes to make way for the interstates. In some cases, it destroyed entire neighborhoods. The former Bronzeville and Borchert Field neighborhoods were virtually eliminated. These neighborhoods had been populated by German Americans in the early 1900s, but they were primarily Black neighborhoods when the county built the freeway system. Thus, thousands of Black Milwaukeeans lost their homes.

State and city leaders at the dedication of Wisconsin's first expressway, a seven-mile stretch of Interstate Highway 94 in Waukesha County in 1958. The women in the photo are wearing sashes that say "Miss Concrete" and "Miss Blacktop." | *WHI Image ID 1873*

The freeways allowed white middle-class families to move to the suburbs. Streetcars did not operate that far outside the city, so people had to buy cars. However, many Black Americans could not afford cars. Once again, they were confined to the city. By the mid-1950s, the streetcars and interurban train stopped running due to declining ridership. From that point on, many Black Americans had to walk or take buses.

Zoning laws also contributed to segregation. Many suburbs required residents to build houses on large lots. In Franklin and Mequon, for example, residents had to build houses on at least half an acre of land. Brookfield required houses to be at least one hundred feet from the street. This made property more expensive. Many people, including most Black Americans, could not afford to buy property in the suburbs at all. Some suburbs gave tax breaks to companies to get them to relocate from the city. They created new industrial districts and business parks. When factories and businesses moved to the suburbs, the jobs moved with them. This meant there were fewer jobs available in the city. The people who lived there faced widespread poverty.

In 1948, voters elected Frank Zeidler (brother of the previous mayor, Carl Zeidler) as the mayor of Milwaukee. He was a socialist. Zeidler had a solution to segregation. He wanted to build public housing at the edge of the city. He wanted everyone, regardless of race or income, to be able to live there. But the Common Council and the state government opposed the idea. Essentially, they wanted the new neighborhoods to be white and middle class. Thus, by 1953, more than 98 percent of Milwaukee's Black Americans lived in the central city on Milwaukee's north side.

Annexation and Suburbanization

Frank Zeidler served as mayor from 1948 until 1960. He was the last socialist mayor of any city in the United States. He was also a stark contrast to his brother, Carl. Carl had been an outgoing, charming bachelor who got by on his personality. Frank, by comparison, was a family man known for his intellect. He believed government should improve people's lives. He also more than doubled the size of the city during his twelve years in office.

A Milwaukee family inside their new bomb shelter in 1952 | *WHI Image ID 1941*

Frank Zeidler was mayor during one of the worst parts of a period known as the Cold War. This was not a war like World War II, with multiple battlefronts and fighting. Instead, the Cold War was a period of tense relations and rivalries between the US and the Soviet Union. The two countries had very different types of government. The US was a democracy, while the Soviet Union was communist. The people of both countries deeply distrusted each other's form of government.

During the Cold War, the US and the Soviet Union were both developing nuclear weapons. Americans feared the Soviet Union might bomb them. Milwaukee's city government built fallout shelters in public buildings where people could go during an atomic bomb attack. Neighborhood leaders called block wardens coordinated efforts with the police. They hosted civil defense talks and films that were meant to prepare civilians to respond to attacks. They even held city-wide practice drills in case of nuclear attack. Every family received evacuation guides.

Zeidler read a book by nuclear physicist Ralph Eugene Lapp. Lapp had worked on the Manhattan Project (the US government program that developed the first atomic bomb). Lapp argued that American cities should spread out their population to minimize death and destruction in the event of a nuclear attack. Lapp said cities should build smaller cities several miles away from the downtown area. The main city would connect to these "satellite cities" by freeway. Along the way, there would be museums, parks, golf courses, and open green space, all of which would help block any fires that would break out if a nuclear attack happened.

Zeidler set his sights on Greendale as a possible satellite city for Milwaukee. It was ten miles from downtown. It had 572 housing units, all still owned by the federal government. It also had room for at least another three thousand families. The federal government announced that it would sell the land to private individuals. Zeidler partnered with Arthur Marcus, a Greendale resident. Marcus was also a veteran and a member of the American Legion, a veterans' service organization. Marcus formed the American Legion Community Development Corporation (ALCDC) in 1948 to try to buy all the residences in Greendale. He and Zeidler believed that public housing was good for the middle class as well as low-income people. Under their plans, the city would keep annexing land until it reached Greendale's border. Meanwhile, ALCDC would buy the land Greendale was located on from the federal government and sell it to the city. Thus, Milwaukee would have its own satellite community. It would build thousands of public housing units, furthering both defensive and socialist goals.

Greendale residents panicked. They feared they would lose their homes. They urged their congressman and President Truman not to sell to ALCDC. Then, Marcus died unexpectedly. Without him, ALCDC dissolved in 1951. The federal government decided to sell the homes in Greendale to individual residents instead.

Zeidler, meanwhile, made plans to move the city westward. The city had annexed five miles of land along Hampton Avenue in 1946, before Zeidler was mayor. The "Hampton strip" connected the city to the Village of Butler. Butler is located just over the county line in Waukesha County. Zeidler advertised city services. The city would have paved streets and sidewalks. It also would have given Butler fire and police protection, water and sewer service, and regular garbage collection. It would have built schools and libraries. Once in Waukesha County, Zeidler hoped to annex 9.6 square miles of land, just beyond Butler, for a satellite city. However, a group from the Town of Wauwatosa sued the city. It portrayed the city as a bully trying to gobble up land. Farmers in the towns of Brookfield and Menomonee complained that they had nothing in common with people in the city. The residents of the village were torn. They wanted city services, but they also liked their independence. Finally, in 1950, they voted to build their own storm sewer. One year later, the state supreme court ruled that the city's annexation along Hampton Avenue had not been legal. The state legislature gave suburbs annexation powers. Thus, the city would have a harder time annexing land in the future, and it would be easier for new suburbs to form.

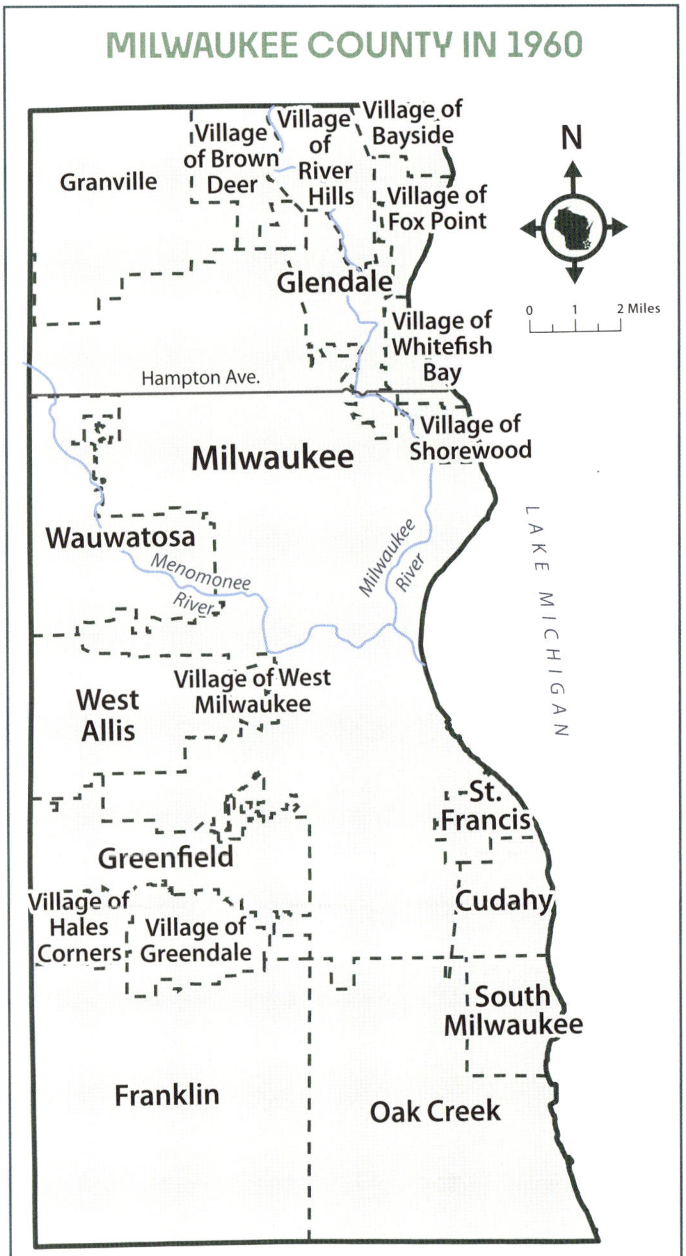

Map by Colter Sikora

St. Francis was the first of the new wave of suburbs to incorporate. St. Francis was in the Town of Lake and was named after the St. Francis seminary. Wisconsin Electric's Lakeside Power Plant was located there. The plant was the main source of property taxes for Lake. St. Francis incorporated as a city in 1951. It took the power plant and the tax money with it. The remaining townspeople in Lake had to absorb the tax burden. Milwaukee offered to annex the Town of Lake. It offered city services and lower taxes. Residents of Lake voted to join the city in 1954. Milwaukee gained thirteen thousand people and 9.35 square miles of land.

Hales Corners and Brown Deer were the next two suburbs to incorporate. Seneca and William Hale were brothers who had arrived in the area in 1837. Each man occupied one corner of the intersection near the current site of Highway 100 and Janesville Road. So did their father, Ebenezer. "Hales Corners" was, therefore, a logical name. White settlers also lived in Brown Deer in the 1830s. According to one legend, the animal in question jumped through a saloon door, breaking up a card game. The patrons yelled out, "brown deer!" The name stuck. Both villages were farm communities until the big wave of suburbanization in the 1950s. Hales Corners incorporated in 1952. Brown Deer did the same in 1955.

Hales Corners' incorporation did not cause controversy. Brown Deer's, on the other hand, prompted a legal battle. Brown Deer was in the northeast corner of the Town of Granville. Mayor Frank Zeidler wanted to annex the entire town. The issue went to trial, and the court ordered a referendum. The people of Brown Deer voted overwhelmingly in favor of incorporation. Then, a race to annex Granville began between the new village and the city. A court awarded 4.5 square miles of Granville to Brown Deer in 1962. The other sixteen square miles went to Milwaukee. It was the largest annexation in city history.

The city extended water lines to its new neighborhoods. Eventually, it could not keep up with demand. The city ordered residents not to water their lawns more frequently than every other night. Violators were subject to a fifty-dollar fine and thirty days in jail. The city opened a second water treatment plant at Sixth Street and Howard Avenue in 1962.

Zeidler wanted to continue annexing land. However, he was running out of options. The northern suburbs blocked him. Glendale incorporated in 1950. Bayside followed in 1953. They and their neighbors, Fox Point and River Hills, divided what was left of the Town of Milwaukee in 1954.

Growing to the south was not an option either. In 1955, the state legislature passed the "Oak Creek law." It allowed the agricultural Town of Oak Creek to incorporate as a city. Its neighbor, Franklin, did the same a year later. The two "cities" had only 2 percent of the county's population. However, they occupied more than one-quarter of the county's land. The Town of Greenfield was all that remained to annex. Zeidler sent recruiters to Greenfield to annex territory block by block and sometimes house by house. What remained of the town incorporated as the City of Greenfield in 1957. Communities in Waukesha and Ozaukee Counties incorporated about the same time. Thus, they blocked further annexation. Frank Zeidler said the city was surrounded by an "iron ring" of suburbs.

By 1957, the year this photo was taken, Milwaukee's suburbs were well established. Many white, middle-class families could afford modest homes with yards, a car, and even higher-end consumer goods like this boat. | *WHI Image ID 2073*

The city could no longer expand, but it still had plenty of space. Middle-class, mostly white families moved to new neighborhoods in recently annexed areas. They bought small houses with two or three bedrooms. As they acquired more money and had more children, many moved into bigger homes. In the prewar era, neighborhoods had one major ethnicity. However, the new neighborhoods were multiethnic. Soon, the old ethnic traditions began to fade. Life in the new neighborhoods was also more anonymous, as people drove cars instead of walking from place to place.

Zeidler still wanted to build public housing. Many business groups criticized public housing as "socialist," which they meant as an insult. However, they had a hard time criticizing Zeidler when he asked for funding to build three housing projects for veterans. In 1948, the city built Northlawn and Berryland on the north side and Southlawn on the south side. Westlawn, on the northwest side of the city, opened for low-income residents in 1951. With 726 housing units, it was the biggest housing project in city history.

Milwaukee County Executive John Doyne throws a pitch during pregame ceremonies as the Brewers open the 1970 baseball season at County Stadium. | *WHI Image ID 137723*

As city services expanded, so did county services. Traditionally, the county oversaw the courts and social services. Over time, it also became responsible for the parks, the zoo, the airport, and Milwaukee County Stadium. Zeidler proposed merging the city, suburban, and county governments. He wanted to increase efficiencies and lower costs. The suburbs, however, wanted to maintain their independence. Some suburbanites said they did not want their tax money to go to programs for low-income city residents. The state refused to agree to the merger.

Instead, the state ended up strengthening the county government. The county was in charge of so many things that the part-time board of supervisors could no longer oversee them all. The county created the position of county executive in 1960. John Doyne was Milwaukee's first. Under his leadership, the county built the freeway system, a new public museum building, the Milwaukee Regional Medical Center, and the Milwaukee Art Museum. It expanded social services and access to health care. It also took over the public transit system. William "Bill" O'Donnell succeeded Doyne in 1976. He continued Doyne's policies.

The Postwar Economic Boom

During the late 1940s and early 1950s, there were a lot of young families across the United States. They wanted to fill their homes with consumer goods. Demand for these goods created more factory jobs. Factory workers continued to unionize. Sometimes, the unions went

Labor union leaders and members gather during a strike by Milwaukee factory workers in 1946. | *WHI Image ID 2954*

on strike for better wages and conditions. The average industrial worker's weekly pay was $47 in 1946. It increased to $67 in 1950 and $93 in 1956. That increase was more than twice the rate of inflation. Workers had more money to spend than ever before. Quality of life improved for many people.

As young middle-class families made more money, they were able to move out of their temporary housing. Some bought newly built homes in the outlying parts of the city and in the suburbs. They drove between home and work and other destinations. Driving offered a degree of freedom that public transit did not. Most families owned a car by 1965, and 29 percent owned two. Horse travel and streetcars disappeared. The city government sold its last horse, Dolly, in 1957. The last streetcar ran in 1958.

Southgate Shopping Center around 1966 | *WHI Image ID 41145*

Shopping centers were becoming major destinations. Every metropolitan area had one or more. Southgate was Milwaukee's first. It opened in 1951 at Twenty-Seventh Street and Morgan Avenue. It was the brainchild of Kurtis Froedtert. Froedtert owned a malting company that provided barley to breweries. Prior to Southgate's construction, shoppers parked on the street or in small parking lots. Then they walked several blocks between stores. But Southgate had a parking lot big enough for two thousand cars. From the lot, shoppers could access twenty stores, including a Gimbels department store and a Krambo supermarket, the largest supermarket in Milwaukee. Southgate's opening celebration included Polish and Italian folk dancers, polka bands, fireworks, and other attractions. It was so exciting that sixty thousand people visited on its first day. Traffic was tied up for hours.

Other shopping centers followed, each one bigger than the last. Bayshore opened in Glendale in 1954. It had thirty-eight stores, including a Krambo and a Kohl's Food Store. It also had a Walgreens and several other national chains. Its location next to Interstate 43 was ideal for shoppers. Eventually, it added Sears, Boston Store, and Chapman's department stores. (All three stores are gone today.) The Capitol Court shopping center, which opened in 1956, was even bigger. It was located between Sixtieth Street, Capitol Drive, and Fond du Lac Avenue. It had sixty stores, including Schuster's, Chapman's, J. C. Penney, Woolworth's, and Kohl's Food Store. Kurtis Froedtert opened Westgate (now Mayfair) shopping center in 1958. It had seventy stores, including Gimbels and Marshall Field's.

Shopping centers were convenient, but they hurt traditional retail. Downtown, North Third Street, and West Mitchell Street lost businesses. People had no reason to shop in an old neighborhood when shopping centers were closer to people's homes.

But the shopping centers' success did not last forever. They faced new competition from shopping malls. Malls were fully enclosed and climate controlled. Brookfield Square mall opened in 1967 in Brookfield. Southridge Mall opened in 1970 in Greendale. It was the largest mall in Wisconsin, more than ten times the size of the original Southgate. It was two stories tall and had five department stores. It had an indoor parklike structure at its center with a fountain, benches, and an aviary. Future US Senator Herb Kohl, of the Kohl's Food Store family, owned both Southridge and Northridge. To compete with the malls, the shopping centers became enclosed. Even so, they eventually became victims of the changing retail landscape. (Today, more people prefer to shop at big-box stores or online. Few malls have survived. Some have added restaurants and other businesses to make up for the loss in shoppers.)

Businesses increased their advertising to try to lure shoppers into stores. Much of this advertising was broadcast on the radio or

This photo taken in a Wisconsin retail store shows what TVs looked like in 1956. | *WHI Image ID 8635*

television. The *Milwaukee Journal* began transmitting a radio signal in 1927 under the call letters WTMJ. The "TMJ" stood for *The Milwaukee Journal*. Its first television broadcast was in 1947 on channel 3. WTMJ-TV was the first television station in Wisconsin and the fifteenth in the United States.

Watching television during the middle of the twentieth century was a lot different from today. Few people owned their own set at first. Typically, a crowd gathered in front of a department store window and watched whatever was on the screen. There was no regular program schedule. Some television shows ran for only five minutes. Many shows did not have regular broadcasts with weekly episodes either. Programming did not run twenty-four hours per day. Everything was live. Anything that moved was worth watching. One show, *Meet Your Neighbor*, consisted of a television camera in the lobby at WTMJ. The host would simply interview people as they walked into the building.

Sports broadcasting quickly became popular. Milwaukeeans liked watching wrestling, boxing, and high school and professional basketball games. Some people thought fans would not attend sporting events if they could watch at home. As it turned out, television had the opposite effect. It actually created new fans. Attendance at games increased. In 1948, the minor league Milwaukee Brewers started paying WTMJ-TV to broadcast their games. The station added *Bowling with the Champs* in 1955. It ran for almost forty years.

Programming expanded over time. WTMJ signed a contract with the National Broadcasting Corporation (NBC) in 1948. It has had network programming ever since. WTMJ moved to channel 4 in 1951. It broadcast weather reports and church services that year. By the end of the decade, Milwaukee viewers had four channels to choose from. They were WTMJ, channel 4 (NBC); WITI-TV, channel 6 (no affiliate); WTVW/WISN, channel 12 (ABC); and WXIX, channel 18 (CBS).

The networks had developed regular schedules by the mid-1950s. Their programs replaced most local shows. Variety shows were very popular. They offered singing, dancing, and sketch comedy. The *Texaco Star Theatre* (1948–1956) with Milton Berle was one of the earliest such shows. Eventually, Westerns dominated the airwaves. There were more than thirty of them in 1959. Situation comedies, such as *I Love Lucy* and *Leave It to Beaver*, also aired in the 1950s. Cooking shows and soap operas that aired during the daytime targeted homemakers.

Local stations still produced children's programming. One show on WTMJ-TV featured an announcer reading the Sunday comics to children to help them learn to read. Children's cowboy shows were especially popular. On *Foreman Tom's B-Square Ranch*, Foreman Tom introduced Western films. He also taught children to be good little "cowpokes" with the B-Square Ranch Club pledge: "Be happy, be healthy, be friendly, fair, helpful, handy, trusty, and square."

Children at the zoo in 1955, when it was located at Washington Park | *WHI Image ID 49011*

Mayor Frank Zeidler wanted the city to pay for public broadcasting. He thought the city could use it for educational purposes. It took him four years to convince the Common Council that spending tax money on television was a good idea. Today, Milwaukee is one of the only cities that has two public broadcasting stations instead of one. The Milwaukee Vocational School (now the Milwaukee Area Technical College, or MATC) runs both. Channel 10, WMVS, began broadcasting in 1957. Channel 36, WMVT, began in 1963.

The city continued to spend money on building projects. Milwaukee Arena opened in 1950. It is still located next to the Milwaukee Auditorium (later renamed the Milwaukee Theatre and now the Miller High Life Theatre). The arena doubled the city's convention space. It also hosted professional basketball and hockey teams. The 1952 American Bowling Congress tournament was the arena's first major sporting event. It ran for eighty-five days on forty bowling lanes.

The city and county governments invested in many other building projects to improve residents' quality of life. The county opened the Milwaukee Art Museum and War Memorial Center in a shared space on Lake Michigan in 1957. In 1958, it moved the zoo from Washington Park to the west end of the city. The new zoo was much larger than the old one. It allowed its animals to live in natural-looking habitats instead of cages. Additionally, the Wisconsin Teachers College and

HISTORY IN PERSON

The Milwaukee Art Museum and War Memorial Center

One of Milwaukee's most striking landmarks is the Milwaukee Art Museum and War Memorial Center. The iconic winged pavilion, designed by the Spanish architect Santiago Calatrava, opened in 2001, but the site's history goes back much further. Milwaukee has had art exhibitions and galleries since at least the 1880s. The most significant was the Layton Art Gallery. In the early 1900s, the Milwaukee Art Association saw a need for a larger museum and opened the Milwaukee Art Institute on Jefferson Street. Following World War II, the city built a war memorial at the current site on the lakefront. The midcentury-style building was dedicated in 1957. The Layton Art Gallery and Milwaukee Art Institute combined and moved there. Since then, the facilities have continued to expand, becoming one of the most popular destinations in Milwaukee. When you visit, think about how different parts of the center represent the eras of Milwaukee history in which they were built.

The War Memorial Center, photographed sometime after 1956 | *WHI Image ID 53921*

University of Wisconsin's Extension center merged into the University of Wisconsin–Milwaukee in 1956.

One building project was risky. Milwaukee had an excellent minor league baseball team at Borchert Field, but fans wanted a major league team. In 1952, the county built a new stadium near the Veterans Administration hospital. It could seat thirty-six thousand fans and had space for expansion. The county gambled that the stadium would lure a team to Milwaukee. The following year, the bet paid off. The Boston Braves announced they were moving to Milwaukee.

Milwaukee fans loved their team. Professional athletes did not make much money back then, so fans gave the players gifts. They gave traditional Milwaukee gifts such as beer, cheese, and sausage. They also gave them clothes, jewelry, pens, and even outboard motors. Out-of-town news reporters were puzzled by Milwaukee's devotion to the Braves. They could not understand why ten thousand fans would greet the team at the airport after a routine road trip.

Two fans at County Stadium, home of the World Series–champion Milwaukee Braves, in 1957 | *WHI Image ID 10853*

They played up Milwaukee's rural reputation by reporting that fans rang cowbells in the stands.

The Milwaukee Braves finished in second place in the National League in 1953. By 1957, they were in the World Series. They played the New York Yankees. One of the Yankees called Milwaukee "bush league," meaning "second rate" or minor league. Milwaukeeans were insulted and infuriated. Each team won three of the first six games. It all came down to Game 7. Braves ace Warren Spahn was supposed to pitch, but he came down with influenza. Lew Burdette, who had pitched just three days before, was called in. Burdette pitched the entire game, and the Braves beat the Yankees, 5–0. It was Burdette's third complete game of the series and second shutout. Braves player Hank Aaron led both teams with a .393 batting average. He had eleven hits, including three home runs. A sign in Milwaukee proudly proclaimed "Bushville Wins." Fans danced in the streets. The victory parade drew 150,000 spectators. It was the single biggest public event in Milwaukee history at the time.

Hank Aaron in his Milwaukee Braves uniform | *WHI Image ID 26365*

Often, after a team is a world champion, fans will expect it to keep winning. When the Braves didn't meet those expectations, attendance declined slightly. New owners bought the team in 1962. They moved the team to Atlanta after the 1965 season. In 1970, Major League Baseball would return to Milwaukee when Bud Selig brought the Seattle Pilots to the city to become the Brewers.

A Renewed Conservatism

Frank Zeidler was mayor for twelve years (1948–1960). He was a socialist who thought government should improve people's lives. Conservatism, however, proved to be more popular by 1960. Conservatives favor limiting the government's involvement in the economy and solving social problems. This preference for conservatism played out in the city's media, housing, politics, and labor practices.

Frank Zeidler was a thoughtful man. He played piano and translated Shakespeare into modern English for his children. He had served on the Milwaukee school board. He was also a quiet man. He preferred to take his wife and children on a walk rather than attend a party. He did not smoke, he disliked hunting and fishing, and he rarely attended a baseball game. Zeidler carried around a notebook to write down concerns that the people of Milwaukee shared with him. When possible, he would address those concerns with the appropriate city official. Then, he would write a letter explaining the resolution to the person who had brought up the issue.

Pretty much everyone liked Zeidler. However, not everyone liked his politics. Many people confused socialism with communism. The *Milwaukee Sentinel* was a conservative newspaper that strongly opposed Zeidler, calling him a communist. The *Milwaukee Journal* was more moderate, but it was still biased. For example, in the 1948 election, the paper referred to Zeidler as a socialist, but it did not use political labels for his opponent, Henry Reuss. That selective use of language made Reuss sound like a better candidate. The newspaper also had a policy of placing Reuss's name ahead of Zeidler's in news stories. That way, people who did not have time to read the entire article never got to Zeidler's name.

People read more national magazines in the 1950s than ever before. Corporations owned most of the magazines. Many corporations followed a conservative agenda. *Reader's Digest*, for example, mixed homespun advice with stories about traditional values. Next to those stories, readers found articles that praised business or condemned socialism. *Reader's Digest* had 9.5 million subscribers in 1951.

Joseph McCarthy (right) speaks at a hearing in 1946. | *WHI Image ID 3614*

At this same time, many people watched Senator Joseph R. McCarthy on television. McCarthy was a Wisconsin senator. He claimed to have a list of more than two hundred people in the US State Department who were disloyal to the United States. He said they were communist. He had no proof of this, however. McCarthy conducted hearings in the US Senate in 1954 intended to separate the loyal from the disloyal. The hearings were broadcast on television. Eager viewers watched the compelling drama. The hearings destroyed the reputations and careers of many people who were falsely accused.

In Milwaukee, the Affiliated Taxpayers' Committee (ATC), a business group, strongly objected to Zeidler's public housing agenda. They said public housing was nothing but communism. They also said it was immoral to give people housing. They thought people should have to save money to buy their own homes. They had a negative opinion of people who lived in poverty. ATC started a petition to require a referendum to prevent public housing. They ran full-page advertisements in both major city newspapers in 1951. The advertisements urged people to sign the petition, saying that voting was a patriotic, American thing to do. These advertisements confused many people who signed the petition. They thought they were supporting voter rights. They actually were in favor of public housing. Still, the referendum went forward, and ATC won. This halted the development of public housing in the city.

Frank Zeidler wanted to use public housing to promote racial **integration**. Alderman Milton McGuire disagreed. He ran against Zeidler in the 1956 mayoral race. McGuire claimed Zeidler liked Black Americans too much. One of his campaign slogans was "Milwaukee needs an honest white man for mayor." He told white people false stories about Black violence, gangs, and drugs. He warned them that racial integration would decrease their property values. Zeidler received anonymous letters threatening his family. Still, Zeidler won the election by 11 percent of the vote. Black Americans voted heavily for him. In the same election, voters elected attorney Vel Phillips to the Common Council. She became the first woman and first Black American on the Common Council.

Vel Phillips in 1953, the year she ran for a seat on the Milwaukee Public Schools board. She lost that race but within two years was elected to the Common Council. | *WHI Image ID 51783*

Labor unions also supported Zeidler and socialist and Democratic causes. Unions were very strong in the 1950s. More than one-third of all workers belonged to one. Milwaukee unions were among the strongest in the United States. They usually got what they wanted, with or without a strike. Wages were at record highs.

Conservative businessmen across the US tried to break the unions. In 1947, industrial leader Walter Harnischfeger testified before Congress in support of the Taft-Hartley Act. This was a law that placed limits on strikes. It also required unions to represent workers who did not join the union. The idea was simple—if workers could get the benefits of the union without joining the union, then they would not pay to join. If there were fewer dues-paying union members, then the unions would have less money to donate to socialists or Democrats who ran for office. As a result, the Republicans would win more offices. In 1953, Harnischfeger's company made $3.1 million in profits. Union officials claimed that he and other industrialists put profits ahead of employees.

Zeidler supported unions in the private sector. However, he did not approve of unions for public (government) employees. He worked well with them, but he reminded them that public employees in Milwaukee received better pay and benefits than public employees in most other cities. He thought they should work not for money but for the greater good.

In 1959, organized public employees convinced the state of Wisconsin to pass a law that allowed them to negotiate, or bargain, for their pay, benefits, and working conditions. Wisconsin was the first state to do so. The law lasted until its repeal in 2011.

Primary Sources

The Cold War

The Cold War was a time of fear for many. It was also a time of intense competition. The US and the Soviet Union raced to develop new technologies. Some of these were weapons technologies. Others were focused on space exploration. In 1957, the Soviet Union became the first country to launch a satellite, called Sputnik, into orbit around Earth. The US responded by creating NASA and launching its own space missions.

In these documents, Milwaukee students and teachers share some of their thoughts about life during the Cold War. Read the documents, think about how you might feel in the same situation, and then answer the questions that follow.

STUDENT EDITORIAL, 1951

If we should hear the order, "Attention! Attention! Our city is about to be attacked by enemy planes—proceed to your nearest air raid shelter and wait for further instructions," what would we do?

We all hope that we shall never hear the above words, but we have learned from past experience that "hoping" is not enough. We realize that aircraft and guided missiles of today can strike swiftly and at long range—and with deadly precision. Today, the threat of a sudden, devastating world war is constantly hanging over our heads, and we must prepare now for a surprise attack by air.

Nationally, our air force must have a bigger and stronger defensive arm of many planes and a network of coastal radar stations on constant duty. Locally, we need an efficient air raid alarm system that can be heard anywhere by anyone. The congested downtown area and other shopping areas need air raid shelters.

The citizens must know what to do in case of air attack. Newspapers and radio can play an important part in keeping us informed about steps to be taken when under attack. The air raid wardens in each block must know their job and enforce all safety regulations.

Care must be especially taken to alert the elementary and high schools as soon as possible so the boys and girls may be given ample time to proceed to their assigned air raid shelters without getting panicky and causing undue turmoil and congestion.

Only if plans have been well worked out and the public informed about them, can panic and costly errors be avoided. The schools can have regular and effective drills.

But—let's hope we never need them.

Source: "Danger—Are We Prepared?," *The Craftsman*, Milwaukee Boys' Technical High School, April 27, 1951.

TEACHER'S EDITORIAL, 1953

Very vital to a free people is an understanding of our democratic goals and processes. Every citizen needs to have a core of information about the American way of life with its emphasis on the worth of the individual, the privilege of personal beliefs and the right to change those beliefs. Only through continued education can such concepts as the democratic way of life, social justice and world peace be fully understood.

Attitudes are the result of one's perception of values, purposes and motives in life. They provide the driving force which leads the individual to action. Among the attitudes which are important in democratic citizenship and therefore important for the school to develop are:

a. A desire to learn and to explore and to develop one's own capacities and interests

b. Pride in wholesome achievement and good workmanship

c. An open-mindedness which respects the point of view and fine qualities of others

d. An inclination to engage harmoniously with others in day to day activities

e. An appreciation of the importance of wholesome family living

f. An appreciation of the need for the conservation of human and material resources

g. A recognition of the need for limitations on individual and group freedom in order that greater liberties may be enjoyed by all

h. A respect for private and public property

i. A desire to become economically self-sustaining

j. A willingness to assume responsibilities both of leadership and followership

k. An appreciation of the inter-dependence of various economic and social groups and their contributions to the welfare of the community, the nation and the world

l. A willingness to be of service in all human relationships that advance the welfare of the group

Source: "Building Good Citizens" (1953), file 14, box 2, Milwaukee Public Schools Collection (MSS 1680), Milwaukee County Historical Society, Milwaukee, Wisconsin.

TEACHER'S EDITORIAL, 1957

The recent achievements of the Russian scientists have caused many different reactions among the people of the United States. To many of us it was quite inconceivable that the people of any other nation could possibly equal or surpass our achievements in any area of human endeavor. Suddenly to be confronted with the realization that in one single phase of science the Russians had temporarily moved ahead of us, brought consternation to every section of our country. Inevitably our educational system was scrutinized, comparisons were swiftly drawn between the strong points of Soviet education and the so-called weak points of American Ed.

Very often in human life we go along in our tranquil way, thinking we are pretty good, doing as well, or perhaps a little better than our neighbors, when suddenly we are awakened by a jolt that could send us into a panic.

This was nearly so in the U.S. when Russia launched the Sputnik. American citizens said, "Where are our scientists, why have we lagged behind, something must be wrong with our school system." . . .

The [Russian] school child works a good deal harder than the average American child; he goes to school 6 hours 6 days a week for about 213 days a year as compared to our 190 days in the U.S. Home work adds hours to his work. . . .

It may be difficult for the schools to expect pupils to take on a greatly increased education work load when the trend at the adult level is in the direction of a shorter work week with the distractions of the movie star, television comedian, the sports figure, the prize fighter and other extra curricular diversions, and it will be increasingly difficult for teachers and principals to cope with these facts. . . .

[Superintendent] Vincent acknowledged curricula at all levels must be strengthened. The abilities and aptitudes of pupils must be better identified and broadened, opportunities made available for their full development. The provisions for effective teaching must be improved. The profession of teaching must be made more attractive. The adequate financing of the total program must be assured. The future is bright, said Mr. Vincent, with intensified interest in schools, in scholarship, in intellectual accomplishment. We may be on the verge of a massive break through in the entire field of education.

Source: Norma Z. Coke, "Milwaukee Schools vs Sputnik," January 1, 1957, Public Education Records, box 50, City Club of Milwaukee Records, 1909–1975, Milwaukee Manuscript Collection AS, Wisconsin Historical Society, Milwaukee Area Research Center, Golda Meir Library, University of Wisconsin–Milwaukee.

STUDENT LETTER TO THE EDITOR, 1959

Those of us who have lived in America all our lives may not realize how fortunate we are to be able to choose our own career. We take it for granted that some day we will be able to work at the job of our choice.

In Russia, the people have no choice. They are forced to do the type of work the government wants them to do. Because we have the liberty to choose our life's vocation, most of us will work hard to prepare for it. The enthusiasm will be much greater than if we had to prepare for a job we disliked.

Unfortunately, there are those who do not use this freedom to their advantage. They do not study properly while they are in school, and when it is time to get a job they can't find one. However, those people who have a sincere desire to get the fullest benefits out of life will follow an old familiar saying—"Work Before Pleasure."

All of us should put ourselves into that category so we can say, "I am proud to live in a democracy."

—Judith Voland, Shorewood High School

Source: "Democracy Brings Freedom of Choice," *Milwaukee Sentinel*, May 2, 1959.

- **What was it like to grow up and attend school during the Cold War? How does it compare to what it's like growing up today?**
- **What are some differences between students' and teachers' points of view on the Soviet Union in the 1950s?**
- **What did you learn about the Soviet Union from these sources? Do you think these are reliable sources of information about the Soviet Union? Why or why not?**
- **What else do you want to find out about life during the Cold War? Where would you begin your research?**

CHAPTER 9

A City in Transition
1960–1988

CHAPTER QUESTIONS

- How did the quality of life improve for some residents during this time? How did it decline for others? What people or groups were most responsible for these improvements and declines?
- What was it like to be a Black or Latin American person living in Milwaukee during this time?
- What role did different groups play in Milwaukee's civil rights movement?
- What are the lasting achievements of the civil rights movement in Milwaukee?
- What effect did city officials have during this period?

Milwaukee continued to mirror national trends in many ways between 1960 and 1988. Like they did in many other cities across the country, people in Milwaukee fought for social and political equality, including Black Americans, Latin Americans, American Indians, women, and members of the lesbian, gay, bisexual, and transgender (LGBT) community. Like other northern cities, Milwaukee deindustrialized in the 1970s and 1980s. The loss of jobs had devastating consequences for the economy and schools. Suburbanization continued. Milwaukee, however, still offered vibrant cultural experiences. As the city's slogan said in the 1980s, Milwaukee was "a great city on a Great Lake."

Demonstrators march in Waukesha in support of the Equal Rights Amendment (ERA) in 1980. | *WHI Image ID 132296*

A New Mayor and a New Police Chief

Frank Zeidler did not run for a fourth term as mayor in 1960. Voters elected state Senator Henry W. Maier, a Democrat, as the city's new mayor. He served for a record twenty-eight years. People called him "Mayor Maier." That title might seem as normal as "Mayor Hoan" or "Mayor Zeidler." However, people pronounced it run together as if it was one word. Maier kept tight control over the city. Social conservatives liked him. He cultivated a strong image in the media. He used a lot of radio and television commercials during his campaigns. He was the first Milwaukee mayor to hire a press secretary. He also brought the media along when he made public appearances.

Maier portrayed himself as a man of action. One of the first things he did as mayor was reorganize all city departments. He wanted to end their overlapping authority and make them more efficient. He worked with the county to build the Marcus Performing Arts Center and other county-funded facilities within the city. Thus, the city received benefits that the entire county paid for.

Maier did not react well to criticism. For example, in 1960, the *Milwaukee Journal* criticized the mayor and Common Council for not doing enough to help people who lived in the central city. Maier then broke off relations with the *Journal*'s television station WTMJ-TV channel 4. He held press conferences on WISN-TV channel 12 instead. He also criticized the *Journal*'s writing quality until he left office.

Maier's record on racial equality was not very good. His critics said he did little to relieve poverty in the central city. He opposed the civil rights movement, and in 1967 he banned protest marches for thirty days. However, police chief Harold Breier's record on civil rights was even worse. The fire and police commission appointed him in 1964. By state law, Breier had the job for life. He enforced racial segregation in the police department. He also allowed the use of excessive force against people of color.

Mayor Maier and police chief Harold Breier took a "law and order" approach to policing that emphasized strict enforcement of laws and harsh penalties for law breakers. The two men came to power during the civil rights movement, which began in the 1950s and continued into the 1960s. However, the city was slow to implement civil rights laws. Milwaukee civil rights advocates used nonviolent protest methods. They wanted to integrate neighborhoods and schools. But many working-class white people wanted to leave things the way they were. They also wanted a crackdown on the protests. They were the dominant majority, and Maier and the Common Council gave them what they wanted.

Similar tensions and protests were happening across the country in the summer of 1967. In Milwaukee, the tensions flared late on Saturday, July 29. A dance had just ended at the social center of St. Francis Church on Fourth and Brown Streets. The church was in a high-poverty central city neighborhood. Two women got into a fight in the parking lot. A crowd of about 350 people formed. Some people in the crowd threw bottles and other objects. The police arrived in riot gear. The crowd dispersed. There was little property damage, and things seemed to quiet down.

However, the next night, the police received a report of a Black youth breaking windows on Third Street. Rumors circulated that the police arrived and beat up the youth. A crowd gathered at Third and Walnut Streets around 10:00 p.m. Some people in the crowd started throwing rocks through the windows of white-owned businesses. Others engaged in looting and set fires. People threw rocks at the firefighters when they tried to put out the fire. People also fired multiple shots and set more fires between State and Burleigh Streets.

About 1:30 a.m., a white man drove a station wagon through the neighborhood around Second and Center Streets. He shouted profanity, threats, and racial slurs at the Black residents. John Tucker, a janitor at Shorewood High School, was in his home nearby. One of his neighbors told him the white man had shot at her. Tucker grabbed his shotgun, ran outside, and returned fire. The police sent five white officers to the scene in plain clothes and an unmarked car. Tucker did not know they were police officers. He thought they were going to attack him. He shot and killed one of the officers and wounded several others. The police threw tear gas into Tucker's house. He was arrested and was later charged with murder. Other outbursts of violence broke out around the neighborhood. The next day, a seventy-seven-year-old woman was found dead, shot in the head, at a different location. A forty-three-year-old woman died of a heart attack while running from her apartment.

Mayor Maier was concerned that the situation might worsen. Other cities, such as Los Angeles and Detroit, had recently experienced riots that lasted several days. He asked Governor Warren Knowles to send in the National Guard. He also declared a state of emergency. He imposed a citywide curfew. He lifted it from 4:00 to 6:00 p.m. the next day. People rushed to stores to buy food. The next day, August 1, the mayor lifted the curfew during daytime hours. Night workers needed a permit to go out during the curfew. That night, the police saw some young people lighting a paint store on fire. The police shot Clifford McKissick, a Black college student. They claimed he was one of the perpetrators and that he refused to halt when ordered to do so. Witnesses disputed the officers' reports. They said McKissick was sitting on his porch when he heard noises behind his house and ran to investigate, and that's when the police shot him. McKissick died on the way to the hospital. His death prompted anger, fear, and more protests in the city's Black community.

The mayor gradually relaxed the curfew. He lifted it entirely on August 9. Four people had been killed between July 30 and August 1. There were also more than one hundred injuries, including forty-four injured police officers. Police arrested more than seventeen hundred people, mostly for curfew violations. There was about a half million dollars in property damage. Many white people called the incident a riot. They praised Maier and Breier for keeping them safe. In reality, there were only a few hundred people in one neighborhood engaged in any disruptive behavior. It was not like the incidents in other cities, where thousands of people had rioted in multiple neighborhoods.

Breier was so popular with white people that council members were afraid to criticize him. In the 1980s, however, there were a number of scandals in the police department. Breier made a racist remark in an interview about Black youth and crime. The police beat a white man to death. A Black man died in police custody. Two on-duty police officers were killed. An officer allegedly murdered her husband's ex-wife. These and other events damaged the reputation of the police department and the city of Milwaukee. The state decided Breier needed oversight. It transferred some of his powers to the fire and police commission in 1984. Breier retired that same year rather than serve in a diminished role.

Milwaukee's Civil Rights Movement

Milwaukeeans played an active part in the civil rights movement. Black Americans took the lead in the early 1960s. From the late 1960s through the early 1980s, Latin Americans and American Indians organized for change as well. Milwaukee also had a youth movement that rejected the values of its parents' generation. By the end of this period, women and the LGBT community also made strides in fighting for their rights and improving life in the city.

Alderwoman Vel Phillips was one of Milwaukee's early civil rights leaders. She wanted to end housing discrimination. In 1962, she introduced an open housing (also called fair housing) ordinance to the Common Council. It would have prohibited people from refusing to sell or rent a home to someone because of their race. However, the rest of the Common Council's aldermen voted against it. Phillips tried several more times over the next few years, but she lost each vote.

Father James Groppi (at far right) and members of the NAACP Youth Council demonstrate outside the Eagles Club in March of 1966.
| WHI Image ID 53595

Other Black Americans organized into groups that promoted integration. The Milwaukee NAACP Youth Council was one prominent group. Banker and activist Ardie Clark Halyard had founded the Youth Council in 1947. Most of its members were young adults, and some were white. The Youth Council staged its first public protests in 1963.

Father James Groppi became the Youth Council's adviser in 1965. He was a white Catholic priest at St. Boniface Church, which was located in the central city neighborhood. In spring 1966, Groppi and the Youth Council protested against the Fraternal Order of Eagles Club. The club had a policy of admitting only white people. That summer, the Youth Council protested in front of the houses of aldermen who belonged to the Eagles Club. The national Eagles group voted to keep the whites-only policy. (Eagles chapters were desegregated in the 1980s.)

Groppi and the Youth Council moved on to other battles. Their most public action was a march across the Sixteenth Street viaduct in August 1967, not long after the shootings and unrest in the central city neighborhood. The viaduct symbolized the racial division within the city. It separated the Black north side of Milwaukee from the Polish south side. On Monday, August 28, 1967, almost two hundred Youth Council members and supporters, some of them white, marched across the bridge to protest segregation. A hostile crowd of more than five thousand white people waited on the south side of the bridge. They screamed racist slurs at the marchers. They threw eggs, rocks, bricks, and bottles. Still, Groppi and the Youth Council held a second march the next night. Again, the marchers were harassed, but they didn't give up. The marches continued for two hundred consecutive nights until March 1968. On April 4, Martin Luther King Jr. was assassinated. One week later, the federal government passed the Fair Housing Act. Then, on April 30, the

Protesters at a 1967 rally for fair housing in Milwaukee
| WHI Image ID 97930

HISTORY IN PERSON

James E. Groppi Unity Bridge

In 1988, Milwaukee mayor John Norquist and the Common Council changed the name of the Sixteenth Street viaduct to the James E. Groppi Unity Bridge. A historic marker below the bridge notes, "Today the bridge is a symbol of racial and ethnic unity. Protestors met again on the bridge in 2003 calling for an end to street violence. That time they came from both the North and South sides in a show of unity." Many other groups have organized marches across the bridge, both to remember the open housing marches and to bring attention to the social and racial justice issues of today.

The James E. Groppi Unity Bridge | *WHI Image ID 157191*

Milwaukee Common Council finally passed its own open housing ordinance. It was stronger than the federal law.

The open housing law was an important victory. However, discrimination and unequal treatment of minority groups persisted. The Fair Housing Act did nothing to address segregated schools. In 1954, the US Supreme Court had considered the case of *Brown v. Board of Education of Topeka*. The court ruled that school districts could not assign students to schools with the goal of separating students by race. *Brown v. Board of Education* did not apply to Milwaukee Public Schools (MPS). MPS assigned students to schools closest to their homes. Segregated neighborhoods, therefore, produced segregated schools. But MPS did not tell people where they had to live. Therefore, it claimed it was not at fault for school segregation.

Cornelius Golightly was the only Black American on the Milwaukee school board in the mid-1960s. There were fifteen people on the board. Golightly was one of seven who were known for being liberals, or people who believe government should be actively involved in solving social problems. He wanted to end school segregation even if MPS was not at fault. He demonstrated that white high schools had a wider array of courses than Black high schools. The conservative majority, which included Milwaukee school superintendent Harold Vincent, did not want to listen to him. They stated they were trying to improve Black schools and that desegregation was unnecessary.

Attorney Lloyd Barbee was the most vocal critic of the conservatives. Barbee was from Memphis, Tennessee. He joined the NAACP at age twelve. He earned a law degree from the University of Wisconsin, then moved to Milwaukee in 1962. He then began researching school segregation. In 1964, he formed the Milwaukee United School Integration Committee (MUSIC).

Lloyd Barbee at the Wisconsin State Capitol in 1964 | *WHI Image ID 26539*

MUSIC organized two marches and a one-day school boycott in May 1964. Rather than attend MPS, students went to one of thirty "freedom schools" held in Black churches. Perhaps as many as 60 percent of the city's Black students participated in the boycott. So did some white students. The schools taught Black American history and culture. They functioned like other schools. Students engaged in reading, writing, group discussions, and singing. They attended lectures and films too. Volunteers from the Black community served as teachers and principals. So did a few white people. Marilyn Morheuser, a white woman who had been a teaching nun, wrote the curriculum. In 1963, she had moved to Milwaukee to become Barbee's chief lieutenant. She was also the editor of the *Milwaukee Star*, a Black community newspaper.

Barbee took his struggle to court in 1965. He sued the school board on behalf of the parents of thirty-two Black American students and nine white students. *Amos et al. v. Board of School Directors of the City of Milwaukee et al.* was the official name of the case. Barbee had to prove that school segregation was not just a result of neighborhood segregation. He had to prove that MPS deliberately separated students by race. He did so in five ways.

Barbee's first piece of evidence was about school boundary lines. MPS divided the city into several elementary school districts. There was one school for every neighborhood. Each elementary school was part of a junior high school district. It was also part of a senior high school district. MPS adjusted school boundaries when it saw that a school had too many students. It moved some blocks from one district to an adjacent district. Some districts had both Black and white families. In those cases, MPS made sure to attach white blocks to another white district. Thus, the original school went from a mixed population to an entirely Black population.

Second, Barbee showed that MPS built schools in Black neighborhoods when there was plenty of room in white schools on the south side. He said MPS should have bused Black American students to those schools.

Barbee's third and fourth arguments were interrelated. He analyzed hundreds, perhaps thousands, of students' transfer applications. He found that MPS allowed white students to transfer out of mixed-race schools and into white schools. All a white student had to say was that they were afraid to go to school. Barbee also found that the district allowed Black American students to transfer only to other Black schools, if it gave them transfers at all. Similarly, MPS allowed white teachers to leave Black schools if they reported feeling unsafe. Black American teachers ended up at the schools no one else wanted. Those schools were Black schools.

Finally, there was the idea of "intact busing." This was, in Barbee's view, the most blatant tool that MPS used to maintain segregation. It was supposed to temporarily relieve overcrowding at Black elementary schools. MPS bused teachers and students "intact" as a classroom to a different school. Usually, the receiving school was white. MPS did not allow the bused children to mix with children at the receiving school. Then, the children rode the bus back to their neighborhood school at the end of the day. Sometimes they even had to ride the bus back for lunch. In those cases, they made four trips in a day. Superintendent Vincent claimed he kept the children separate because the busing was temporary. He said it would not be fair to break up their friendships when space became available again at the sending school. MUSIC countered Vincent by forming human chains around "intact" buses. Barbee surveyed teachers who participated in intact busing. Most of them said their students felt isolated. They said the students did not feel accepted at either school. Students also missed a lot of learning time while on the bus. Based on this evidence, Barbee concluded that intact busing was psychologically damaging.

People march down a Milwaukee street to protest school segregation in 1964. | *WHI Image ID 98959*

The initial trial lasted until 1976. Barbee won the case. The school board hired a new superintendent, Lee McMurrin, in 1975. He devised a plan for integration. He assigned a different college focus or career specialty to each of the fifteen high schools. Students could attend any high school they wanted to. McMurrin used a massive busing plan to transport students to their new schools. He also assigned specialties to several junior high school and elementary schools. At the elementary level, MPS became a national leader in fine arts, language immersion, bilingual education, and Montessori education.

Some white families liked these new opportunities. However, others did not accept having Black children in white schools. Some parents said the new students did not behave well or were too far behind in school. Some white families left MPS and put their children in private schools. Others moved to the suburbs. Additionally, the white birthrate had fallen by the 1980s. Therefore, there were fewer white students available for integration. (The legacy of segregation can be seen in Milwaukee schools even today. In the 2019–2020 school year, only about 10 percent of all MPS students were white. Statewide, 69 percent of the student population was white.)

Black Americans also had mixed opinions about this program. Some parents thought the new school specialties were wonderful. However, others wanted to keep their children in neighborhood schools. Too few Black children volunteered for busing. MPS closed some of their neighborhood schools and now the children had no choice. They had to attend a south-side school. In some cases, MPS reopened closed schools as "citywide" schools. Students from the neighborhood could not attend them unless they met admissions criteria. Some people in the Black community resented what they saw as a takeover of their schools. A man named Howard Fuller became their chief spokesperson. He organized protests against the conversion of neighborhood schools to citywide status. Fuller was successful in his efforts. He would later serve as superintendent of MPS.

Just like in other American cities, Black people were not the only community fighting for civil rights in Milwaukee. The city's Latin American population had been growing since the 1920s. By 1970, there were between eight thousand and ten thousand Latin Americans living in Milwaukee. About 65 percent of them were Mexican. Another 25 percent were Puerto Rican. Most Latin Americans worked in manual labor. However, they also built a business district at Sixth Street and National Avenue.

As the Latin American population grew, it became more politically active. In 1962 in California, Cesar Chavez founded the United Farm

Workers. It was (and still is) a nationwide labor union for farmworkers. Three years later, white religious leaders formed United Migrant Opportunity Services (UMOS) in Waukesha County. UMOS addressed the needs of migrant and seasonal farmworkers—people who lived in Mexico and the southwestern states but traveled to the Midwest during certain times of year to plant and harvest crops. Many migrant farmworkers who came to Wisconsin were Latin American.

Latin American children walk in a parade in Milwaukee in 1969. | *WHI Image ID 128551*

United Farm Workers and UMOS both tried to get better pay, safer working conditions, and shorter workdays for their members. In 1968, a group of Latin American leaders took over control of the UMOS organization. The group's board selected Jesus Salas, a labor activist and union organizer, as UMOS's director. UMOS moved to the south side of Milwaukee and began offering adult education classes. In 1969, UMOS opened offices in other parts of southeastern Wisconsin. In 1970, the group led a march to demand better housing for migrant farmworkers. By 1972, UMOS was providing emergency food and medical services to more than four thousand people. It began offering legal services the following year.

The Latin American Union for Civil Rights (LAUCR) was another important group in Milwaukee. LAUCR protested police brutality and tried to stop immigration officials from harassing immigrants. It asked the city government to stop cutting social services. In addition, LAUCR wanted the Spanish language and Latin American culture to be taught in schools and colleges. It helped start the city's first Cinco de Mayo festival. Founders of LAUCR also started *La Guardia*, a bilingual newspaper published from 1969 until 1982.

Roberto Hernandez, Ezequiel Guzman, and a third man, name unknown, work on an issue of *La Guardia* newspaper in 1969. | *WHI Image ID 91127*

History in Focus

Potawatomi Casino Hotel

Although the Potawatomi once had a thriving community in the Menomonee Valley, they were mostly pushed out by white settlers. Forced to relocate by the US government, most of the Potawatomi people who remained in Wisconsin went to live on the Forest County Potawatomi Reservation in the northern part of the state. In 1990, the Forest County Potawatomi reclaimed a piece of the Menomonee Valley. The nation purchased a piece of industrial land near downtown Milwaukee that had previously belonged to them. In 1991, the Potawatomi opened a bingo hall on the land. Many Native nations open casinos on their land as a way to provide income and employment to their members. This was the first casino in the country to be opened on nonreservation land. The highly successful casino has expanded over the years to include slot machines, a hotel, and a spa. With profits from the casino and hotel, the Potawatomi nation has made many donations to local charities and community needs.

The number of Native peoples living in Milwaukee grew again during World War II. Like other groups, members of Native nations pursued equal treatment in society. The American Indian Movement (AIM) started in Minneapolis in 1968. A Milwaukee branch was formed that same year and included members of the Brotherton, Ho-Chunk, Menominee, Potawatomi, Ojibwe, Oneida, and Stockbridge-Munsee nations, along with some others. AIM helped urban American Indians get jobs, better housing, and health care. It provided counseling for alcohol and drug addiction. AIM also tried to stop police harassment.

Like similar groups, AIM staged protest marches to bring attention to its causes. In 1971, twenty to thirty AIM members seized the abandoned Coast Guard station at Milwaukee's McKinley Beach. They claimed they could do so under an 1868 treaty. The treaty said all abandoned government property would revert back to American Indian nations. The US government agreed to give the land to AIM.

By 1971, three Milwaukee Oneida women had created a small independent school. They felt the public school system wasn't serving Native students well. They hired Dorothy LePage, a Menominee woman just finishing her education degree, to be their school's director. After AIM took over the old Coast Guard station, the Indian Community School and its twenty-six students moved in. The school has a long and complex history, and at times it has struggled financially. But today the Indian Community School is thriving. It moved into its current building, in the suburb Franklin, in 2007. Its students are from more than forty tribal nations.

Protesting War and Expanding Equality

By the late 1960s, much of the civil rights advocacy work in Milwaukee transformed into protests against the Vietnam War. In 1968, five Catholic priests and nine other men raided the downtown Selective Service office. They seized thousands of draft records. They then took them to a parklike spot across the street and burned them. They sang hymns and read from the Bible as the police arrested them. Two years later, more than one thousand young adults took over buildings at the University of Wisconsin–Milwaukee (UWM) as a protest against the war.

Young people called **hippies** also condemned the Vietnam War. Hippies were part of a national movement in the 1960s and 1970s called the counterculture movement. Generally, hippies rejected their parents' values. They supported civil rights for people of color. They rejected consumerism. They embraced Eastern religions and listened to new forms of rock and folk music. Brady Street became their main street in Milwaukee. It had low-cost housing and was close to UWM. Restaurants and record stores that catered to hippies lined the street. Many hippies read *Kaleidoscope*, an underground newspaper published in Milwaukee from 1967 until 1971. It presented the hippie perspective on social and political issues. It also offered reviews of art, music, and literature.

The hippies held many of their gatherings at Water Tower Park on the east end of North Avenue. Local residents and the administration at St. Mary's Hospital did not want them there. They wanted the area quiet at night. The police tried to impose a 10:00 p.m. curfew, but the hippies ignored it. On July 13, 1970, police officers wearing helmets and armed with clubs cleared the area. They arrested some of the hippies. Other hippies went into St. Mary's for medical attention. The next day, a group of young militants called "yippies" hid rocks in the bushes of the park. When the police came back that night, one yippie yelled "Charge!" An ugly confrontation ensued. A lot of people were hurt, and several windows were broken.

A new feminist movement also took off in the late 1960s. It had its roots in earlier women's rights movements, including suffrage. Kathryn Clarenbach, a Wisconsin native, was a founding member of the National Organization for Women (NOW) in 1967. NOW wanted women to have access to birth control and abortion. It also wanted laws to guarantee equal pay for equal work. In 1968, the Milwaukee chapter staged a sit-in at a men's club. It also staged protests at bridal fairs and beauty pageants, events the group considered sexist.

There were several other feminist groups in Milwaukee. Women published *AMAZON*, Milwaukee's feminist newspaper, from 1971 until 1984. Other groups started shelters for women who had experienced violence at home. They also campaigned for the Equal Rights Amendment to the US Constitution. (This proposed amendment would have guaranteed equal rights to all people in the country, no matter their sex. It has never been passed.) Women's groups established Take Back the Night, a march against sexual violence toward women. The first Take Back the Night march in Milwaukee was in 1979. The march is now an annual event. It has expanded to protest sexual violence against people of all genders.

The LGBT community also made significant progress in the period between 1960 and 1988. LGBT people have always been in Milwaukee. However, most did not openly identify themselves as being gay or lesbian until after 1949, when Milwaukee's first gay bar opened. At that time, most straight people did not view being lesbian or gay as a sexual orientation. They thought it was immoral behavior. LGBT people who chose to live openly were discriminated against and harassed. Some were physically attacked. Police could arrest, fine, or beat people who engaged in same-sex acts. In 1960, Milwaukeean Elroy Schulz, a gay man, died after being injured while he was in police custody. And in 1961, a riot broke out at the Black Nite, a gay bar on North Plankinton Avenue. Four servicemen entered the bar and started a fight. The men were kicked out and later came back with a bigger group to continue the brawl. Seventy-five bar patrons-fought back. Police arrested the servicemen. Charges against them were later dropped.

By 1963, there were at least eight gay bars and restaurants in Milwaukee. Most were downtown, off Brady Street, or in the Third Ward. LGBT people across the country continued to fight for their rights. Events that happened in New York City in June 1969 brought national and global attention the gay rights movement. A police raid of New York's Stonewall Inn, a gay bar, led to days of demonstrations and calls for change. Some straight people became more accepting of LGBT people in the 1970s. Many became active supporters of LGBT people's rights. In 1982, Wisconsin passed Assembly Bill 70, a law that made it illegal to discriminate against gay and lesbian people in housing or employment. Wisconsin was the first state to create legal protections for LGBT people. It took several years and the work of many people, including politicians, religious leaders, and citizens, to pass this law.

More LBGT bars and other establishments opened in the city throughout the 1970s, many of them in Walker's Point. Gay pride gatherings began taking place in the city in the late 1970s and early 1980s, including a Lesbian and Gay Pride Week in June 1980. The Milwaukee Lesbian/Gay Pride Committee formed in 1988. A year later, they held a two-mile Pride parade followed by a rally that five hundred people attended. It is considered the forerunner to the city's annual PrideFest events. By 1996, Milwaukee's PrideFest was big enough to move to the Summerfest grounds. Milwaukee now has one of the largest PrideFests in the United States.

The 1960s: An Era of Progress?

Milwaukee's geography changed a lot in the 1960s. Some changes were positive. Others were negative. On the positive side, the county and city both sponsored new building projects. But on the negative side, some people lost their homes to make room for these changes. At the same time, white residents took new opportunities to move to the suburbs. The Milwaukee area became more segregated than ever before.

The county opened new public buildings in the 1960s. It finished a new building for the public museum in 1962 and added new buildings to the county zoo in 1963. Additionally, it built the Mitchell Park Horticultural Conservatory between 1964 and 1967. Nicknamed "the Domes," these buildings feature three kinds of environments for plants: tropical, desert, and temperate. The temperate dome environment is similar to Wisconsin.

The city also continued to try to improve residents' quality of life. It tore down entire blocks of run-down homes. It replaced them with neighborhoods like Halyard Park and Parkview. These neighborhoods attracted middle-class Black Americans. However, many low-income residents had to leave their homes because costs were too high.

Constructing new housing destroyed old neighborhoods. Groups organized to save beautiful old buildings. They rescued the Pabst Theater, the Pabst Mansion, and a few other gems. In 1974, Ann Tylenda organized volunteers to form Historic Milwaukee, Incorporated (HMI). HMI raises awareness about historic buildings. It also sponsors daily

The Domes at Mitchell Park Conservatory in the late 1960s | *WHI Image ID 135176*

HISTORY IN PERSON

Pabst Mansion

Beer baron Frederick Pabst built the Pabst Mansion as a family home in 1892. His descendants sold the building in 1908. For decades, the house served as the center for the Roman Catholic Archdiocese of Milwaukee. It was sold again in 1975 and nearly torn down before historic preservation groups saved it. The mansion has been carefully restored. Since 1978, the building has been open to the public as a museum. Visitors can tour the museum and get a sense of what it looked like in 1892, when it was home to one of Milwaukee's wealthiest families.

The Pabst Mansion in 2016 | *Carol M. Highsmith Archive, Library of Congress, Prints and Photographs Division*

and weekly tours and weekend events. Tylenda did not have a lot of money. However, she showed what ordinary people can do. In 1981, the city created the Historic Preservation Commission. It determines whether a property or neighborhood is worth saving.

White middle-class people continued to move to outlying areas of the city. New neighborhoods formed in what had been the towns of Lake and Granville. Other people moved out to the suburbs.

Milwaukee suburbs came in two types prior to the 1960s. Some were industrial suburbs. They included Cudahy, South Milwaukee, West Allis, and West Milwaukee. Residents lived in small homes. They worked in nearby factories or other businesses. The "bedroom community" was the other type of suburb. These included Bayside, Fox Point, River Hills, Shorewood, and Whitefish Bay. Generally speaking, the people in these suburbs worked in Milwaukee. They commuted to and from their jobs. These suburbs were wealthier than the industrial variety. Their residents tended to live in larger homes.

Then, in the 1950s, new suburbs incorporated. They had characteristics of both industrial suburbs and bedroom communities. These suburbs included Franklin, Glendale, and Oak Creek. They had big office parks or industrial parks. They also had the larger homes that people associated with suburbs. Except for Glendale, they also had a lot of farmland. As the farmers retired, they often sold their land to developers. These developers built new subdivisions or retail space.

These new suburbs developed into edge cities. Edge cities are areas that function as self-contained communities. They have homes, businesses, shopping, restaurants, and entertainment all near each other. In other words, one can live, work, shop, eat, and find recreational opportunities without leaving the community.

These and other suburbs attracted white, middle-class people. Economic and racial segregation increased. In 1970, 39 percent of all people in Milwaukee and Waukesha Counties lived in neighborhoods that were economically segregated. By 1990, the number increased to 55 percent. That change was greater than that of any other metropolitan area in the United States. In addition to Black Americans, the city had significant numbers of Latin American and Asian American residents. American Indians, who once dominated the area, made up about 1 percent of the population by the 1990s.

Just as it had in the first half of the twentieth century, the racial divide in housing led to a racial divide in schools. The state started the Chapter 220 program to promote racial integration between school districts. Twenty-three suburban school districts around Milwaukee agreed to enroll students of color from the city. MPS also allowed white suburban students to attend its schools. Very few suburban families volunteered. Over time, MPS lost most of its white students.

Deindustrialization and Its Consequences

Milwaukee was called the "Machine Shop of the World" in the early twentieth century. But Milwaukee fell hard in the 1970s and 1980s. The city lost its major industries. It experienced a major decline in the academic success of its schools. It witnessed the rise of gangs.

The American Midwest deindustrialized throughout the 1970s and 1980s. Factories closed. Manufacturers moved jobs from northern cities to the American South, Mexico, or overseas, often to China. Workers in these places accepted much lower wages than workers in the old industrial regions of the United States. Milwaukee was hit hard. It lost 40 percent of its manufacturing jobs between 1960 and 1985. That percentage was higher than any other large city in the United States. Allis-Chalmers left the city. Other Milwaukee-based companies, such as Allen-Bradley, A. O. Smith, and small-engine manufacturer Briggs and Stratton, cut jobs or relocated. Even the

Schlitz, Pabst, and Blatz breweries had closed by the 1990s. They could not compete with Anheuser-Busch in St. Louis and several small, independent brewers that became popular.

When people are unemployed, they have little money to spend. If people do not spend money, then more people lose their jobs. By 1980, 37 percent of Milwaukeeans were living in poverty. That number was higher than 50 percent in northside neighborhoods near closed factories. By 1987, more than half of all MPS students received free or reduced-price lunch, a program offered to families below a certain income level. At some schools, more than 80 percent of students qualified for these lunch programs. There were also many more single-parent households. Single-parent families made up 7.4 percent of all MPS families in 1960, but they made up 40.4 percent of MPS families in 1985. Many more people received welfare benefits. Even if they found new jobs, those jobs paid much less than jobs in factories had.

As businesses left the city, property tax revenue fell. The city had less money to spend, so the city and school district cut services. In 1980, voters elected Ronald Reagan president of the United States. He reduced federal aid to cities and public schools. People who did not have much to begin with now had even less.

Eventually, new jobs developed. However, many of them required high levels of skill in reading, mathematics, or technology. The average unemployed person did not have those skills. Worse, many of those jobs were in the suburbs. Unemployed people who lived in the central city had no way to get to them. (While the area where less affluent families lived on Milwaukee's north side was small in the 1960s, by the 1980s and 1990s it had grown much larger.) The county buses either did not run out to the suburbs or ran infrequently, and many people living in the central city did not own automobiles.

Poverty caused families to move around a lot. If a family could not pay their rent, they had to move. For families with children, changing homes often meant changing schools. For example, during the 1985–1986 school year, Palmer Street School (now Carver Academy) was one of the schools in MPS with a high level of poverty. It had 710 students at the beginning of that year. By the end of the year, 296 students had left the school, and 290 had transferred into it. In one sixth-grade class, only six of twenty-eight students had been at the school since kindergarten. Changes like these made it harder for children to learn.

Many young people in the city left school before graduating and turned to gangs. Gangs provided a sense of belonging and a group of friends. Since illegal gang activities provided a source of income, many gang members remained unemployed. Few ever returned to school.

Poverty and gangs contributed to a decline in student achievement throughout MPS. But some residents saw the school district's leadership as part of the problem too. Howard Fuller, the man who had organized protests against the conversion of neighborhood schools to citywide status, criticized Superintendent McMurrin. Fuller had never liked McMurrin's integration plan. He did not like MPS's policy of closing Black schools. He argued that this meant Black students, not white students, lost their schools and were forced to ride buses. Fuller wanted Black schools to be under Black leadership. Other residents thought the school district should allow children to attend private schools at public expense. (Private schools cost a lot of money to attend.) Ultimately, McMurrin resigned in 1987. He became superintendent of a small district in Ohio.

McMurrin had spent twelve years as Milwaukee superintendent. One year after he resigned, Henry Maier retired as mayor. Maier had served a record-setting twenty-eight years in that office. Thus, two influential city administrators left public life. A new era began.

Primary Sources

Continuity and Change

These primary sources show a variety of ways Milwaukee has changed—or not changed—in recent decades, from the 1960s and into the twenty-first century. Look closely at each and answer the questions that follow.

MILWAUKEE CENSUS DATA

	1960	1980	2000
White	675,572	453,576	298,556
Black American	62,458	145,832	222,902
Other	3,294	10,693	36,436
Asian and Pacific Islander	no data available	no data available	17,865
American Indian	no data available	no data available	5,203
Two or more races	no data available	no data available	16,140

Source: US Bureau of the Census

HISTORIC PHOTOGRAPH, 1967

Young adults in Milwaukee practice for a debutante event in 1967. Debutantes were young women who were "introduced" into society at formal events. Usually this meant the young women were introduced to young men as eligible for marriage. | *WHI Image ID 129886 © Milwaukee Journal-Sentinel*

HISTORIC PHOTOGRAPH, 1970

Milwaukee's first female parking enforcement officer writes a ticket while a male officer observes. When this photo was taken in 1970, a woman doing this job was called a "meter maid." | *WHI Image ID 146101 © Milwaukee Journal-Sentinel*

HISTORIC PHOTOGRAPH, 1976

Artists work on a mural at Fifth and National in Milwaukee in 1976. | *WHI Image ID 128555*

NONPROFIT WEBSITE, 2020

Leaders Igniting Transformation (LIT) is a youth of color led independent nonprofit. Founded in 2017, LIT engages in values-based issue and electoral organizing, direct action, advocacy for public policy, and leadership development. On campuses and communities in Milwaukee's key geographies, we organize young people to build independent political power for social, racial and economic justice.

In Spring of 2019, high school LIT members conducted interviews with School Board candidates, co-hosted several community forums, canvassed in their communities, and got 8 out of the 9 candidates to endorse the Youth Power Agenda. Since then, students have been meeting with School Board members to advocate for the school district they deserve. Less than two months after the election, we reached our biggest victory yet; a $600,000 divestment from the security and policing budget and reinvestment into mental health resources for students.

Source: Leaders Igniting Transformation, accessed April 11, 2020, https://www.litmke.org and https://www.litmke.org/high-school-organizing.

- **What are some of the ways these sources show Milwaukee has changed since the 1960s? In what ways has Milwaukee stayed the same?**
- **Which of the sources show a theme of continuity? Which show a theme of change?**

CHAPTER 10

CHAPTER QUESTIONS

- Who are Milwaukeeans today? How are they similar to or different from other people in Wisconsin?
- What makes Milwaukee a place many people want to live?
- What challenges does Milwaukee still face?

Modern Milwaukee

1988–2020s

By 1988, Milwaukee had one of the highest levels of poverty in the United States. Compared to 1960, almost half of its manufacturing jobs were gone. Also in 1988, new city, county, and school district leaders took over. Each initiated many changes—some successful, and some not. Toward the end of the twentieth century and into the twenty-first, city leaders have tried to remake Milwaukee's image into a world-class city that would attract visitors. The city has had to innovate in order to move forward. By the 2020s, Milwaukee still has a lot of problems with poverty. However, it is in a better position today to address these than it was in previous decades.

Downtown Milwaukee in 2016 | *Carol M. Highsmith Archive, Library of Congress, Prints and Photographs Division*

New Leaders for a Changing City

In 1988, Milwaukee chose new leaders for the city, the county, and the public schools. The city got a new mayor, a new county executive, and a new school superintendent. All three tried to move Milwaukee forward. Not all of their efforts were successful.

After Mayor Maier retired in 1988, Martin Schreiber ran for mayor against John Norquist. It was a race between the old Milwaukee and the new. On one hand, Schreiber was a north-side German Lutheran. He was a former state senator and governor. His father had been on the Common Council for thirty-two years, including twelve years as council president. John Norquist, on the other hand, was originally from New Jersey. His father was a Presbyterian minister. The family moved around a lot until they settled on the south side of Milwaukee. Norquist had been elected as a state senator in 1982. He was ten years younger than Schreiber. He beat Schreiber with 55 percent of the vote and became the new mayor of Milwaukee.

The county executive race that year was also the old versus the new. Bill O'Donnell, who had been on the county board since 1948, ran for a fourth term. He was sixty-six years old. He liked to say his favorite vacation spot was his front porch. Dave Schulz ran against him. Schulz had grown up in Milwaukee. He had been budget director for the city of Chicago and Milwaukee County. He took over as Milwaukee's parks director in 1985. Schulz was very outgoing. He launched a television campaign to encourage more people to use the parks. One of his commercials featured him sliding down a water slide in his swim trunks. Schulz beat O'Donnell by a two-to-one margin.

After MPS superintendent Lee McMurrin left Milwaukee in 1987, Hawthorne Faison filled in for a year. The school board gave the permanent job to Dr. Robert Peterkin in 1988. Faison and Peterkin were the first Black Americans to lead MPS.

Both Norquist and Schulz ran great campaigns, and hopes were high for Peterkin. However, governing is harder than campaigning. Norquist was very successful as an administrator. Schulz and Peterkin were not. In some ways, Mayor Norquist was a conservative Democrat. He cut taxes. He also privatized some city services to reduce costs. However, Norquist did not cut the police department's budget. He wanted to "get tough on crime." Norquist believed in the "new urbanism." This is the idea that cities should create walkable neighborhoods with lots of shared public spaces. For example, in 1988, the

The Milwaukee River in 2016 | *Carol M. Highsmith Archive, Library of Congress, Prints and Photographs Division*

Third Ward was a mostly deserted warehouse district. Norquist encouraged development in the neighborhood, and today it has expensive condominiums, restaurants, theaters, and art galleries. Residents can live, eat, and shop all in the same place. Others can work downtown and live only a short distance away. These kinds of neighborhoods can lure young people away from suburbs.

Norquist also convinced the county to tear down the Park East freeway. He replaced the freeway with new streets that connect downtown to neighborhoods like Haymarket and Brewer's Hill. Soon, new condominiums, apartments, and offices sprang up in those areas. The Milwaukee Riverwalk connects these neighborhoods to downtown and the Third Ward. The Riverwalk is lined with restaurants.

Not everyone liked Norquist and the changes he made. The downtown development was impressive, but it primarily attracted white people with money. Some Black leaders criticized Norquist for not helping their community. Others criticized him for tearing down the Park East freeway. They did not like him spending money on the Riverwalk either. Ultimately, though, both projects were successful.

Marvin Pratt | *Milwaukee VA Medical Center via Wikimedia Commons*

Norquist also wanted to build a light-rail line. It would have connected downtown Milwaukee to Brookfield with stops in between. However, Norquist could not secure the funding and approvals he needed. He also had public disputes with other city officials. Then, in 2000, one of Norquist's aides accused him of sexual harassment. The city reached a **settlement** with her. Norquist agreed not to run for a fifth term. He resigned in 2003 to take a job with the Congress for the New Urbanism in Chicago.

After Norquist resigned, Common Council president Marvin Pratt became acting mayor. He was the first Black American to lead the city of Milwaukee. In 2004, voters elected Congressman Tom Barrett, a white Democrat, as mayor. Under Barrett's leadership, the downtown area continued to redevelop. In 2018, the city started operating a streetcar to make it easier for residents and visitors to get from place to place downtown. The Forest County Potawatomi provided a $12 million sponsorship for the streetcar, using income from the Potawatomi Hotel and Casino. This allowed the city to offer streetcar rides for free.

A streetcar on St. Paul Avenue at Broadway in Milwaukee in 2019 | *David Wilson via Wikimedia Commons*

Leadership at the county level has had many ups and downs since the late 1980s. County Executive Dave Schulz took office in 1988, the same year as Mayor Norquist. But Schulz was not as successful as Norquist. He got into public disputes with the county board and other local officials. He left office in 1992. Tom Ament followed him. Like Norquist, Ament cut taxes. He also sold the county hospital to its neighbor, Froedtert Hospital, in 1995. Ament asked the county board to approve a new pension plan. It rewarded hundreds of senior county workers, including Ament, with big retirement bonuses. The bonuses totaled $900 million. When taxpayers found out how much they would be paying retired workers under the plan, many were angry. Ament resigned rather than face a recall election, in which voters were likely to reject him.

Voters elected Republican Scott Walker to replace Ament. Walker cut spending. He slashed the number of buses in the public transit system and cut money for county parks, among other changes. The county turned over many welfare programs to the private sector. Walker's leaner style of governing appealed to many Wisconsinites. Voters elected Walker governor of Wisconsin in 2010.

After Walker became governor, Lee Holloway and Marvin Pratt (who had also served as acting mayor) each briefly filled the role of acting county executive. They were the first Black Americans to hold that position. Then, in 2011, voters chose Chris Abele, a white man, as the new county executive. He identified as a Democrat, but he limited spending. He had several disputes with the county board. He wanted more authority over county operations. Republicans controlled state government. They sided with Abele. The state cut the county board's pay to part-time status. It took away their health care benefits. It also shortened their terms from four years to two years. Finally, it transferred some of the board's powers to the county executive. In 2020, voters elected David Crowley, a Black man, as county executive.

As for the schools, Robert Peterkin inherited a lot of problems when he became superintendent in 1988. MPS had major problems with violence and gangs. Students' test scores, attendance, and grades were lower than they had ever been. It was hard to find teachers who wanted to teach in that situation.

One of Peterkin's solutions was to start an immersion program for Black American boys. They were the group that was most at risk of dropping out of school. Peterkin felt they needed intensive help. Critics said it was a return to segregation. Still, the school board approved two schools for the new immersion program. Victor Berger Elementary School became Martin Luther King Elementary School. Fulton Middle School became Malcolm X Academy. However, both were open to all children regardless of race or gender. Peterkin wanted to recruit a staff of mostly Black men. He thought they would be good role models. But the staffing plan would have denied jobs to other qualified teachers already at those schools. The teachers' union and school board blocked it. Peterkin lost enthusiasm for his job. He resigned in 1990. (King Elementary is still open today. However, Malcolm X Academy closed in 2008.)

North Division High School seniors on graduation day in 1989 | *WHI Image ID 129810 © Milwaukee Journal-Sentinel*

Dr. Howard Fuller became the superintendent in 1991. Fuller made controversial reforms. He allowed principals to have control over their budgets. Many of them cut art, music, and physical education teachers. They also reduced the number of guidance counselors, psychologists, social workers, and librarians. They put the money they saved into core subject areas. Fuller also wanted to turn some schools over to private operators as charter schools. The teachers' union objected, saying that public schools should be run by public school teachers and principals, not private companies that use non-union labor.

Fuller's relationship with the teachers' union worsened in the mid-1990s. He transferred teachers to other schools without following the union's contract. He kept pushing for charter schools. In 1995, the teachers' union helped elect four school board directors. All four rejected the expansion of charter schools. Fuller resigned in frustration two weeks later.

About the same time, the state gave MPS more competition. In 1993, the state government made it easier to start charter schools. It also expanded the Milwaukee school voucher program. In 1990, the state had started a pilot voucher program in Milwaukee. A small number of low-income students could apply for a voucher to pay for tuition at a private school. In 1995, Wisconsin expanded vouchers to include religious schools. In 2011, it let middle-class children have vouchers. Many parents enjoyed having more choices. But critics said these schools pushed children out if they had disabilities or behavior problems. Those students ended up going back to MPS schools.

Generally speaking, charter schools have to follow many of the same rules that public schools follow. However, voucher schools are private schools. As such, they are free from some other regulations. For example, they can hire teachers who do not have teaching licenses. Initially, some of the schools hired teachers without high school diplomas. Academic results have been mixed. In general, well-established private schools have done about as well as MPS. Some have done slightly better. In other cases, the schools have performed worse than MPS.

Finally, in 1997, the state created a third competitor for MPS and other districts. It passed an open enrollment law. The law allows students to attend any public school in Wisconsin as long as the school or district is willing to take them. Suburban schools generally like the program because the state pays them for each student they take from outside their districts.

After Fuller's resignation, several others filled the role of superintendent. Spence Korte served as superintendent from 1997 until 2002. In 2000, he and the school board implemented a radical plan for neighborhood schools. MPS built new schools and expanded others. Korte boosted the number of kindergarten through eighth-grade (K–8) schools from ten to forty-seven and closed most middle schools. The plan cost $100 million but failed to attract students. Some schools sat vacant.

The next superintendent, William Andrekopoulos, created small high schools of fewer than five hundred students. Some of the high schools were housed in former elementary or middle schools that had closed. A few of the small high schools were successful, but most were not. Several small schools were more expensive for the district to run than a few large ones. They also offered fewer sports, clubs, and elective classes. These schools did not attract enough students to stay open. By 2013, most of the small schools had closed.

Andrekopoulos retired in 2010. Dr. Gregory Thornton (2010–2014), Dr. Darienne Driver (2014–2018), and Dr. Keith Posley (2018–present) have served since then. In 2019, only about 55 percent of Milwaukee children went to MPS schools. The rest attended voucher schools, charter schools, or suburban schools. Many of the schools are severely underenrolled today. Graduation rates and test scores in MPS remain lower than the state average.

Unemployment and Poverty in a Changing Economy

Factories continued to close across the United States in the 1990s and the 2000s. A lot of people lost their jobs. Poverty took a heavy toll on Milwaukeeans.

The gap between those with the most money and the least money grew. At one time, most workers in the Milwaukee area had been employed in factories. These jobs paid well because workers joined unions. By 2009, less than 20 percent of people in Milwaukee worked in factories. By 2012, only 11 percent of Milwaukee workers belonged to unions. Without strong unions, it became hard for workers to improve their pay. Worker wages were almost flat between 1990 and 2011. They increased only 8.7 percent. By comparison, the top twenty-five corporate executives got raises of more than 300 percent.

Like a lot of other cities, Milwaukee transitioned to a postindustrial economy. Many of the new jobs did not pay nearly as well as factory work had. Jobs in technology and science paid better, but unemployed factory workers did not have the skills to hold these jobs. They also could not get to them, since many of the good jobs were located in the suburbs and beyond the reach of the county bus system. A few employers chose to relocate from the suburbs to the Menomonee Valley or downtown. A few others helped pay for buses to transport workers from the city.

Poverty was related to geography. In 2009, 9.6 percent of Milwaukee-area residents were unemployed. That percentage did not include the people who had given up trying to find jobs. The unemployment rate was even higher in the city. By 2010, 26.3 percent of people in the city were experiencing poverty. The poverty rate among Black Americans in Milwaukee had been 29.4 percent in 1979. By 2010, it was 35.9 percent. In 2014, the 53206 zip code, on the city's north side, was the lowest-income zip code in the United States.

It is hard for people to pay rent when they do not have jobs. Between 2009 and 2011, more than one in eight Milwaukee renters moved against their will. There were about sixteen thousand evictions in each of those years. In some cases, landlords gave their tenants only a few hours to get out of their homes. In other cases, tenants came home to find their belongings on the street. In addition to those formal evictions, there were almost as many "informal evictions." Landlords used informal evictions when they did not want the hassle of getting a court order. Sometimes, landlords paid families a couple hundred dollars to leave before the lease expired. Other landlords refused to make repairs or even removed the home's front door. These landlords made living conditions so horrible that renters left on their own.

Children celebrate their heritage during Ethnic Pride Day in Milwaukee in 1989. The event was part of a program providing home-based education and support to families with children under age five. | *WHI Image ID 7196*

Some of the evicted tenants experienced homelessness or stayed in shelters. Others moved in with friends or family until they could find a place to live. Some children were separated from their parents as a result of eviction. Children changed schools as they changed homes. The lack of stability interfered with learning.

There were some modest signs of racial integration during this time. Some white people moved into the city. They wanted to live in or near downtown. These neighborhoods gentrified. **Gentrification** occurs when people fix up an urban neighborhood that has deteriorated. It attracts new residents who have high incomes. They can spend their money on restaurants and entertainment. Most developers like gentrification. They can buy properties for very little and sell them at high prices. Many city officials like gentrification because the new residents pay high property taxes. The city can use those taxes to pay for services that benefit all city residents. However, many people oppose gentrification. They point out that renters lose their homes when landlords sell to developers.

The Brewer's Hill neighborhood is one example of gentrification. The neighborhood fell on hard times after World War II. Older white residents moved to the edges of the city or to the suburbs. Some sold their homes to absentee landlords. The landlords rented to Black Americans and allowed the homes to fall into disrepair. The city tore down many of the homes. It destroyed almost seven hundred housing units in Brewer's Hill from 1950 to 1970. Gentrification of the neighborhood began in 1975. Ron Radke purchased an old mansion in Brewer's Hill when he was only twenty-two years old. He began to fix up the house. Within a few years, other young white people did the same thing. They liked the old homes. Over the next twenty years, developers converted old factories to new, expensive condominiums. They also built several new housing units at the eastern edge of the neighborhood. Families moved into once-vacant homes. Today, children play in front yards. The neighborhood association sponsors community events. Storefronts are reopening on Dr. Martin Luther King Drive.

Many other neighborhoods have gentrified in the past several decades. The Third Ward has been the most notable example. It used to be the home of Irish and Italian immigrants. By 1980, the

The Historic Third Ward neighborhood in 2016 | *Carol M. Highsmith Archive, Library of Congress, Prints and Photographs Division*

neighborhood had only seventy-four residents listed in the census. All but a few factories had closed. Most of the warehouses were empty. In 1976, a group of businesspeople began promoting the Third Ward. The neighborhood is directly south of downtown businesses. Its buildings are made of brick and have exposed beams and other nice features. Investors began to rehabilitate the buildings, turning former warehouses and factories into apartment buildings and condos. The Milwaukee Institute of Art and Design moved into one in 1992. Today, the Third Ward boasts live theater, art galleries, and fashion boutiques. It is also home of the Milwaukee Public Market, a collection of locally owned food vendors. Restaurants feature cuisine from all over the world. The area has attracted professionals with a higher income and education level than other neighborhoods. By 2020, the population of the neighborhood had grown to more than a thousand.

History in Focus

Changing Riverwest

This chart shows how the population by race and the per capita (per person) income changed from 2000 to 2010 in Riverwest Census Tracts 70, 71, 79, 80, and 107. How did this area change during this time period? What do these changes tell you about the effects of gentrification?

	2000	2010
Black population	26.2%	17.2%
White population	58.8%	71.1%
Per capita income	$15,174	$23,192

Source: US Bureau of the Census

Today's Riverwest neighborhood is home to people of all races, classes, and sexual orientations. A blend of activists, artists, and musicians have lived in the neighborhood since the 1970s. Brady Street on the Lower East Side revived in the late 1980s. Its business association lured new restaurants and resale shops to the area. By the early 2000s, Bay View had also gentrified. This neighborhood attracts higher-income families with children. As Bay View filled, developers next looked to Walker's Point, which lies between Bay View and the Third Ward. By the 2010s, those developers were converting old factories and warehouses into new residences. They also built new apartment buildings on vacant land. The city is working to redevelop the Harbor District next. It is located between Lake Michigan and Walker's Point.

Milwaukee artist Marina Lee created a public art installation, including this sculpture called *Izy Bird*, as part of a revitalization project in the Brady Street neighborhood. | *Carol M. Highsmith Archive, Library of Congress, Prints and Photographs Division*

A New Identity

In the twenty-first century, Milwaukee still has many problems with schools, poverty, and racism. But city leaders have tried to remake Milwaukee's image as a world-class city in the arts, entertainment, and technology.

Today Milwaukee has more than a dozen museums. There are also a number of museums in nearby suburbs. The Milwaukee Art Museum, located on the lakefront, draws more than four hundred thousand visitors each year. It has more than thirty thousand works of art. The museum is part of the War Memorial Center, which has exhibits about veterans of American wars. Other art museums in the city include the Charles Allis Art Museum, the Haggerty Museum of Art, the Lynden Sculpture Garden, and the Villa Terrace Decorative Arts Museum.

The Milwaukee Public Museum has displays on American Indian history and culture and other cultures from around the world. Other exhibit topics include prehistoric animals, Milwaukee history, butterflies and other insects, and a rain forest. Discovery World Science and Technology Museum is located next to Lake Michigan. It features an aquarium, a flight simulator, a model railroad, and other interactive exhibits. Nearby is the Betty Brinn Children's Museum, designed for children ages ten and younger.

The Milwaukee Art Museum's Quadracci Pavilion, designed by the Spanish architect Santiago Calatrava | *Carol M. Highsmith Archive, Library of Congress, Prints and Photographs Division*

There are also several museums in Milwaukee with a specific focus. They include:

- America's Black Holocaust Museum
- Grohmann Museum (human labor/work)
- Harley-Davidson Museum
- Jewish Museum Milwaukee
- Milwaukee County Historical Society
- Milwaukee Fire Historical Society and Museum
- Mitchell Gallery of Flight
- National Bobblehead Hall of Fame and Museum
- Pabst Mansion
- Wisconsin Black Historical Society/Museum

Milwaukee is a great place to enjoy theater, music, and film. The Milwaukee Repertory Theater ("the Rep") is the city's most active theater company. It has three performance venues downtown and gives more than six hundred performances in a typical year. It is best known for its annual production of *A Christmas Carol*. The Broadway Theatre Center in the Third Ward includes three performance companies and three theaters. The Marcus Performing Arts Center hosts several Broadway shows each year. It is also the home of Black Arts MKE, the Bronzeville Arts Ensemble, the Florentine Opera, and the Milwaukee Ballet. The Milwaukee Symphony Orchestra played there until 2020, when it moved to the former Warner Grand Theater. Potawatomi Casino Hotel opened in the Menomonee Valley in 1991. Its complex includes theaters for concerts and other live performances. Additionally, the Milwaukee Film Festival shows hundreds of films to more than seventy thousand spectators each year. The annual MKE Black Theatre Festival offers plays and workshops at locations across the city each August. And Latino Arts hosts a variety of Hispanic culture and arts programs throughout the year.

Milwaukee is one of the best cities in the United States for children's performing arts. First Stage presents several productions featuring students from grades pre-K through twelve every year. Young dancers can train at the Milwaukee Ballet School and Academy, and young musicians perform in the Milwaukee Youth Symphony Orchestra. They are two of the largest training companies of their kinds in the United States.

Milwaukee has the largest array of outdoor festivals in the United States. Summerfest is the world's largest music festival. It happens at Henry Maier Festival Park, which is on Lake Michigan just south

Fans gather at Summerfest around 1982. | *WHI Image ID 99183*

of the art museum and Discovery World. It features more than eight hundred acts on eleven stages, running over several summer weekends. The city hosts other festivals on the Summerfest grounds, including PrideFest, Polish Fest, German Fest, Irish Fest, Black Arts Fest MKE, and Mexican Fiesta. State Fair Park in the western suburb West Allis hosts Milwaukee Hmong New Year. Churches and neighborhoods sponsor festivals too. They go on every weekend from late spring until early autumn.

City and county parks are also popular. Milwaukee County has one of the highest rates of parkland per capita among urban counties in the United States. The county also has more than one hundred miles of hiking trails. Along the lakeshore, a series of trails connects bikers and pedestrians to Bradley Beach, McKinley Harbor, the art museum, Discovery World, and Lakeshore State Park next to the Summerfest grounds. Additionally, Lake Michigan is popular for sailing and swimming. Public beaches dot the shoreline.

Sports have always been popular in Milwaukee, for both participants and fans. In 1988, Jane Bradley Pettit donated a new basketball arena to Milwaukee. Pettit was a descendant of the Bradley family that started the Allen-Bradley manufacturing company. The arena was named the Bradley Center and was home to the Milwaukee Bucks basketball team. The Bucks moved to a new arena, the Fiserv Forum, in 2018. Baseball continues to entertain fans in Milwaukee as well. Milwaukee County Stadium, on the west side of the city, was home

Miller Park in 2016. The stadium's name changed to American Family Field in 2021.
| Carol M. Highsmith Archive, Library of Congress, Prints and Photographs Division

to the major league Milwaukee Braves and then the Brewers. It was replaced by Miller Park in 2001. Renamed American Family Field in 2021, Milwaukee's major league ballpark has the only clamshell roof in baseball.

Both the Fiserv Forum and American Family Field were built in part using public tax money. Not everyone wanted to spend tax money on sports arenas. However, elected officials and others wanted to keep the teams in Milwaukee, so they advocated for the projects. The city is also home to the Milwaukee Admirals hockey team, indoor and outdoor soccer teams, and sports teams at the University of Wisconsin–Milwaukee and Marquette University.

Milwaukee has invested in technology as well. By 2009, MPS had engineering programs in seventeen schools. Additionally, the US Department of Labor Job Corps came to the city in 2010. It trains low-income young people for jobs in manufacturing, construction, and health care. Milwaukee also leads the world in freshwater research. More than 120 water-related companies are located in southeastern Wisconsin. The University of Wisconsin–Milwaukee's School of Freshwater Sciences is the only school of its kind in the United States.

Some of the old manufacturers still operate in Milwaukee. They include Harley-Davidson and Rockwell Automation. A. O. Smith is the largest manufacturer of water heaters in North America. Johnson Controls makes automobile seats, batteries, and industrial controls. Walter

Harnischfeger's company is now part of Komatsu, a Japanese company. It still makes mining equipment in West Milwaukee. Milwaukee County and the six surrounding counties are home to more than four thousand high-tech, design, and creative industry companies. Those businesses employ more than sixty-seven thousand people. As of 2020, they accounted for about 4.2 percent of all jobs in the area. Nationally, only about 3.7 percent of workers were in those fields.

Milwaukee is home to other nationally known companies. Northwestern Mutual sells insurance and other financial services. The ManpowerGroup is the largest employer of temporary workers in the world. Miller Brewing, now owned by an international beverage company, still brews beer in Milwaukee, and Kohl's department stores has its headquarters in Menomonee Falls.

The 2020 US Census reported that Black Americans owned 12.3 percent of the small businesses in Milwaukee. The number of businesses owned by people of color in the city is rising. And organizations have formed to support them. One example is Sherman Phoenix, in the Sherman Park neighborhood. It is both a nonprofit organization and a retail market. It leases space to dozens of Black-owned businesses and helps them grow their companies. In the historic Bronzeville arts and cultural district, Bronzeville Collective MKE sells and promotes handcrafted goods made by Black, brown, and LGBT people. The African American Chamber of Commerce of Wisconsin and the Wisconsin Black Chamber of Commerce, both based in Milwaukee, also support Black-owned businesses. Similar organizations in the city work to help Latino, American Indian, and Hmong business owners.

The city's new image attracts visitors. In 2016, twenty-three million tourists came to the Milwaukee area. They spent more than

Milwaukee's Lake Michigan beachfront | *Carol M. Highsmith Archive, Library of Congress, Prints and Photographs Division*

$5 billion. They put fifty thousand people to work. The hotel industry is booming. Visitors can take city tours. Some tours focus on history and architecture. Others focus on food or Lake Michigan.

Milwaukee has also attracted new residents. Although many other US cities are larger, some people consider Milwaukee to be one of the best places for young, educated people to live. It has everything a big city offers but in a smaller environment. People who decide to make Milwaukee their home spend money at local businesses and pay taxes. They attract other people who do the same. Business opportunities improve. The city uses the tax money to improve services.

While this prosperity is good for the city and some residents, not everyone has the same opportunity to enjoy it. Milwaukee continues to struggle with poverty and racism. In 2020, Milwaukee's poverty

History in Focus

Black Lives Matter Protests

City leaders have tried to transform downtown Milwaukee and its adjacent neighborhoods into places in which people with high incomes want to live, work, and spend money. Critics of gentrification say the city does not invest enough money into central city neighborhoods. The residents of these central city neighborhoods are overwhelmingly people of color.

In 2013, a movement called Black Lives Matter began across the United States. The movement did not seek to claim that Black lives are more important than other lives. Rather, its members called attention to racism and discrimination that people of color face on a daily basis. Members spoke out against police brutality against Black men and women and what they saw as a justice system that was unfair to people of color.

In 2020, the COVID-19 pandemic swept across the United States. Many Americans confined themselves to their homes to prevent the spread of the disease. Schools and most places of employment closed. A disproportionate number of those who died from COVID-19 were people of color. Then, on May 25, a police officer murdered a Black man named George Floyd in Minneapolis, Minnesota. Anger over Floyd's death, compounded by anger over the way the COVID-19 pandemic was handled, boiled over.

Black Lives Matter protests broke out throughout the United States. Hundreds of people participated in protests in downtown Milwaukee. Initially, there was property damage associated with the Milwaukee protests. Some people were arrested. But leaders of the Black Lives Matter movement quickly distanced themselves from the people who broke store windows and looted. They saw to it that future protests would remain peaceful.

rate was 24 percent, more than double the national rate. More than 40 percent of the city's children were living in poverty. Extreme poverty can cause trauma, hopelessness, and loss of opportunities.

Into the Future

The residents of Milwaukee have enjoyed many signs of progress in modern times. As the city heads deeper into the twenty-first century, it is tempting to predict what the future holds. But predictions about the future do not always come true. On the first day of the twentieth century (January 1, 1901) the staff of the *Milwaukee Herold and Seebote*, a newspaper, speculated about life in the year 2000. Consider the following predictions they made:

- The city will have an extensive subway system.
- Mass transit will be at least as popular as automobiles.
- Mass transit will have an express delivery service.
- Telephone service will be cheap and abundant.
- Most people will eat in public kitchens instead of at home.
- Public laundries will replace washing clothes at home (the worst piece of housework).
- There will be more working women.
- Daycare will be free if mothers have to work.
- All people will use public baths.
- Hospitals will always have room for patients.
- Laws will require children to attend schools.
- The city will be decorated with sculptures and paintings.
- There will be libraries all over the city.

Which predictions actually came true? Which did not? What predictions do you have for the city of Milwaukee?

Primary Sources

The Debate over Gentrification

These excerpts from news articles and interviews show a variety of views on the changes that began happening in Milwaukee neighborhoods in the late twentieth and early twenty-first centuries. Use these sources to answer the questions that follow.

WTMJ ARTICLE, 2020

Just like turning a house into a home, it takes a special mixture of ingredients to make a street into a neighborhood. However, Desha Wilson says he feels like the things that make up his neighborhood are disappearing.

"To me it changed dramatically. I mean, you see how it is now. It's all quiet. You don't really see anybody out there. (There) was a time you'd come over here there'd be people outside. Everybody (on) the porch, 'Hey, how you doing?' Everybody talking to each other," he said. . . .

Wilson has lived in his Riverwest home for 37 years and seen a lot of his childhood neighbors leave.

"I would say it is a gentrification thing," he said. "You come across Holton this way east (and) you don't really see too many black families no more."

But Desha isn't sitting idly by as his neighborhood changes. He wants to bring a sense of community back to his block.

"I'm working on a non-profit organization. I basically want to do it for the kids," he said. "Where I can maybe feed the homeless and have some of the neighborhood kids come help me just to get things going."

By engaging the neighborhood to participate in community volunteerism, this Riverwest veteran hopes he can reignite a sense of belonging and togetherness in his Riverwest neighborhood.

Source: James Groh, "My Block: A Neighborhood Changed by Gentrification," TMJ4.com, January 16, 2020, https://www.tmj4.com/news/my-block/my-block-a-neighborhood-changed-by-gentrification.

URBAN MILWAUKEE ARTICLE, 2018

Real estate developer Kalan Haywood Sr. grew up in the Brewers Hill neighborhood when it was "99.99 percent people of color, both black and Latino." He and his mother still live in the recently gentrified neighborhood near downtown. Some of the changes they have seen are for the better—their daily exposure to street prostitution has stopped—but many changes are not. Most of their new neighbors are transplants with no sense of the neighborhood's history, Haywood said.

As the two sat on their porch last summer, most passersby barely gave them a nod. "Why do they look at us like we're the visitors?" asked Haywood's mother, who has lived in the neighborhood since she was a child.

Source: Andrea Waxman, "Panel Grapples with Gentrification and Low-Income Minorities," *Milwaukee Neighborhood News Service*, October 2, 2018, https://urbanmilwaukee.com/2018/10/03/city-faces-gentrification-issue.

PERSONAL INTERVIEW, 2020

"I like living in Bay View because it's a safe neighborhood with lots to do. It has cafés, shops, bowling alleys, and the beach. However, gentrification is pushing Black, brown, and low-income people out of their homes, which is, of course, bad. I can't think of a way it has personally affected me, but I am sure it has indirectly. I used to live in Walker's Point. The rent there has been increasing. Our landlord increased the rent a couple of times when we were there."

—Jaya Sims, age nineteen

Source: Interview with author, April 21, 2020.

BIZTIMES ARTICLE, 2013

Today, Walker's Point is experiencing a renaissance with no need for a re-branding. The neighborhood's proximity to downtown and the Third Ward, the low cost of real estate, the availability of numerous old buildings and vacant sites, combined with the gritty authenticity of this old industrial Milwaukee neighborhood, has made Walker's Point a hot spot for development and the city's newest cool neighborhood.

"You can see improvement everywhere you look," [Ursula] Twombly, [a board member of the Walker's Point Association] said. . . .

Walker's Point has become a major dining destination in Milwaukee and several restaurants and bars have opened there during the last three years.

Source: *BizTimes* Staff, "Walker's Point Emerges as One of Milwaukee's Hottest Neighborhoods," *BizTimes*, October 14, 2013, https://biztimes.com/walkers-point-emerges-as-one-of-milwaukees-hottest-neighborhoods.

BIZTIMES ARTICLE, 2019

Milwaukee aldermen have approved a new pilot program that aims to prevent displacement in neighborhoods around the downtown area by requiring certain new residential projects to set aside some units for nearby residents.

Meeting Tuesday, the Milwaukee Common Council voted without objection to support the creation of the Anti-Displacement Neighborhood Preference Policy. According to a report from the Department of City Development, this policy would require 20% of city-assisted affordable units within a multi-family development to be prioritized for residents who live in the ZIP code where the development is located.

Source: Alex Zank, "Milwaukee Aldermen Approve Policy Aimed at Preventing Displacement in Neighborhoods Near Downtown," *BizTimes*, August 1, 2019, https://biztimes.com/milwaukee-aldermen-approve-policy-aimed-at-preventing-displacement-in-neighborhoods-near-downtown.

- **Which primary source most strongly supports gentrification, and which most strongly opposes gentrification?**
- **What could be considered two positive characteristics and two negative characteristics of gentrification?**

Glossary

abolitionist: A person who wants to stop slavery

anarchist: A person who believes in the absence of government and the denial of authority

annexed: When land is added to a city or town government to increase that city or town's size

archaeologist: A person who studies the material remains of past human life and activities, such as tools, pottery, and monuments

assimilate: To take on the cultural traditions of a dominant group

boomtown: A town with a recent, rapid increase in population and business

boycott: To refuse to have dealings with a person, store, organization, or group to attempt to force its acceptance of certain conditions

cede: To give up

clan: A subdivision of the members of an American Indian nation

conformity: Behavior that meets the conventions and expectations of a dominant group

gentrification: When part of a city experiences an increase in middle-class or wealthy residents, often displacing low-income residents

incorporated: When a town or city receives a charter from the state and can elect its own local government officials

integration: When referring to race, the combining of people from multiple racial identities

labor union: An organization of workers that seeks to improve members' work environment in regards to wages, benefits, and working conditions

missionary: A person who has undertaken a mission to spread their religion to other groups

monopoly: When one person or company has control over an entire product or service, giving consumers no choice

oral histories: Stories and histories that are shared through spoken word rather than written records

ordinance: A law passed by a local (city, county, village, or town) government

population density: The number of people living in a particular unit of area

prosperity: A period of economic well-being and success

public housing: Low-cost housing that is funded in part by the government

ration book: Books issued during wartime containing stamps that civilians could exchange for items that were in short supply such as sugar, meat, and cooking oil

recall: A procedure that allows an elected official to be removed from office by a vote of the people

referendum: A vote by the people on a single political question

reparations: Money or materials paid by a country that a lost a war to the winner to make up for damage done during the war

repeal: The removal of a previously enacted constitutional amendment

restrictive covenant: A law controlling the use of land

schooner: A sailing vessel with two or more masts

scrip: A document used as evidence that the owner is entitled to receive something, such as money or land

secede: To withdraw from an organization, such as the United States

sedition: Speech and actions that are intended to inspire rebellion against the government

segregation: When referring to race, the separation of people based on racial identity

speakeasy: A place where alcohol is sold illegally

stalemate: A contest or battle that ends in a draw; neither side wins or loses

stock market: Where investors buy and sell shares of companies

strike: When a group of workers refuses to work to try to convince employers to agree to their conditions

suburb: A small community located next to or close to a larger city

tannery: A place where animal hides and skins are treated, or tanned, and turned into leather to be used in products

temperance: Choosing not to drink alcohol

treaty: An agreement between countries, such as the United States and American Indian nations

voyageur: A man employed by a fur company to transport goods to and from trading posts

wigwam: A type of home made by certain Native peoples that has an arched frame covered by bark, mats, or hides

zoning: The act of separating a city or town into zones reserved for different purposes

Selected Bibliography

Anderson, Margo, and Victor Greene, eds. *Perspectives on Milwaukee's Past*. Urbana and Chicago: University of Illinois Press, 2009.

Barton, E. E. *Industrial History of Milwaukee: The Commercial, Manufacturing and Railway Metropolis of the North-West*. Milwaukee: Elmer E. Barton, 1886.

Bruce, William George, ed. *History of Milwaukee City and County.* Vol. 1. Chicago and Milwaukee: S.J. Clarke Publishing, 1922.

Buck, James S. *Pioneer History of Milwaukee: From the First American Settlement in 1833, to 1841, with a Topographical Description as It Appeared in the State of Nature, Illustrated, with a Map.* Milwaukee: Milwaukee News Company, 1876. Rev. ed. Milwaukee: Swain & Tate, Book and Job Printer, 1890.

Buenker, John D., ed. *Milwaukee in the 1930s: A Federal Writers Project City Guide.* Madison: Wisconsin Historical Society Press, 2016.

Callaway, Rolland L., with Steven Baruch. *The Milwaukee Public Schools: A Chronological History, 1836–1986.* Thiensville, WI: Caritas Communications, 2008. CD-ROM.

Encyclopedia of Milwaukee, https://emke.uwm.edu.

Flower, Frank A. *History of Milwaukee, Wisconsin: From Prehistoric Times to the Present Date, Embracing a Summary Sketch of the Native Tribes and an Exhaustive Record of Men and Events for the Past Century; Describing in Elaborate Detail the City As It Now Is; Its Commercial, Religious, Educational and Benevolent Institutions; Its Government, Courts, Press, and Public Affairs; Its Musical, Dramatic, Literary, Scientific and Social Societies; Its Patriotism During the Late War; Its Development and Future Possibilities and Including Nearly Four Thousand Biographical Sketches of Pioneers and Citizens.* Chicago: Western Historical Co., 1881.

Friedlander, Ted. *The Story of Clothing Manufacturing in Milwaukee, from 1843 to 2004.* Milwaukee: T. Friedlander, 2003.

González, Sergio M. *Mexicans in Wisconsin.* Madison: Wisconsin Historical Society Press, 2017.

Gurda, John. *Milwaukee: A City Built on Water.* Madison: Wisconsin Historical Society Press, 2018.

Gurda, John. *Milwaukee: City of Neighborhoods.* Milwaukee: Historic Milwaukee, Inc., 2015.

Gurda, John. *The Making of Milwaukee,* 3rd ed. Milwaukee: Milwaukee County Historical Society, 2008.

Indigenize Milwaukee Mapping Project, Marquette University Indigeneity Lab, https://indigenizemilwaukeeproject.github.io/map/#2.

Janik, Erika. *Odd Wisconsin: Amusing, Perplexing, and Unlikely Stories from Wisconsin's Past.* Madison: Wisconsin Historical Society Press, 2007.

Jones, Meg. *World War II Milwaukee.* Charleston, SC: The History Press, 2015.

Kannel, Jeff. *Make Way for Liberty: Wisconsin African Americans in the Civil War.* Madison: Wisconsin Historical Society Press, 2020.

Leavitt, Judith Walzer. *The Healthiest City: Milwaukee and the Politics of Health Reform.* Princeton, NJ: Princeton University Press, 1982. Reprint, Madison: University of Wisconsin Press, 1996.

Loew, Patty. *Indian Nations of Wisconsin: Histories of Endurance and Renewal,* 2nd ed. Madison: Wisconsin Historical Society Press, 2013.

McBride, Genevieve G. *On Wisconsin Women: Working for Their Rights from Settlement to Suffrage.* Madison: The University of Wisconsin Press, 1993.

McCarthy, John M. *Making Milwaukee Mightier: Planning and the Politics of Growth, 1910–1960.* DeKalb: Northern Illinois University Press, 2009.

Prigge, Matthew J. *Damn the Old Tinderbox! Milwaukee's Palace of the West and the Fire that Defined an Era.* Madison: Wisconsin Historical Society Press, 2019.

Rodriguez, Joseph A., and Walter Sava. *Latinos in Milwaukee.* Charleston, SC: Arcadia, 2006.

Skenandore, Opal. "Reminiscences of Oneida Life in Milwaukee, 1920–1975." In *A Nation within a Nation: Voices of the Oneida in Wisconsin,* L. Gordon McLester III and Laurence Hauptman, eds. Madison: Wisconsin Historical Society Press, 2010.

Still, Bayrd. *Milwaukee: The History of a City*, 2nd ed. Madison, WI: State Historical Society, 1965.

Takach, Michail. *LGBT Milwaukee.* Charleston, SC: Arcadia Publishing, 2016.

Trotter, Joe William, Jr. *Black Milwaukee: The Making of an Industrial Proletariat, 1915–45*. 2nd ed. Urbana: University of Illinois Press, 2007.

Wells, Robert W. *This Is Milwaukee*. Garden City, NY: Doubleday, 1970.

Widen, Larry. *Entertainment in Early Milwaukee*. Charleston, SC: Arcadia, 2007.

Wisconsin 101, https://wi101.wisc.edu.

Source Notes

Chapter 1: Before It Was Milwaukee

10: "those runegates in Milwakie . . .": Robert W. Wells, *This Is Milwaukee* (Garden City, NY: Doubleday, 1970), 4.

Chapter 2: A Frontier Town

16: "seemed to pierce your very soul": Robert W. Wells, *This Is Milwaukee* (Garden City, NY: Doubleday, 1970), 15.

22: "the first rapids in the same . . .": The Enabling Act of Wisconsin, August 6, 1846.

Chapter 4: An Industrial City

57: "a brilliancy equal . . ." and "surrounded by a glass globe . . .": *Milwaukee Sentinel*, April 6, 1880.

Chapter 6: Socialism in an Age of War and Peace

93: "It takes more than that to kill a bull moose": Theodore Roosevelt, "It Takes More Than That to Kill a Bull Moose," Speech, Milwaukee, Wisconsin, October 14, 1912, The Theodore Roosevelt Association, Oyster Bay, New York.

96: "Every effort will be made . . .": "Patriots Urged to Unite," *Milwaukee Journal*, September 9, 1917.

Chapter 7: Struggles through Depression and War

115: "a new deal for the American people": Campaign Address at Madison Square Garden, New York City, October 31, 1936, Speeches of President Franklin D. Roosevelt, 1933–1945; Collection FDR-PPF: Papers as President, President's Personal File, 1933–1945, Franklin D. Roosevelt Library, National Archives and Records Administration, Washington, DC.

129: "If anyone harms one of those eggs . . .": Gordon MacQuarrie, "They're Here! 3 Junior Gerties Unshelled; One Seems Likely to Come to No Good End." *Milwaukee Journal*, May 31, 1945.

129: "In 1900, Milwaukee was home to 862 Black Americans . . ." and other population statistics: Joe William Trotter Jr., *Black Milwaukee: The Making of an Industrial Proletariat, 1915–45*, 2nd ed. (Urbana: University of Illinois Press, 2007), 5, 41, 149.

Chapter 8: A New Metropolis

139: "iron ring": John Gurda, *The Making of Milwaukee*, 3rd ed. (Milwaukee: Milwaukee County Historical Society, 2008), 342.

Index

Please note that page numbers in **bold** in this index indicate illustrations.

About the Author

James Nelsen is a high school social studies teacher in Milwaukee. He works at Golda Meir School, a public magnet school for college-bound students in grades 3 through 12. As a lifelong resident of Milwaukee, he finds the history of the city fascinating, from its early days in the mid-nineteenth century to the modern challenges of urban life today. As a teacher, he enjoys researching the history of education from colonial times to the present. He has a PhD in urban history from the University of Wisconsin–Milwaukee. When not teaching or researching, he enjoys spending time with his family, exploring his city, and following his beloved Milwaukee Brewers baseball team.

Photo by Stephanie Nelsen